THE AMERICANS WITH DISABILITIES ACT

A PRACTICAL GUIDE FOR MANAGERS

THOMAS D. SCHNEID
ATTORNEY AT LAW
ASSOCIATE PROFESSOR
EASTERN KENTUCKY UNIVERSITY

VNR VAN NOSTRAND REINHOLD
NEW YORK

Library of Congress Catalog Card Number 92-16477
ISBN 0-442-01281-0

Printed in the United States of America

Van Nostrand Reinhold
115 Fifth Avenue
New York, New York 10003

Chapman and Hall
2-6 Boundary Row
London, SE1 8HN, England

Thomas Nelson Australia
102 Dodds Street
South Melbourne 3205
Victoria, Australia

Nelson Canada
1120 Birchmount Road
Scarborough, Ontario MIK 5G4, Canada

16 15 14 13 12 11 10 9 8 7 6 5 4 3 2 1

Library of Congress Cataloging-in-Publication Data

Schneid, Thomas D.
The Americans with Disabilities act : a practical guide for managers / by Thomas D. Schneid.
p. cm.
Includes index.
ISBN 0-442-01281-0
1. Handicapped—Employment—Law and legislation—United States. 2. Discrimination against the handicapped—Law and legislation—United States. 3. Handicapped—Legal status, laws, etc.—United States. I. Title.
KF3469.S36 1992
344.73' 0159—dc20
[347.304159]
92-16477
CIP

Table of Contents

Preface

The Americans with Disabilities Act has been called an Emancipation Proclamation and Bill of Rights for people with disabilities.[1] Advocates for the disabled heralded this legislation for bringing nationwide attention to and protection against discrimination on the basis of disability. Business organizations counter that the Americans with Disabilities Act is another governmental intrusion into their workplace, an additional cost burden in an already weak economy, and will generate an onslaught of costly litigation. No matter which position you should advocate, the Americans with Disabilities Act is the most sweeping social legislation to be experienced by the private sector business community in the United States since the Civil Rights Act of 1964 and the Occupational Safety and Health Act of 1970.

Until recently, the general public was not aware of the passage of this new legislation, nor the breadth and depth of the discrimination against disabled individuals within our nation that generated the call for such expansive legislation. The Americans with Disabilities Act was not an "overnight sensation" but is the result of years of patchwork legislation by Congress and several state legislatures to eliminate discrimination against disabled individuals in the workplace.

The Americans with Disabilities Act is, however, the first disability discrimination legislation that will impact the vast majority of both public and private sector employers.

By 1994, more than 51,000 employers in the public and private sectors will be required to comply with the requirements of the Americans with Disabilities Act. Protection under the Act will be afforded to an estimated 45 million disabled individuals. Employers must realize that many of the fundamental aspects of daily life, such as employment and public accommodations, will now be subject to this expansive social legislation and the enforcement thereof by the federal government.

Covered employers are well advised to prepare to achieve and maintain compliance with this sweeping civil rights legislation.

I

HISTORY OF DISABILITY LEGISLATION

EARLY ATTEMPTS AT LEGISLATION

Since the beginning of this country, individuals with disabilities have fought against discrimination in education, employment, and many other areas. Throughout the many years, many individuals and organizations have attempted to correct the discrimination against disabled individuals through litigation and proposed legislation. In the 1960s and early 1970s, a substantial increase in litigation in the area of disability discrimination was experienced along with a national organizing effort by many different groups to highlight the plight of disabled individuals. As an outgrowth of the Civil Rights Act of 1964 providing rights and protections in the areas of race, color, religion, and national origin, many commentators and organizations noted that individuals with disabilities were also in need of civil rights and of similar protections against discrimination.[1]

In 1971, Representative Charles Vanik (D-Ohio) introduced a bill to amend Title VI of the Civil Rights Act of 1964 to prohibit discrimination based on "physical or mental handicap" in federally assisted programs.[2] A companion bill introduced by Senator Hubert Humphrey (D-Minn) and Senator Charles Percy (R-Ill) was offered in the Senate.[3] Despite the cosponsorship of sixty members of the House and twenty members of the Senate, no hearings were held and these bills died in committee.

In 1972, Representative Vanik attempted to include physical or mental handicap into the Civil Rights Act through a separate bill. This bill attempted to amend Title VII of the Civil Rights Act to bar discrimination in employment. This bill also died in committee.

In the subsequent years, numerous other attempts were made to amend the Civil Rights Act to include handicap or disability discrimination without success.

PRE-ADA FEDERAL LAWS IN THE PUBLIC SECTOR

Although Congress was unsuccessful in amending the Civil Rights Act to include discrimination against disabled individuals, several other nondiscrimination laws were enacted to protect disabled individuals. As of the 1983 U.S. Commission on Civil Rights Report, twenty-nine federal statutory prohibitions of discrimination against individuals with disabilities existed.[4] From 1983 to the enactment of the Americans with Disabilities Act (known as the ADA) in 1990, Congress enacted several laws that prohibited discrimination against disabled individuals, but only within the perimeters of the federal government, federal contractors, and recipients of federal financial assistance. These laws included the Architectural Barriers Act of 1968, the Education for All Handicapped Children Act (EAHCA) in 1975, the Developmental Disabilities Bill of Rights (DDABRA) in 1975, the Voting Accessibility Act of 1984, and the Rehabilitation Act of 1973. Congress did, however, include such prohibition against discrimination in two areas of legislation, namely the Fair Housing Amendments Act of 1988 and the Air Carriers Access Act, which directly impacted the private sector.

These pre-ADA laws did not provide the expected impact in reducing discrimination against individuals with disabilities. As can be seen from the structure and language used in the Americans with Disabilities Act, these laws did serve as the foundational basis through which Congress designed and built the ADA.

2

The Beginning of the ADA

Congress first considered comprehensive civil rights legislation for individuals with disabilities during the 100th Congress as a direct result of the recommendations made by the National Council on Disability. In April 1988, identical bills were introduced in the House (H.R. 4408) by Representative Tony Coelho (D-Cal) and in the Senate (S. 2345) by Senator Lowell Weicker.

The House Subcommittee on Select Education and the Senate Subcommittee on the Handicapped held a joint hearing on September 27, 1988. At this hearing, Senator Edward Kennedy (D-Mass), the Chairman of the Labor and Human Resources Committee, announced that passage of a bill to prohibit discrimination against disabled individuals would be the top priority in the next Congressional session. Additional emphasis was provided in this area through the testimony of members of the President's Commission on the Human Immunodeficiency Virus regarding the need to protect from discrimination individuals who have contracted the AIDS virus.

Of major importance is the fact that during this election year of 1988, the Democratic candidate for president, Governor Michael Dukakis (D-Mass), and the Republican candidate, then Vice President George Bush, both endorsed the concept of a comprehensive federal law to bar discrimination against individuals with disabilities not only in the public sector but in the private sector as well.

SENATE BILL

On May 9, 1989, Senator Tom Harkin (D-Iowa) and Representative Coelho (D-Cal) jointly introduced identical civil rights bills for individuals with disabilities (S. 933 and H.R. 2273). These bills received strong support with twenty-three Democrats and nine Republicans cosponsoring the Senate bill and seventy-four Democrats and eleven Republicans cosponsoring the House bill.

Initial hearings on the Senate bill were held before the Senate Labor and

Human Resources Committee and before the Senate Subcommittee on the Handicapped (later called the Subcommittee on Disability Policy). The Bush administration provided qualified support to the Senate Bill but expressed concern over the scope, enforcement procedures and remedies, and potential cost. This bill received zealous support from a number of disability rights organizations, the Leadership Conference on Civil Rights, the AFLCIO, several labor organizations, and religious organizations. Reservation regarding this bill was expressed by representatives of small business, the construction industry, and private bus companies.

ATTORNEY GENERAL'S OPINION

On June 22, 1989, then Attorney General Richard Thornburgh testified before the Senate Labor and Human Resources Committee regarding the proposed legislation. Mr. Thornburgh praised the "comprehensive character" of the proposed legislation but expressed reservations regarding the proposed scope and remedies, stating that the scope and remedies should not exceed the parameters set forth in the Civil Rights Act of 1964.

In the following weeks, the sponsoring senators and the White House negotiated a substitute bill. On August 2, 1989, the Senate Labor and Human Resources Committee unanimously approved a substitute bill that eliminated jury trials, compensatory damages, or punitive damages against employers found guilty of intentional discrimination. The substitute bill provided the same rights and remedies as found in the Civil Rights Act of 1966 (known as Section 1981) and the same enforcement mechanism as found under Title VII of the Civil Rights Act of 1964.

On September 7, 1989, the amended version of the ADA passed the Senate by a vote of 76–8. Several amendments were proposed, including the exclusion categories, the "good faith effort" consideration, and tax credits.

HOUSE BILL

The House moved substantially more slowly than the Senate due to the fact that the proposed bill was referred to four different committees for review and as a result of a vigorous campaign against the proposed bill by small business. The House Education and Labor Committee was the first committee to offer a substitute bill. The substitute bill provided for the use of "site-specific factors," use of the same complaint procedure as the Rehabilitation Act, and called for the removal of punitive damages among other items.

The introduction of the Civil Rights Act of 1990 (S. 2104; H.R. 4000) in February of 1990 caused additional delays. The proposed Civil Rights Act of 1990 would significantly amend Title VII of the Civil Rights Act of 1964 and provide for jury trials and allow for compensatory and punitive damages against employers for intentional discrimination. With the Bush Administration and Congress at odds, Representative F. James Sensenbrenner, Jr. (R-Wis) offered an amendment to limit the remedies under the ADA to reinstatement, back pay, and equitable relief. This amendment was defeated by the House in a 227–192 vote. The House also defeated several other amendments, including an amendment to exclude HIV-positive and other infectious diseases from inclusion under the ADA.

CHAPMAN AMENDMENT

On May 17, 1990, Representative Jim Chapman (D-Texas) introduced an amendment that would allow employers to transfer employees with AIDS or infected with HIV from food-handling positions if the transfer resulted in no loss of pay or benefits. After vigorous debate, this amendment passed by a margin of twelve votes, setting up a direct confrontation with the Senate version of the proposed ADA.

TRANSPORTATION AMENDMENT

The House defeated two amendments to the public transportation section of the proposed ADA that would have eased the requirements for all new buses and commuter trains purchased by local transit authorities regarding accessibility of disabled individuals in wheelchairs. An amendment by Representative Lipinski would have permitted commuter trains to provide one accessible car on every train, unless demand dictated, to be wheelchair accessible. This amendment was soundly defeated by a vote of 290–110. An amendment by Representative Shuster would allow the Secretary of Transportation the ability to grant cities with a population of 200,000 or less a waiver from the wheelchair accessibility requirements on new public transit busses. This amendment was defeated 266–148.

CONFERENCE COMMITTEE AND COMPROMISE

A joint House-Senate Conference Committee was appointed to review the differences between the House and Senate versions of the ADA. The major issues surrounded the Chapman Amendment and how the ADA would effect Congress itself (known as the Grassley Amendment). After substantial debate, and unable to obtain approval of the joint conference report, the Conference Committee accepted a motion by Senator Wendell Ford (D-Ky) to recommit the bill to conference with instructions to remove the provisions permitting the Senate to be sued under the ADA in federal court. On July 10, Senator Ford successfully amended the Civil Rights Act of 1990 to provide that the Senate could be sued for discrimination under the ADA and other civil rights laws but all claims should be investigated and resolved by the Senate Committee on Ethics. No appeal to federal court from the decision of the Ethics Committee is permitted under this Amendment.

Senator Helms offered an amendment to retain the Chapman amendment regarding the transfer of individuals infected with AIDS from food-handling jobs. Senator Hatch then introduced an amendment under which Health and Human Services would be required to publish annually a list of communicable and infectious diseases. Employers in the restaurant and other food-related industries would be allowed to transfer from food-handling jobs any individual who possesses any of the diseases specified on the Health and Human Services list. Additionally, state and local public health ordinances related to food handling would not be preempted by the ADA.

The Senate defeated the Helms proposal by a vote of 61–39 but accepted the Hatch amendment 99–1. The conference committee then approved the Hatch Amendment. The House defeated an amendment by Representative Dannemeyer designed to get the Chapman Amendment back into the ADA by a vote of 224–180.

The House adopted the conference report by a vote of 377–28 and the next day the Senate approved the conference report by a vote of 91–6. On July 26, 1990, President Bush signed the Americans with Disabilities Act into law.

3

OVERVIEW AND IMPACT

With the signing of the Americans with Disabilities Act of 1990 by President Bush, discrimination against qualified individuals with physical or mental disabilities in all employment settings became prohibited and additional amendments to the Rehabilitation Act of 1973 were provided. In the estimate of a number of commentators, the ADA will be the most important law in terms of its impact on employment practices in the workplace since the passage of the Occupational Safety and Health Act of 1970 and the Civil Rights Act of 1964.

From most estimates, the Americans with Disabilities Act will afford protection to approximately 43 million to 45 million individuals, or approximately one in five Americans. In terms of the affects on the American workplace, the estimates of protected individuals when compared to the number of individuals currently employed in the American workplace (approximately 200 million) provides that employers can expect that approximately one in four individuals currently employed or potential employees could be afforded protection under the ADA.

ADA ANTICIPATED AFFECTED POPULATION

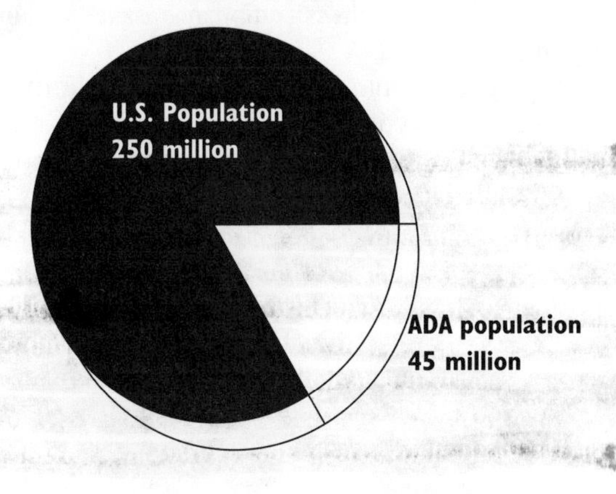

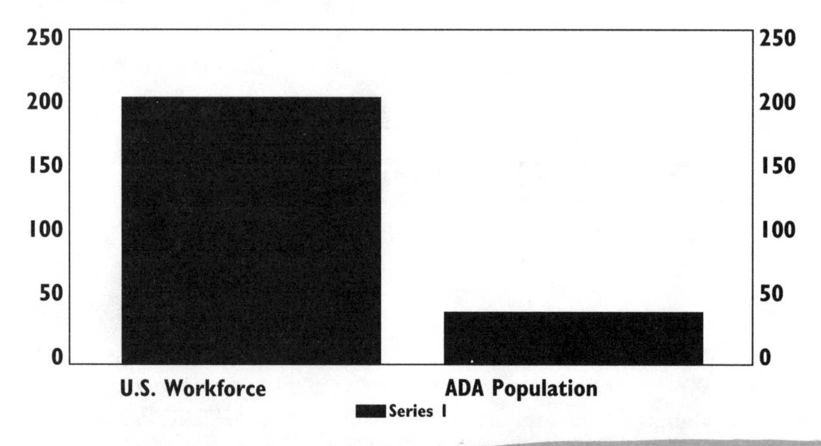

Covered employers should be aware that approximately 67 percent of the estimated 43 million to 45 million individuals who will be afforded protection under the ADA are currently unemployed.[5] According to a poll conducted by Lewis-Harris in 1986, 82 percent of all individuals with disabilities would give up government subsidies and benefits in favor of a full-time job.[6] It is the responsibility of the covered employer or entity to prepare their workplace to insure compliance with all facets of the ADA. In the estimate of most commentators, between 12,000 and 20,000 ADA-related claims will be filed with the EEOC by protected individuals against employers and other covered entities who do not achieve an acceptable level of compliance and thus discriminate, knowingly or unknowingly, against qualified individuals with disabilities. Given the broad scope of the ADA and the direct effects that the ADA has on a substantial number of policies, procedures, and practices utilized by most businesses and operations, covered employers must become knowledgeable in all aspects of the ADA and address compliance issues within the specified perimeters provided under the ADA.

The ADA is divided into five titles, of which all titles appear to possess the potential of substantially impacting a covered public or private sector organization. Title I contains the employment provisions that protect all individuals with disabilities in the United States, regardless of national origin and immigration status. Title II prohibits discrimination against qualified individuals with disabilities or excluding qualified individuals with disabilities from the services, programs, or activities provided by public entities. Title II includes the transportation provisions. Title III, entitled "Public Accommodations," requires that goods, services, privileges, advantages, or facilities of any public place be offered "in the most integrated setting appropriate to the needs of the individual."[7] Title III additionally covers transportation offered by private entities. Title

IV addresses telecommunications and requires that telephone companies provide telecommunication relay services, and that television public service announcements produced or funded with federal money include closed captions. Title V includes the miscellaneous provisions and notes that the Americans with Disabilities Act does not limit or invalidate other federal and state laws providing equal or greater protections for the rights of individuals with disabilities. It also addresses related insurance, alternate dispute, and congressional coverage issues.

Title I of the ADA goes into effect for *all* employers and industries engaged in interstate commerce with twenty-five or more employees on July 26, 1992, and on July 26, 1994, the ADA will become effective for all employers with fifteen or more employees.[8] Just as law enforcement organizations were not exempt from the ADA's predecessor, the Rehabilitation Act of 1973, most law-enforcement organizations will be subject to the ADA mandates. Title II, which applies to public services,[9] and Title III, which concerns requiring public accommodations and services operated by private entities, become effective on January 26, 1992,[10] except for specific subsections of Title II that went into effect immediately on July 26, 1990.[11] A telecommunication relay service required by Title IV must be available by July 26, 1993.[12]

Title I prohibits covered employers from discriminating against a "qualified individual with a disability" with regard to job applications, hiring, advancement, discharge, compensation, training, and other terms, conditions, and privileges of employment.[13]

Section 101(8) defines a "qualified individual with a disability" as any person

> who, with or without reasonable accommodation, can perform the essential functions of the employment position that such individual holds or desires . . . consideration shall be given to the employer's judgement as to what functions of a job are essential, and if an employer has prepared a written description before advertising or interviewing applicants for the job, this description shall be considered evidence of the essential function of the job.[14]

The Equal Employment Opportunity Commission (EEOC) provides additional clarification of this definition: "an individual with a disability who satisfies the requisite skill, experience and educational requirements of the employment position such individual holds or desires, and who, with or without reasonable accommodation, can perform the essential functions of such position."[15] Congress did not provide a specific list of disabilities covered under the ADA because "of the difficulty of ensuring the comprehensiveness of such a list."[16] Under the ADA, an individual has a disability if he/she possesses:

(A) a physical or mental impairment that substantially limits one or more of the major life activities of such individual;
(B) a record of such an impairment; or
(C) is regarded as having such an impairment.[17]

This definition parallels the language defining an "individual with a handicap" in the Rehabilitation Act.[18] The Senate Report describing the meaning of a qualified individual with a disability states that the definition "is comparable to the definition used in regulations implementing Section 501 and Section 504 of the Rehabilitation Act of 1973."[19] Additionally, the U.S. Department of Justice issued regulations implementing Section 504 of the Rehabilitation Act that expanded the language in the Rehabilitation Act and provided specific examples of covered impairments.[20] Thus, the case law developed under the Rehabilitation Act of 1973 may possibly be utilized for guidance in this area.

For an individual to be considered "disabled" under the ADA, the physical or mental impairment must limit one or more "major life activities." Under the U.S. Justice Department's regulations issued for Section 504 of the Rehabilitation Act, "major life activities" is defined as "functions such as caring for one's self, performing manual tasks, walking, seeing, hearing, speaking, breathing, learning and working."[21] Congress clearly intended to have the term "disability" construed broadly. However, this definition includes neither simple physical characteristics, nor limitations based on environmental, cultural, or economic disadvantages.[22]

A substantial issue under the Rehabilitation Act, and one left unclarified under the ADA, is whether a condition is covered when it limits the individual's access to one or more types of employment but otherwise does not limit the individual's employability or otherwise impair a major life activity. The Rehabilitation Act case most often cited in is E. E. Black, Limited v. Marshall.[23] In finding that working was a major life activity, the Black court listed the following factors for determining whether a individual's impairment substantially limits employment opportunities:

- The number and types of jobs from which the impaired individual is disqualified
- The geographical area to which the applicant has reasonable access
- The applicant's own job expectations and training
- The criteria or qualifications in use generally
- The types of jobs to which the rejection would apply.

The second prong of this definition is "a record of such an impairment disability." The Senate Report and the House Judiciary Committee Report each stated:

> This provision is included in the definition in part to protect individuals who have recovered from a physical or mental impairment which previously limited them in a major life activity. Discrimination on the basis of such a past impairment would be prohibited under this legislation. Frequently occurring examples of the first group (i.e. those who have a history of an impairment) are people with histories of mental or emotional illness, heart disease or cancer; examples of the second group (i.e. those who have been misclassified as having an impairment) are people who have been misclassified as mentally retarded.[24]

In interpreting the record-of-impairment section of Section 504 of the Rehabilitation Act, the U.S. Court of Appeals in *Allen v. Heckler*[25] stated, in regard to providing coverage to former patients in a psychiatric hospital: "Although plaintiffs are no longer institutionalized, the (Rehabilitation) Act recognizes that discrimination also occurs against those who at one time had a disabling condition. The handicap that these people face is the continuing stigma of being a former psychiatric patient; this disability does not disappear on discharge from the hospital." Other courts have found that a record of various physical impairments including hepatitis B,[26] heart disease,[27] and shoulder dislocation[28] fulfilled this portion of the definition.

The third prong of the statutory definition of a disability extends coverage to individuals who are "being regarded as having a disability." The ADA has adopted the "regarded as" test utilized for Section 504 of the Rehabilitation Act:

> "Is regarded as having an impairment" means (A) has a physical or mental impairment that does not substantially limit major life activities but is treated...as constituting such a limitation; (B) has a physical or mental impairment that substantially limits major life activities only as a result of the attitudes of others toward such impairment; (C) has none of the impairments defined (in the impairment paragraph of the Department of Justice regulations) but is treated . . . as having such an impairment.[29]

Under the EEOC's regulations, this third prong covers three classes of individuals:

- Persons who have physical or mental impairments that do not limit a major life activity but who are nevertheless perceived by covered entities (employers, places of public accommodation) as having such limitations (for example, an employee with controlled high blood pressure that is not, in fact, substantially limited, is reassigned to less strenuous work because of his employer's unsubstantiated fear that the individual will suffer a heart attack if he continues to perform strenuous work. Such a person would be "regarded" as disabled).[30]
- Persons who have physical or mental impairments that substantially limit a major life activity only because of a perception that the impairment causes such a limitation (for example, an employee has a condition that periodically causes an involuntary jerk of the head, but no limitations on his major life activities. If his employer discriminates against him because of the negative reaction of customers, the employer would be regarding him as disabled and acting on the basis of that perceived disability.)[31]
- Persons who do not have a physical or mental impairment but are treated as having a substantially limiting impairment (for example, a company discharges an employee based on a rumor that the employee is HIV-positive.

Even though the rumor is totally false and the employee has no impairment, the company would nevertheless be in violation of the ADA).[32]

Thus, a "qualified individual with a disability" under the ADA is any individual who can perform the essential or vital functions of a particular job with or without the employer accommodating the particular disability. The employer is provided the opportunity to determine the "essential functions" of the particular job before offering the position through the development of a Written Job Description. This written job description will be considered evidence to which functions of the particular job are essential and which are peripheral. In deciding the "essential functions" of a particular position, the EEOC will consider the employer's judgment, whether the written job description was developed prior to advertising or beginning the interview process, the amount of time spent on performing the job, the past and current experience of the individual to be hired, relevant collective bargaining agreements, and other factors.[33]

The Congressional intent of this provision is to insure the courts provide some consideration to the employer's judgment as to what functions of a particular job are essential.[34] As under the Rehabilitation Act where job descriptions have been found to be relevant,[35] covered organizations may also be able to introduce into evidence internal studies, reviews, and other pertinent information prepared in the normal course of business.

The EEOC defines the term "essential function" of a job as meaning "primary job duties that are intrinsic to the employment position the individual holds or desires" and precludes any marginal or peripheral functions that may be incidental to the primary job function.[36] The factors provided by the EEOC in evaluating the "essential functions" of a particular job include the reason the position exists, the number of employees available, and the degree of specialization required to perform the job.[37]

Congress was particularly concerned about the treatment of the disabled individual, who, as a matter of fact or employer prejudice, was believed to be a direct threat to others. To address this issue, Congress provided that any individual who poses a direct threat to the health and safety of others that cannot be eliminated by reasonable accommodation may be disqualified from the particular job.[38] The term "direct threat" to others is defined by the EEOC as "a significant risk of substantial harm to the heath and safety of the individual or others that cannot be eliminated by reasonable accommodation."[39] The determining factors to be considered include the duration of the risk, the nature and severity of the potential harm, and the likelihood the potential harm will occur.[40]

Additionally, the EEOC's Interpretive Guidelines stated:

> [If] an individual poses a direct threat as a result of a disability, the employer must determine whether a reasonable accommodation would either eliminate the risk or reduce it to an acceptable level. If no accommodation exists that would either eliminate the risk or reduce the risk, the employer may refuse to hire an applicant or may discharge an employee who poses a direct threat.[41]

Title I of the ADA additionally provides that if an employer does not make reasonable accommodation for the known limitations of a qualified individual with disabilities, it is considered to be discrimination. Only if the employer can prove that providing the accommodation would place an undue hardship on the operation of the employer's business can discrimination be disproved.

Section 101 (9) defines a "reasonable accommodation" as:

(a) making existing facilities used by employees readily accessible to and usable by qualified individuals with disabilities; and
(b) job restriction, part-time or modified work schedules, reassignment to a vacant position, acquisition or modification of equipment or devices, appropriate adjustments or modification of examinations, training materials, or policies, the provision of qualified readers or interpreters and other similar accommodations for qualified individuals with disabilities.[42]

The EEOC further defines "reasonable accommodation" as:

(1) Any modification or adjustment to a job application process that enables a qualified individual with a disability to be considered for the position such qualified individual with a disability desires, and which will not impose an undue hardship on the . . . business; OR
(2) Any modification or adjustment to the work environment, or to the manner or circumstances which the position held or desired is customarily performed, that enables the qualified individual with a disability to perform the essential functions of that position and which will not impose an undue hardship on the . . . business; OR
(3) Any modification or adjustment that enables the qualified individual with a disability to enjoy the same benefits and privileges of employment that other employees enjoy and does not impose an undue hardship on the . . . business.[43]

In essence, the employer is required to make "reasonable accommodations" for any/all known physical or mental limitations of the qualified individual with a disability unless the employer can demonstrate that the accommodations would impose an "undue hardship" on the business or the particular disability directly affects the safety and health of the qualified individual with a disability or of others. Included under this section is the prohibition against the use of qualification standards, employment tests, and other selection criteria that tend to screen out individuals with disabilities, unless the employer can demonstrate the procedure is directly related to the job function. In addition to the modifications to facilities, work schedules, equipment, and training programs, employers must initiate an "informal interactive (communication) process" with the qualified individual to promote voluntary disclosure of specific limitations and restrictions by the qualified individual to enable the employer to make appropriate accommodations to compensate for the limitation.[44]

Job restructuring within the meaning of Section 101(9) means modifying a job such that a disabled individual can perform its essential functions. This does not mean, however, that the essential functions themselves must be modified.[45] Examples of job restricting may include:

- Eliminating nonessential elements of the job
- Redelegating assignments
- Exchanging assignments with another employee
- Redesigning procedures for task accomplishment
- Modifying the means of communication that are used on the job.[46]

Section 101(10)(a) defines "undue hardship" as "an action requiring significant difficulty or expense, when considered in light of the following factors":

(i) the nature and cost of the accommodation . . .
(ii) the overall financial resources (and workforce) of the facility . . . involved . . .
(iii) the overall financial resources . . . number of its employees; the [structure of the parent entity]; and
(iv) the type of operation . . . including the composition . . . and functions of the workforce . . . administrative or fiscal relationship [between the entity and the parent].[47]

The EEOC has proposed that rules providing the factors of overall size of the operation, the structure and function of the workforce, the geographical location, and the "impact of the accommodation upon the operation of the site, including the impact on the ability of the other employees to perform their duties and the impact on the site's ability to conduct business" be considered.[48]

Section 102(c)(1) of the ADA provides the prohibition against discrimination through medical screening, employment inquiries, and similar scrutiny. Underlying this section was Congress's conclusion that information obtained from employment applications and interviews "was often used to exclude individuals with disabilities—particularly those with so-called hidden disabilities such as epilepsy, diabetes, emotional illness, heart disease and cancer—before their ability to perform the job was even evaluated."[49] This section expanded regulations issued under the Rehabilitation Act related to preemployment inquiries.[50]

Under Section 102(c)(2), employers are generally *prohibited* from conducting preemployment physical examinations of applicants and are also prohibited from asking the prospective employee if he/she is a qualified individual with a disability. Employers are further *prohibited* from inquiring as to the nature or severity of the disability even if the disability is visible or obvious. But employers may ask any candidate for transfer or promotion who has a known disability whether he/she can perform the required tasks of the new position if the tasks are job-related and consistent with business necessity. An employer is also permitted to inquire as to the applicant's ability to perform the essential job functions prior to employment. The employer should use the written job descriptions as evidence of the essential functions of the position.[51]

Employers may require medical examinations *only* if the medical examination is specifically job-related and is consistent with business necessity. Medical examinations are permitted *only after* the applicant with a disability has been *offered* the job position. The medical examination may be given *before* the applicant *starts* the particular job and the job offer *may be conditioned* on the results of the medical examination *if all* employees are subject to the medical examinations and if information obtained from the medical examination is maintained in separate confidential medical files. Employers are permitted to conduct voluntary medical examinations for current employees as part of an ongoing medical health program but again the medical files must be maintained separately and in a confidential manner.[52]

The ADA does not prohibit employers from making inquiries or requiring medical examinations or "fit for duty" examinations when there is a need to determine whether an employee is still able to perform the essential functions of the job or where periodic physical examinations are required by medical standards or federal, state, or local law.[53]

The employer may test job applicants for alcohol and controlled substances prior to an offer of employment under Section 104(d). This testing procedure for alcohol and illegal drug use is not considered a medical examination as defined under the ADA. Employers may additionally prohibit the use of alcohol and illegal drugs in the workplace and may require that employees not be under the influence while on the job. Employers are permitted to test for alcohol and controlled-substance use by current employees in their workplace to the limits permitted by current federal and state law. The ADA requires all employers to conform to the requirements of the Drug-Free Workplace Act of 1988. Thus, most existing preemployment and postemployment alcohol and controlled-substance programs that are not part and parcel of the preemployment medical examination or ongoing medical screening program will be permitted in their current form.[54]

Individual employees who choose to use alcohol and illegal drugs are not protected under the ADA; however, employees who have successfully completed a supervised rehabilitation program and are no longer using or addicted are offered the protection of a qualified individual with a disability under the ADA.[55]

Of importance to restaurants, cafeteria operations, meat packers, and other food related functions is Section 103(d)(1). This compromise section was designed specifically for *food handling employees*. The Secretary of Health and Human Services is required to develop and publish a list of infectious or communicable diseases that can be transmitted through the handling of food.[56] If an employee possesses one or more of the listed diseases, and if the risk cannot be eliminated through reasonable accommodation by the employer, the employer may refuse to assign the employee to or remove the employee from the job involving food handling.[57]

Section 103(d)(1) is the result of much debate over whether employers may refuse to allow employees with AIDS or who have tested positive for the HIV virus to work in the food-service industry. The language adopted did not decide the question but left this issue to the Secretary of Health and Human Services, who must decide whether AIDS and HIV positive should be included on the list of infectious or communicable diseases.[58]

Title II of the ADA is designed to prohibit discrimination against disabled individuals by public entities. This title covers the provision of services, programs, activities, and employment by public entities. A public entity under Title II includes:

- a state or local government;
- any department, agency, special purpose district or other instrumentality of a state or local government; and
- the National Railroad Passenger Corporation (Amtrak), and any commuter authority as this term is defined in section 103(8) of the Rail Passenger Service Act.[59]

Title II of the ADA prohibits discrimination in the area of ground transportation including buses, taxis, trains, and limousines. Air transportation is excluded from the ADA but is covered under the Air Carriers Access Act.[60] Covered organizations may be affected in the purchasing or leasing of new vehicles and in other areas such as the transfer of disabled individuals to hospitals or other facilities. Title II requires covered public entities to insure that new vehicles are accessible to and usable by the qualified individual, including individuals in wheelchairs. Thus vehicles must be equipped with lifts, ramps, wheelchair space, and other modifications unless the covered public entity can justify that such necessary equipment is unavailable despite a good-faith effort to purchase or acquire this equipment. Covered organizations may want to consider alternative methods to accommodate the qualified individual such as use of ambulance services or other alternatives.

Title III of the ADA builds upon the foundation established by the Architectural Barriers Act and the Rehabilitation Act. This title basically extends the existing prohibitions against discrimination in facility construction financed by the federal government to apply to all privately operated public accommodations. Title III focuses on the accommodations in public facilities, including such covered entities as retail stores, law offices, medical facilities, and other public areas. This section requires that goods, services, facilities, and so on of any public place be provided "in the most integrated setting appropriate to the needs of the qualified individual with a disability" except where the qualified individual with a disability may pose a direct threat to the safety and health of others that cannot be eliminated through modification of company procedures, practices, or policies. Prohibited discrimination under this section includes prejudice or bias against the qualified individual with a disability in the "full and equal enjoyment" of these services and facilities.[61]

The ADA makes it unlawful for public accommodations not to remove architectural and communication barriers from existing facilities and transportation barriers from vehicles "where such removal is readily achievable".[62] This statutory language is new and is defined as "easily accomplished and able to be carried out without much difficulty or expense,"[63] for example, moving shelves to widen an aisle, or lowering shelves to permit access. The ADA also requires that when a commercial facility or other public accommodation is undergoing a modification that affects the access to a primary function area, specific alterations must be made to afford accessibility to qualified individuals with disabilities.

Congress did not want the ADA to overwhelm, dominate, or inhibit an owner's ability to make needed alterations. The key comparison is the difference between the cost and scope of the alteration for accessibility and the cost and scope of the entire alteration. The U.S. Department of Justice's regulations define disproportionality by providing that alterations made to provide an accessible path of travel will be presumed to be disproportionate to the overall alteration when the cost exceeds 20 percent of the cost of the alteration to the primary function area.[64] Congress did provide a narrow exception in this area when the accommodation is "structurally impracticable."[65]

The term "readily accessible and usable" is a legal term of art derived from previous legislation. The exact criteria imposed by this standard is to be included in the minimum guidelines and regulations issued under the ADA. The committee report provided the following general parameters and definition:

> The term is intended to enable people with disabilities (including mobility, sensory, and cognitive impairments) to get to, enter, and use a facility. While the term does not necessarily require the accessibility to every part of every area of a facility, the term contemplates a high degree of convenient accessibility, entailing accessibility of parking areas, accessible routes to and from the facility, accessible entrances, usable bathrooms and water fountains, accessibility of public and common use areas, and access to the goods, services, programs, facilities, accommodations, and work areas available in the facility.[66]

Title III also requires "auxiliary aids and services" be provided for the qualified individual with a disability, including, but not limited to, interpreters, readers, amplifiers, and other devices (not limited or specified under the ADA) to provide the qualified individual with a disability with an equal opportunity for employment, promotion, and so on.[67] Congress did, however, provide that auxiliary aids and services need not be offered to customers, clients, and other members of the public if the auxiliary aid or service creates an undue hardship on the business. Business and professional firms may utilize alternative methods of accommodating the qualified individual with a disability. This section also addresses modification of existing facilities to provide access to the qualified individual with a disability and requires all new facilities to be readily accessible and usable by the qualified individual with a disability.

Title IV requires all telephone companies to provide "telecommunications relay service" to aid the hearing- and speech-impaired qualified individual with a disability. The Federal Communication Commission has issued a regulation requiring implementation of this requirement by July 26, 1992, and has established guidelines for compliance. This section also requires that all public-service programming and announcements funded with Federal monies be equipped with closed captions for the hearing impaired.[68]

Title V assures that the ADA does not limit or invalidate other federal or state laws that provide equal or greater protection for the rights of individuals with disabilities. A unique feature of Title V is the miscellaneous provisions and the requirement of compliance to the ADA by all members of Congress and all federal agencies. Additionally, Congress required all state and local governments to comply with the ADA and permitted the same remedies against the state and local governments as any other organizations.[69]

Congress expressed their concern that sexual preferences could be perceived as a protected characteristic under the ADA or that the courts could expand the ADA's coverage beyond Congress's intent. Accordingly, Congress included Section 511(b), which contains an expansive list of conditions that are not to be considered within the ADA's definition of disability. This list includes transvestites, homosexuals, and bisexuals. Additionally, the conditions of transsexualism, pedophilia, exhibitionism, voyeurism, gender identity disorders not resulting from physical impairment, and other sexual behavior disorders are not considered qualified disabilities under the ADA. Compulsive gambling, kleptomania, pyromania, and psychoactive substance use disorders from current illegal drug use are also not afforded protection under the ADA.[70]

Individuals extended protection under this section of the ADA include all individuals associated with or having a relationship to the qualified individual with a disability. This inclusion is unlimited in nature, including family members, individuals living together, and an unspecified number of others.[71] The ADA extends coverage to all "individuals," thus the protections are provided to all individuals, legal or illegal, documented or undocumented, living within the boundaries of the United States regardless of their status.[72] Under Section 102(b)(4), unlawful discrimination includes "excluding or otherwise denying equal jobs or benefits to a qualified individual because of the known disability of the individual with whom the qualified individual is known to have a relationship or association."[73] Thus, the protections afforded under this section are not limited only to family relationships; there appear to be no limits on the kinds of relationships or association afforded protection. Of particular note is the inclusion of unmarried partners of persons with AIDS or other qualified disabilities under this section.[74]

As with most regulatory legislation, the ADA requires that employers post notices of the pertinent provisions of the ADA in an accessible format in a conspicuous location within the employer's facilities. A prudent organization may wish to provide additional notification on their job applications and other pertinent documents.[75]

Under the ADA, it is unlawful for an employer to "discriminate on the basis of disability against a qualified individual with a disability" in all areas, including

(1) Recruitment, advertising, and job application procedures;
(2) Hiring, upgrading, promotion, award of tenure, demotion, transfer, layoff, termination, right to return from layoff, and rehiring;
(3) Rate of pay or other forms of compensation and changes in compensation;
(4) Job assignments, job classifications, organization structures, position descriptions, lines of progression, and seniority lists;
(5) Leaves of absence, sick leave, or other leaves;
(6) Fringe benefits available by virtue of employment, whether or not administered by the employer;
(7) Selection and financial support for training including apprenticeships, professional meetings, conferences and other related activities, and selection for leave of absence to pursue training;
(8) Activities sponsored by the employer including social and recreational programs;
(9) Any other term, condition, or privilege of employment.[76]

The EEOC has also noted that it is "unlawful...to participate in a contractual or other arrangement or relationship that has the effect of subjecting the covered entity's own qualified applicant or employee with a disability to discrimination." This prohibition includes referral agencies, labor unions (including collective bargaining agreements), insurance companies and others providing fringe benefits, and organizations providing training and apprenticeships.[77]

A group that has routinely been exempt from such regulation—the insurance industry—is included under the ADA.[78] The ADA requires equal access for the qualified individual with a disability to whatever health insurance coverage the employer provides to all employees. However, the ADA does not affect preexisting condition clauses in insurance policies, so long as the clause does not seek to evade the purposes behind the ADA.[79] This provision may be applicable to law-enforcement organizations in the area of health insurance, disability, and other insurance contracts.

Other notable provisions of the ADA, or lack thereof, include no recordkeeping requirements, no affirmative-action requirements, and no preclusions or restrictions on smoking in the place of employment.

Congress gave the ADA the same enforcement and remedies as Title VII of the Civil Rights Act of 1964 and included the remedies provided under the Civil Rights Act of 1991. As with Title VII, compensatory and punitive damages (with upper limits) have been added as remedies in cases of intentional discrimination, and there is a correlative right to a jury trial. Unlike Title VII, there is an exception where there exists a good-faith effort at reasonable accommodation.[80]

For now, the enforcement procedures adopted by the ADA mirror those of Title VII of the Civil Rights Act. A claimant under the ADA must file a claim with the EEOC within 180 days from the alleged discriminatory event or within

300 days in states with approved enforcement agencies such as the Human Rights Commission. The EEOC has 180 days to investigate the allegation and to sue the employer or issue a right-to-sue notice to the employee. The employee will have 90 days to file a civil action from the date of this notice.[81]

The original remedies provided under the ADA included reinstatement, with or without back pay, and reasonable attorney fees and costs. The ADA also provided for protection against retaliation against the employee for filing the complaint or others who may assist the employee in the investigation of the complaint. The ADA remedies are designed, as with the Civil Rights Act, to make the employee "whole" and to prevent future discrimination by the employer. All rights, remedies, and procedures of Section 505 of the Rehabilitation Act of 1973 are also incorporated into the ADA. Enforcement of the ADA is also permitted by the Attorney General or by private lawsuit. Remedies under these titles include ordered modification of a facility, and civil penalties up to $50,000 for the first violation and $100,000 for any subsequent violations. Section 505 permits reasonable attorney fees and litigation costs for the prevailing party in an ADA action but, under Section 513, Congress encourages the use of arbitration to resolve disputes arising under the ADA.[82]

With the passage of the Civil Rights Act of 1991, the remedies provided under the ADA were modified. Damages for employment discrimination—whether intentional or by practice that has a discriminatory effect—may include hiring, reinstatement, promotion, back pay, front pay, reasonable accommodation, or other action that will make an individual "whole." Payment of attorneys' fees, expert-witness fees, and court costs were still permitted and jury trials were allowed.

Compensatory and punitive damages were also made available where intentional discrimination is found. Damages may be available to compensate for actual monetary losses, for future monetary losses, for mental anguish, and for inconvenience. Punitive damages are also available if an employer acted with malice or reckless indifference. The total amount of punitive damages and compensatory damages for future monetary loss and emotional injury for each individual is limited, based upon the size of the employer.

NUMBER OF EMPLOYEES	DAMAGES WILL NOT EXCEED
15–100	$50,000
101–200	$100,000
201–500	$200,000
501 or more	$300,000

Punitive damages are not available against state or local governments.

In situations involving reasonable accommodation, compensatory or punitive damages may not be awarded if the employer can demonstrate that good-faith efforts were made to accommodate the individual with a disability. (Note: In

March 1992, the Senate Labor and Human Resources Committee approved by voice vote a bill (S. 2062) that would uncap the current damage awards provided under the Civil Rights Act of 1991. If this bill should pass, the damages and remedies currently provided under the ADA may be also be modified.)

Employers should be aware that the Internal Revenue Code may provide tax credits and/or tax deductions for expenditures incurred in achieving compliance with the ADA. As discussed in detail in Chapter IV, Section 20, such programs as the Small Business Tax Credit and Targeted Job Tax Credit may be available upon request by the qualified employers. Additionally, expenses incurred in achieving compliance may be considered a deductible expense or capital expenditure permitting depreciation over a number of years under the Internal Revenue Code.

4

Americans with Disabilities Act

TITLE I: EMPLOYMENT PROVISIONS

The two threshold questions addressed in Title I are which employers and organizations must comply with the ADA, and who is a protected individual under the ADA. These are vitally important issues that must be addressed by employers in order to ascertain whether compliance is mandated and, if so, whether current employees, job applicants, and others who may directly affect your operation are within the protective scope of the ADA.

Question 1: Who Must Comply with Title I of the ADA?

Title I covers all private sector employers that affect commerce, state, local, and territorial governments; employment agencies, labor unions, and joint labor-management committees fall within the scope of a "covered entity" under the ADA.[83] Additionally, Congress and its agencies are covered but they are permitted to enforce the ADA through internal administrative procedures.[84] The Federal government, government-owned corporations, Indian tribes, and tax-exempt private membership clubs—other than labor organizations who are exempt under Section 501(c) of the Internal Revenue Code—are excluded from coverage under the ADA.[85]

Covered employers cannot discriminate against qualified applicants and employees on the basis of disability. Congress did provide a time period to enable employers to achieve compliance with Title I. Coverage for Title I is phased in in two steps according to number of employees to allow additional time to smaller employers.

NUMBER OF EMPLOYEES	EFFECTIVE DATE
25 or more employees	July 26, 1992
15 or more employees	July 26, 1994

State and local governments, regardless of size, are covered by employment nondiscrimination requirements under Title II of the ADA and must comply by January 26, 1992. Certain individuals appointed by elected officials of state and local governments are covered by the same special enforcement procedures as established for Congress.

Similar to the coverage requirements under Title VII of the Civil Rights Act of 1964, an "employer" is defined to include persons who are agents of the employer such as plant managers, supervisors, personnel managers, and others who act for the employer. Thus the corporation or legal entity that is the employer is responsible for the acts and omissions of its managerial employees and other agents who may violate the provisions of the ADA.

In calculating the number of employees for compliance purposes, employers should include part-time employees who have worked for them for twenty or more calendar weeks in the current or preceding calendar year. The definition of "employees" also includes U.S. citizens working outside of the U.S. for U.S.-based corporations. However, the ADA provides an exemption from coverage for any compliance action that would violate the law of a foreign country in which the actual workplace is located.

Employers should be aware that the ADA is worded to afford protection against discrimination to "individuals" rather than "citizens" or "Americans." There is no distinction made under the ADA between individuals with disabilities who are illegal or undocumented and those who are U.S. citizens. ADA protections do not require an individual to possess a permanent resident alien card (known as a "green card"). According to the Judiciary Committee, "as in other civil rights laws . . . the ADA should not be interpreted to mean that only American citizens are entitled to the protections afforded by the Act."[86]

It should be noted that religious organizations are covered by the ADA but such religious organizations may provide employment preference to individuals of their own religion or religious organizations.

After an employer has ascertained that his or her organization or company is a "covered" entity required to comply with the ADA, the second threshold question is which individuals are qualified for protected under the Title I and how these protected individuals can be identified. This question can be addressed by asking the following questions:

- Who is protected by Title I?
- What constitutes a disability?
- Is the individual specifically excluded from protection under the ADA?

Question 2: Who Is Protected by Title I?

The ADA prohibits employment discrimination against "qualified individuals with disabilities" in such areas as job applications, hiring, testing, job assignments, evaluations, disciplinary actions, medical examinations, layoff/recall, discharge, compensation, leave, promotion, advancement, compensation, benefits, training, social activities, and other terms, conditions, and privileges of employment. A qualified individual with a disability is defined as

> an individual with a disability who meets the skill, experience, education, and other job-related requirements of a position held or desired, and who, with or without reasonable accommodation, can perform the essential functions of a job.[87]

Additionally, unlawful discrimination under the ADA includes

> excluding or otherwise denying equal jobs or benefits to a qualified individual because of the known disability of an individual *with whom the qualified individual is known to have a relationship or association.*(emphasis added)

This clause is designed to protect individuals who possess no disability themselves but who may be discriminated against because of their association with or relationship to a disabled person. The protection afforded under this clause is not limited to family members or relatives but extends in an apparently unlimited fashion to all associations and relationships. However, in an employment setting, if an employee is hired and then violates the employer's attendance policy, the ADA will not protect the individual from appropriate disciplinary action. The employer owes no accommodation duty to a nondisabled individual.

Question 3: What Constitutes a Disability?

Section 3(2) of the ADA provides a three-prong definition to ascertain who is and is not afforded protection. A person with a disability is an individual who

TEST 1—has a physical or mental impairment that substantially limits one or more of his/her major life activities;
TEST 2—has a record of such an impairment; OR
TEST 3—is regarded as having such an impairment.

This definition is comparable to the definition of "handicap" under the Rehabilitation Act of 1973. Congress adopted this terminology in an attempt to use the most current acceptable terminology but intended that the relevant case law developed under the Rehabilitation Act be applicable to the definition of "disability" under the ADA.[88] It should be noted, however, that the definition and regulations applying to "disability" under the ADA are more favorable to the disabled individual than the "handicap" regulations under the Rehabilitation Act.

The first prong of this definition includes three major subparts that further define who is a protected individual under the ADA. These subparts—namely (1) a physical or mental impairment (2) that substantially limits (3) one or more of his/her major life activities—provide additional clarification as to the definition of a "disability" under the ADA.

Subpart 1: A Physical or Mental Impairment

The ADA does not specifically list all covered entities. Congress noted that

> it is not possible to include in the legislation a list of all the specific conditions, diseases or infections that would constitute physical or mental impairments because of the difficulty in ensuring the comprehensiveness of such a list, particularly in light of the fact that new disorders may develop in the future.[89]

A "physical impairment" is defined by the ADA as

> [a]ny physiological disorder, or condition, cosmetic disfigurement, or anatomical loss affecting one or more of the following body systems: neurological, musculoskeletal, special sense organs, respiratory (including speech organs), cardiovascular, reproductive, digestive, genito-urinary, hemic and lymphatic, skin, and endocrine.[90]

A "mental impairment" is defined by the ADA as

> [a]ny mental or psychological disorder, such as mental retardation, organic brain syndrome, emotional or mental illness, and specific learning disabilities.[91]

A person's impairment is determined without regard to any medication or assisting devices that the individual may use. For example, an individual with epilepsy who uses medication to control the seizures or a person with an artificial leg would be considered to have an impairment even if the medicine or prosthesis reduced the impact of the impairment.

The legislative history is clear that an individual with AIDS or HIV is protected by the ADA.[92] A contagious disease such as tuberculosis would also constitute an impairment, however the employer would not have to hire or retain a person with a contagious disease that poses a direct threat to the health and safety of others if reasonable accommodation could reduce or eliminate this threat. This is discussed in detail later in this section.

The physiological or mental impairment must be permanent in nature. Pregnancy is considered temporary and thus is not afforded protection under the ADA. Simple physical characteristics, such as hair color, lefthandedness, height, or weight within the normal range are not considered impairments. Predisposition to a certain disease is not an impairment within this definition. Environmental, cultural, or economic disadvantages, such as a lack of education or a prison record, are not considered impairments. Similarly, personality traits such as poor judgment, quick temper, or irresponsible behavior are not considered impairments. Conditions such as stress and depression may or may not be considered impairments, depending on whether the condition results from a documented physiological or mental disorder.[93]

Case law under the Rehabilitation Act, applying similar language as in the ADA, has identified the following as some of the protected conditions: blindness, diabetes, cerebral palsy, learning disabilities, epilepsy, deafness, cancer, multiple sclerosis, allergies, heart conditions, high blood pressure, loss of leg, cystic fibrosis, hepatitis B, osteoarthritis, and numerous other conditions.

Subpart 2: Substantially Limits

Congress clearly intended the term "disability" to be construed broadly, but merely possessing an impairment is not sufficient for protection under the ADA. An impairment is only a "disability" under the ADA if it substantially limits one or more major life functions. An individual must be unable to perform or be significantly limited in performance of a basic activity that can be performed by an average person in America.

To assist in this evaluation, three factors are specified as a test to determine whether an individual's impairment substantially limits a major life activity:

1. The nature and severity of the impairment;
2. The length of time the impairment will last or is expected to last;
3. The permanent and long-term impact, or expected impact, of the impairment.

The determination of whether an individual is substantially limited in a major life activity must be made on a case-by-case basis. The three-factor test should be considered because it is not the name of the impairment or condition that determines whether an individual is protected, but rather the effect of the impairment or condition on the life of the person. Some impairments, such as blindness, deafness, and AIDS, are by their nature substantially limiting, but other impairments may be disabling for some individuals and not for others, depending on the nature of the impairment and the particular activity.[94]

Individuals with two or more impairments, neither of which by itself substantially limits a major life activity, may be combined to impair one or more major life activities. Temporary conditions such as a broken leg, common cold, and sprains or strains are generally not protected because of the extent, duration, and impact of these impairments. If complications arise, however, such temporary conditions may evolve into a permanent condition that substantially limits a major life function.

In general, it is not necessary to determine if an individual is substantially limited in a work activity if the individual is limited in one or more major life activities. An individual is not considered to be substantially limited in working if he/she is only substantially limited in performing a particular job, or is unable to perform a specialized job in a particular area. An individual may be considered substantially limited in working if the individual is restricted in his/her ability to perform either a class of jobs or a broad range of jobs in various classes when compared to an average person of similar training, skills, and abilities. Factors to be considered include

- the type of job from which the individual has been disqualified because of the impairment;
- the geographical area in which the person may reasonably expect to find a job;
- the number and types of jobs using similar training, knowledge, skill, or abilities from which the individual is disqualified within the geographical area; and/or
- the number and types of other jobs in the area that do not involve similar training, knowledge, skill, or abilities from which the individual also is disqualified because of the impairment.[95]

In evaluating the number of jobs from which an individual might be excluded, the EEOC regulations note that it is only necessary to show the approximate number of jobs from which the individual would be excluded.

Subpart 3: Major Life Activities

To be considered a "disability" under the ADA, an impairment must substantially limit one or more major life activities. A major life activity is an activity that an average person can perform with little or no difficulty. Examples include

- walking
- seeing
- speaking
- hearing
- breathing
- learning
- performing manual tasks
- caring for oneself
- standing
- working
- standing
- lifting
- reading
- sitting.[96]

This list of examples is not all-inclusive. All situations should be evaluated on a case-by-case basis.

Test 2 of this definition of disability requires that an individual possess a record of having an impairment as specified in Test 1. Under this test, the ADA protects individuals who possess a history of, or who have been misclassified as possessing, a mental or physical impairment that substantially limits one or more major life functions. A record of impairment would include such documented items as educational, medical, or employment records. It should be noted that merely possessing a record of being a "disabled veteran," or a record of disability under another federal or state program does not automatically qualify the individual for protection under the ADA. The individual must meet the definition of "disability" under Test 1 and possess a record of such disability under Test 2.

The third test of the definition of "disability" concerns an individual who is regarded or treated as having a covered disability even though the individual does not possess a disability as defined under Tests 1 and 2. This part of the definition protects individuals who do not possess a disability that substantially limits a major life activity from the discriminatory actions of others because of their perceived disability. This protection is necessary because "society's myths and fears about disability and disease are as handicapping as are the physical limitations that flow from actual impairment."[97]

Circumstances in which protection would be provided to the individual include

1. When the individual possesses an impairment that is not substantially limiting but the individual is treated by the employer as having such an impairment.
2. When an individual has an impairment that is substantially limiting because of the attitude of others toward the condition.
3. When the individual possesses no impairment but is regarded by the employer as having a substantially limiting impairment.[98]

To acquire the protections afforded under the ADA, an individual must not only be an individual with a disability but must also qualify under the above-noted tests. A "qualified individual with a disability" is defined as a person with a disability who

> satisfies the requisite skills, experience, education and other job-related requirements of the employment position such individual holds or desires, and who, with or without reasonable accommodation, can perform the essential functions of such position.[99]

The employer is not required to hire or retain an individual who is not qualified to perform a particular job.

Question 4: Is the Individual Specifically Excluded from Protection Under the ADA?

The ADA specifically provides a provision that excludes certain individuals from protection. As set forth under Sections 510 and 511(a,b), the following individuals are not protected:

- Individuals who are currently engaged in the use of illegal drugs are not protected when an employer takes action due directly to their continued use of illegal drugs. This includes illegal use of prescription drugs as well as use of illegal drugs. However, individuals who have undergone a qualified rehabilitation program and are not currently using drugs illegally are afforded protection under the ADA.

- Homosexuality and bisexuality are not impairments and therefore are not considered disabilities under the ADA.
- Transvestism, transsexualism, pedophilia, exhibitionism, voyeurism, gender identity disorders not resulting from physical impairment, and other sexual behavior disorders are not considered disabilities and thus are not afforded protection by the ADA.
- Other areas not afforded protection include compulsive gambling, kleptomania, pyromania, and psychoactive substance-use disorders resulting from illegal use of drugs.

A major component of Title I is the "reasonable accommodation" mandate, which requires employers to provide a disabled employee or applicant with the necessary "reasonable accommodations" that would allow the disabled individual to perform the essential functions of a particular job. "Reasonable accommodation" is a key nondiscrimination requirement in order to permit individuals with disabilities to overcome unnecessary barriers that could prevent or restrict employment opportunities.

The EEOC regulations define "reasonable accommodation" as

1. Any modification or adjustment to a job application process that enables a qualified individual with a disability to be considered for the position such qualified individual with a disability desires, and which will not impose an undue hardship on the . . . business; or
2. Any modification or adjustment to the work environment, or to the manner or circumstances which the position held or desired is customarily performed, that enables the qualified individual with a disability to perform the essential functions of that position and which will not impose an undue hardship on the . . . business; or
3. Any modification or adjustment that enables the qualified individual with a disability to enjoy the same benefits and privileges of employment that other employees enjoy and does not impose an undue hardship on the . . . business.[100]

Section 101(9) of the ADA states that reasonable accommodation includes two components. The first is the accessibility component, which sets forth an affirmative duty for the employer to make physical changes in the workplace in order that the facility is readily accessible and usable by individuals with disabilities. This component "includes both those areas that must be accessible for the employee to perform the essential job functions, as well as non-work areas used by the employer's employees for other purposes."[101]

The second component is modification of other related areas. The EEOC regulations set forth a number of examples of modification that an employer must consider:

- job restructuring
- part-time or modified work schedules
- reassignment to vacant position
- acquisition or modification of equipment or devices
- appropriate adjustment or modification of examinations, training materials, or policies
- providing qualified readers or interpreters.[102]

The employer is not bound to make an accommodation for an individual who is not otherwise qualified for a position. In most circumstances, it is the obligation of the individual with a disability to request a reasonable accommodation from the employer. The individual with a disability possesses the right to refuse an accommodation but if the individual with a disability cannot perform the essential functions of the job without the accommodation, the individual with a disability may not be qualified for the job.

An employer is not required to make a reasonable accommodation that would impose an undue hardship on the business.[103] An undue hardship is defined as an action that would require "significant difficulty or expense" in relation to the size of the employer, the employer's resources, and the nature of the operations. Although the undue-hardship limitations will be analyzed on a case-by-case basis, several factors have been set forth to determine whether an accommodation would impose undue hardship. The first is that undue hardship is unduly costly, extensive, or substantial in nature, disruptive to the operation, or would fundamentally alter the nature or operation of the business.[104] Additionally, the ADA provides four factors to be considered in determining whether an accommodation would impose an undue hardship on a particular operation:

1. The nature and the cost of the accommodation needed.
2. The overall financial resources of the facility or facilities making the accommodation, the number of employees in the facility, and the effect on expenses and resources of the facility.
3. The overall financial resources, size, number of employees, and type and location of facilities of the entity covered by the ADA.
4. The type of operation of the covered entity, including the structure and functions of the workforce, the geographic separateness, and the administrative or fiscal relationship of the facility involved in making the accommodation to the larger entity.[105]

Other factors such as the availability of tax credits and tax deductions, the type of enterprise, and so on can also be considered when evaluating an accommodation situation for the undue hardship limitation. Employers should note that the requirements to prove undue hardship are substantial in nature and cannot easily be utilized to circumvent the purposes of the ADA.

The ADA prohibits the use of preemployment medical examinations, medical inquiries, and requests for information regarding workers' compensation claims prior to an offer of employment.[23] An employer, however, may condition a job offer (i.e., make a conditional or contingent job offer) on the satisfactory results of a postoffer medical examination if the medical examination is required of all applicants or employees in the same job classification. Questions regarding other injuries and workers' compensation claims may also be asked following the offer of employment. A postoffer medical examination cannot be used to disqualify an individual with a disability who is currently able to perform the essential functions of a particular job because of speculation that the disability may cause future injury or workers' compensation claims.

If an individual is not employed because the medical examination revealed a disability, the reason for not hiring the qualified individual with a disability must be business related and necessary for the particular business. The burden of proving that a reasonable accommodation would not have enabled the individual with a disability to perform the essential functions of the particular job or that the accommodation would have been unduly burdensome falls squarely on the employer.

As often revealed in the postoffer medical examination, the physician should be informed that the employer possesses the burden of proving that a qualified individual with a disability should be excluded because of the risk to the health and safety of other employees or individuals. In enacting the ADA, Congress was particularly concerned about the treatment of disabled individuals who, as a matter of fact or prejudice, were believed to be a direct threat to the safety and health of others. To address this issue, Congress specifically noted that the employer may possess a job requirement that specifies "an individual not impose a direct threat to the health and safety of other individuals in the workplace."[107] A "direct threat" has been defined as meaning "a significant risk to the health and safety of others that cannot be eliminated or reduced by reasonable accommodation."[108]

The burden of proving this requirement falls upon the employer. The employer must prove that the "person poses a significant risk to the safety of others or property, not a speculative or remote risk, and that no reasonable accommodation is available that can remove that risk."[109] The employer must identify the specific aspect of the disability that is causing the direct threat and "if an individual poses a direct threat as a result of a disability, the employer must determine whether a reasonable accommodation would either eliminate the risk or reduce it to an acceptable level. If no accommodation exists that would either eliminate the risk or reduce the risk, the employer may refuse to hire an applicant or may discharge an employee who poses a direct threat."[110]

In most circumstances, the employer will work closely with the attending physician to ascertain the medical condition of the disabled individual. The physician's evaluation of any future risk must be supported by valid medical analysis and based on the most current medical knowledge and/or best available objective evidence about the individual. The employer should not rely only on the attending physician's opinion, but on the best available objective evidence to support any decision in this area. Other areas of expertise that may be called upon include physicians with particular specialty on a particular disability, advice of rehabilitation counselors, experience of the individual with a disability in previous jobs or other activities, or the various disability organizations. The employer is encouraged to discuss possible accommodations with the individual with a disability.

The direct-threat evaluation is important in evaluating disabilities involving contagious diseases. As discussed later in this chapter, the leading case in this area is *School Board of Nassau County v. Arline*.[111] This case sets forth the test to be used in evaluating a direct threat to others:

- the nature of the risk
- the duration of the risk
- the severity of the risk
- the probability the disease will be transmitted and will cause varying degrees of harm.[112]

For food handlers, Congress specifically addressed the issue of infectious or communicable diseases in the ADA. If an individual has a disease that is on the list published by the Secretary of Health and Human Services, the employer may refuse to assign the individual to a job involving food handling if no other reasonable accommodation exists that would avoid the risks of contamination.[113]

The ADA imposes a very strict limitation on the use of information acquired through postoffer medical examination or inquiry. All medical-related information must be collected and maintained on separate forms and kept in separate files, which must be maintained in a confidential manner with appropriate security and to which only designated individuals are provided access. Medical-related information may be shared with appropriate first-aid and safety personnel when applicable in an emergency situation. Supervisors and other managerial personnel may be informed about necessary job restrictions or job accommodations. Appropriate insurance organizations may acquire access to medical records when required for health or life insurance. State and federal officials may acquire access to medical records for compliance and other purposes.

In the area of insurance, the ADA specifies that nothing within the Act is to be construed to prohibit or restrict "an insurer, hospital, or medical service company, health maintenance organization, or any agent, or entity that administers benefit plans, or similar organization from underwriting risks, or administering such risks that area based on or not inconsistent with State laws."[114] However, an employer may not classify or segregate an individual with a disability in a manner that adversely affects not only the individual's employment but any provisions or administration of health insurance, life insurance, pension plans, or other benefits. In essence, this means that if an employer provides insurance or benefits to all employees, the employer must also provide this coverage to the individual with a disability. An employer cannot deny insurance to, or subject the individual with a disability to, different terms or conditions of insurance based upon the disability alone if the disability does not pose an increased insurance risk. An employer cannot terminate or refuse to hire an individual with a disability because the individual's disability or a family member or dependent's disability is not covered under their current policy or because the individual poses a future risk of increased health costs. The ADA does not, however, prohibit the use of preexisting-condition clauses in insurance policies.

An employer is prohibited from shifting away the responsibilities and potential liabilities under the ADA through contractual or other arrangements. An employer may not do anything through a contractual relationship that it cannot do directly.[115] This provision applies to all contractual relationships, including

- insurance companies
- employment and referral agencies
- training organizations
- agencies used for background checks
- labor unions.

Labor unions are covered by the ADA and have the same responsibilities as any other covered employer. An employer is prohibited from taking any action through a collective-bargaining agreement (i.e., union contract) that it may not take directly by itself. A collective-bargaining agreement may be used as evidence in a decision regarding undue hardship and in identifying the essential elements in a job description.

As with most governmental programs, the ADA provides that all covered entities post notices in an accessible location and in a format accessible to applicants, employees, and others describing the obligations imposed by the ADA.

Although not required under the ADA, a written job description describing the "essential elements" of a particular job is the first line of defense for most ADA-related claims. A written job description that is prepared before advertising or interviewing applicants for a job will be considered as evidence of the essential elements of the job along with other relevant factors.

In order to identify the "essential elements" of a particular job and thus whether an individual with a disability is qualified to perform the job, the EEOC regulations set forth three key factors, among others, that must be considered:

1. The reason the position exists to perform the function.
2. The limited number of employees available to perform the function, or among whom the function can be distributed.

3. The function is highly specialized, and the person in the position is hired for special expertise or ability to perform the job.

A job analysis, usually performed in the development of a written job description, is also not required by the ADA but is highly recommended. A job analysis is the formal process through which the essential job functions are identified and possible reasonable accommodations explored. A job analysis should focus on the purpose of the job and the importance of the actual job function in achieving that purpose.

Employers must be aware that they cannot discriminate against individuals with disabilities in regard to any employment practices or terms, conditions, and privileges of employment under Title I. This prohibition is extremely broad and covers such areas as

- applications
- promotions
- testing
- medical examinations
- hiring
- layoff/recall
- assignments
- termination
- evaluations
- compensation
- disciplinary actions
- leave
- training
- benefits.[116]

Employers should be aware that any type of segregation that limits, classifies, or otherwise adversely affects the employment opportunities or the terms, conditions, or benefits of employment of an individual with a disability or an individual associated with an individual with a disability may constitute discrimination. Employers should also be aware that the exercise of an individual's rights is also protected under the ADA from retaliation, harassment, or coercion.[117]

In conclusion, the purpose of the ADA is to place the individual with a disability on a level playing field with all other individuals in an employer's hiring, promotion, and all other aspects of the employment process. An employer has no obligation to prefer applicants or employees with disabilities over other applicants or employees. The employer's duty under the ADA is to consider the applicant or employee and make employment decisions without regard to an individual's disability or the employer's obligation to provide reasonable accommodation. The employer, after meeting all requirements, simple chooses the most qualified candidate for the particular position.

Compliance with Title 1

To begin compliance efforts, an organization must ascertain whether or not it falls within the perimeters and scope set forth under the ADA. An organization should calculate the number of employees (including part-time employees) and find which effective date, if any, is appropriate.

NUMBER OF EMPLOYEES	EFFECTIVE DATE
25 or more employees	July 26, 1992
15 or more employees	July 26, 1994

For employers with less than fifteen full- or part-time employees, there is no requirement to comply with the ADA at this time.

If you have found that your organization must comply with the ADA, your management team should be made aware of the scope and breadth of the ADA, the potential effects upon your workplace, and the possible penalties. A compliance team or individual should be assigned to insure compliance by the effective date. The appropriate manpower, budget, and other necessary resources should be provided to the compliance team or individual to enable compliance efforts to meet the deadline established under the ADA.

The compliance team should become thoroughly knowledgeable in all aspects of the ADA. The compliance team should review and evaluate all current policies, procedures, and programs that could be impacted by the ADA. Modifications should be initiated when necessary.

The compliance team should evaluate all insurance policies, retirement programs, and any other benefit programs. Additionally, all contractual relationships, including any collective-bargaining agreements, should be evaluated.

All restricted-duty or light-duty programs established for the return to work of injured or ill employees should be closely evaluated. Additionally, all safety- and health-related programs that could impact individuals with disabilities should be evaluated.

Development of written job descriptions identifying the essential elements for each job is a time-consuming task. The compliance team should prepare this necessary evidentiary documentation early in this evaluation stage.

Most hiring procedures will require close evaluation and possible modification. Remember: An employer may not make any preemployment inquires regarding disability nor can an employer require preemployment medical examinations or medical histories prior to an offer of employment. Use of tests or other qualification standards that screen out or tend to screen out individuals with a disability based on the disability must be job-related and consistent with business necessity. Tests or qualification standards must reflect the skills and aptitude of the individual rather than impaired sensory, manual, or speaking skills, unless those are the job-related skills the test is designed to measure. The following twelve areas within the hiring procedure should be closely evaluated.

1. Job Advertisements and Notices

It is advisable that job announcements, advertisements, and other recruitment notices include information on the essential functions of the job. Employers may wish to indicate in job advertisements that they do not discriminate on the basis of disability or other legally prohibited bases, for example: "We are an Equal Opportunity Employer. We do not discriminate on the basis of race, religion, color, sex, age, national origin, or disability." Information concerning job openings should be accessible to individuals with different disabilities. Although there is no obligation for the employer to provide job information in various formats, a prudent employer should make available various written formats upon request.

2. Employment Agencies

If your organization is using employment agencies, the compliance team should inform the agency of their obligation to comply with the ADA. If your organization has a contract with an employment agency, the compliance team may wish to include a provision in the contract requiring the agency to comply with the ADA and other legal nondiscrimination requirements.

3. Recruitment

The ADA is a nondiscrimination law and does not require affirmative-action-type recruiting or hiring. There are no special requirements under the ADA for an employer to recruit individuals with disabilities. However, recruiting activities that have the effect of screening out potential applicants with disabilities may violate the ADA.

4. Application Form

Most application forms currently being used by employers possess numerous questions that are discriminatory on their face. Review and modification of all application forms should be a priority item for the compliance team. These are some examples of questions that may not be asked on applications forms or in job interviews:

- Have you ever had or been treated for any of the following conditions or diseases?(followed by a checklist of various conditions and diseases).
- Please list any conditions or diseases for which you have been treated in the past three years.
- Have you ever been hospitalized? If so, for what condition?

- Have you ever been treated by a psychiatrist or psychologist? If so, for what condition?
- Have you ever been treated for a mental condition?
- Is there any health-related reason you may not be able to perform the job for which you are applying?
- How many days were you absent from work because of illness last year?
- Do you have any physical defects that preclude you from performing certain kinds of work? If yes, describe the defect and specific work limitation.
- Do you have any disabilities or impairments that may affect your performance in the position for which you are applying?
- Are you taking any prescribed medication?
- Have you ever been treated for drug addiction or alcoholism?
- Have you ever filed for workers' compensation insurance?[118]

Employers *may* ask questions to determine whether an applicant can perform a specific job function. The questions should be focused on the ability to perform the job, not the disability. The written job description attached to the application form identifying the essential elements of the job is helpful in describing these functions and will give the applicant the necessary information to request an accommodation. Examples of permitted questions include

- Are you able to perform these tasks with or without an accommodation?
- How would you perform the tasks, and with what accommodation(s)?[119]

5. Job Interview

The job interview possesses the greatest potential for discrimination by members of your management team. It is recommended that the compliance team assemble a written guideline and list of potential questions to be asked in an interview and provide this list to all management team members conducting interviews. Management team members should not be permitted to deviate from this list of approved questions.

The basic requirements regarding preemployment inquiries and the types of questions that are prohibited on job applications apply also to job interviews. An interviewer may not ask questions about the disability, even if the disability is visible or the individual has volunteered information about the disability. The interviewer may obtain more specific information regarding the ability to perform job tasks and about any needed accommodations.

Training for all team members performing interviews is essential to insure compliance. Most employment discrimination against individuals with disabilities is not intentional and is often the result of lack of knowledge. As soon as feasible, prior to the effective date, the compliance team should develop and conduct a training program for all managerial and hourly personnel who will be conducting interviews or other preemployment inquiries.

It is the employer's responsibility to provide necessary accommodations to an applicant to enable the applicant to have an equal opportunity in the interview process. The compliance team may find it helpful to state in the job announcement or on the job application that individuals needing accommodations should request such accommodation in advance.

6. Background and Reference Checks

An employer is prohibited from requesting certain information about the job applicant from a previous employer or other source until after the conditional offer of employment is made to the individual. If an employer uses an outside organization to conduct background or reference checks, the employer must insure the organization is in compliance with the ADA. Before making the conditional offer of employment, the employer is prohibited from asking a previous employer or other source about an applicant's disability, illness, workers' compensation history, or any other prohibited area. A previous employer may be asked about job function, task performance, quality and quantity, attendance record, and other job-related activities that do not relate to disability.

7. Testing

An employer can use any kind of testing to determine job qualifications a long as the test meets the following requirements:

1. If a test screens out or tends to screen out an individual with a disability or a class of such individuals on the basis of disability, it must be job-related and consistent with business necessity.
2. Tests given to people who have impaired sensory, speaking, or manual skills must be given in a format and manner that does not require use of the impaired skill, unless the test is designed to measure that skill.

The burden of proving job-relatedness and business necessity falls upon the employer. The compliance team should evaluate and document all information showing the job-relatedness and business necessity of such tests. The compliance team should be aware that the employer is only required to show that a test is job-related and consistent with business necessity if it screens out a person with a disability because of the disability. If a person was screened out for a reason unrelated to disability, ADA requirements do not apply.

An employer is only required to provide an accommodation if it is informed, before administering the test, that an accommodation will be needed. The responsibility of notifying the employer that an accommodation is needed falls upon the individual with a disability. The compliance team should insure that all applicants are notified concerning their right to request an accommodation. The compliance team may also want to require a specific time period prior to the test for notification of a needed accommodation, and may require that written documentation of the need for an accommodation accompany such request.

8. Drug Testing

The ADA has no effect on employers testing job applicants or employees for drugs or making employment decisions based upon drug tests. The compliance team may structure their program to permit testing for drugs prior to an offer of employment and may discipline, discharge, or refuse to hire individuals who test positive. The compliance team should evaluate the current drug testing program, if any, to insure the accuracy and integrity of such testing. Additionally, the compliance team should evaluate any rehabilitation program being offered by the employer. Remember: Individuals who have completed a qualified rehabilitation program and are not actively using drugs are protected under the ADA.

9. Medical Screening and Inquiries

The compliance team should closely evaluate all medical screening examination procedures currently in place. Remember that the ADA prohibits any medical examination or inquiry until after an offer of employment.

As noted above, the employer is permitted to condition a job offer on the satisfactory results of a postoffer medical examination or medical inquiry if this is required of all entering employees in the same job category. A postoffer medical examination or inquiry does not have to be job-related or consistent with business necessity and questions can be asked regarding previous injuries and illnesses in the medical examination.

The key requirement prior to the initiation of a medical examination is the conditioned offer of employment. The compliance team should develop a procedure through which the conditional offer of employment can be assured. One method is to provide a written conditional offer of employment that is signed and dated by the employer and the applicant at the beginning of the review process. Remember, the only testing that can be performed prior to an offer of employment is drug testing. All medical and other testing should follow the conditioned offer of employment.

For current employees, any medical examination or inquiry must be job-related and necessary for the business. Voluntary wellness and health screening programs are permitted as long as participation is voluntary, the information is maintained in a confidential manner, and the information is not used to discriminate against the employee. Additionally, medical examinations and inquiries required by other federal laws are permitted; however, the medical examination must follow a conditional offer of employment and the employer must comply with all reasonable accommodation requirements.

The compliance team must insure that the information acquired in all medical examinations and medical inquiries is maintained separately from all other files. All medical information must be maintained in a confidential manner.

The physician conducting the medical examination should not be responsible for making employment decisions. The physician's role should be limited to advising the employer about an individual's functional abilities and limitations in relation to job functions, and about whether the individual meets the employer's safety and heath requirements.

The compliance team should inform the physician that any recommendations or conclusions relating to hiring or placement of an individual should focus only on two concerns:

1. Whether the person is currently able to perform this specific job, with or without accommodation; and
2. Whether this person can perform this job without posing a "direct threat" to the health and safety of the person or others.[120]

The compliance team should bear in mind that the physician's opinion should not be relied upon exclusively but the team should structure the evaluation process to use the best available objective evidence.

10. Posting

The compliance team should insure that the necessary posting information is acquired and appropriately displayed in the facility.

11. Planning for Accommodations

The compliance team should develop a plan of action through which to address possible accommodation requests by applicants and employees. Step 1 should include acquiring the request from the individual and discussing potential accommodations. Step 2 should involve analyzing the specific job task involved. Step 3 should involve investigation of all possible accommodation methods. Step 4 should involve evaluation of the undue hardship and the safety and health limitations. Step 5 should involve evaluation of the selected accommodation. Step 6 should involve implementation of the accommodation. And Step 7 should involve the review and modification of the accommodation, if necessary.

The review and evaluation of accommodation requests should involve a team approach. The individual requesting the accommodation should be involved in every step of selecting and implementing the requested accommodation. The compliance team should identify potential sources of assistance—both inside and outside the organization—to assist them in this procedure. Review of the accommodation should be periodical to insure the accommodation is not creating an additional risk of harm for the individual or others working in the area of the accommodation.

12. Review and Audit

The compliance team faces a significant task in insuring compliance with all phases of the ADA. A periodic review and evaluation to insure that all aspects within your compliance program are functioning adequately is essential. Remember, simply asking one wrong question in an interview can lead to a charge of discrimination.

It is recommended that the compliance team assemble an audit instrument through which to evaluate their organization's compliance efforts. During the first two to three years after inception, this audit should be conducted on at least a semi-annual basis. All deficiencies noted in this audit should be slated for immediate corrective action.

The ADA does not require an affirmative action program nor does it mandate a written program of any type. A prudent employer will assemble a written program through which to document all actions and inactions in order to prepare for the filing of any claim of discrimination. The burden of proof under the ADA falls upon the employer. Without documented evidence as to the measures the employer has provided to achieve compliance with the ADA, any defense that could be mounted is tenuous and any hope of a "good faith" showing is minimal.

TITLE II: PUBLIC SERVICES

Title II, designed to prohibit discrimination against disabled individuals by public entities, covers all services, programs, activities, and employment by government or governmental units. Title II adopted all of the rights, remedies, and procedures provided under Section 505 of the Rehabilitation Act of 1973.[122] The effective date for Title II is January 26, 1992.

The public entities to which Title II applies include:

1. a state or local government;
2. any department, agency, special purpose district or other instrumentality of a state or local government; and
3. the National Railroad Passenger Corporation (Amtrak) and any commuter authority as defined in the Rail Passenger Service Act. [39]

The vast majority of Title II's provisions cover transportation provided by public entities to the general public, such as buses and trains. The major requirement under Title II mandates that public entities that purchase or lease new buses, rail cars, taxis, or other vehicles must assure that these vehicles are accessible to and usable by qualified individuals with disabilities. This accessibility requirement includes disabled individuals who may be wheelchair-bound and requires that all vehicles be equipped with lifts, ramps, wheelchair spaces, or other special accommodations, unless the public entity can prove such equipment is unavailable despite a good faith effort to locate the equipment.

All new public transportation facilities, such as rail stations, must be readily accessible and usable by individuals with disabilities. The ADA does not require that current existing facilities be structurally altered by the effective date but any modifications or alterations performed in the future must make the altered portion of any existing facility readily accessible and usable by individuals with disabilities.

Many public entities purchase used vehicles or lease vehicles due to the substantial cost of such vehicles. The public entity must make a good-faith effort to obtain vehicles that are readily accessible and usable by individuals with disabilities. As provided under the ADA, it is considered discrimination to remanufacture vehicles to extend their useful life for five years or more without making the vehicle accessible and usable by individuals with disabilities. Historical vehicles, such as trolley cars, may be excluded if the modification to make the vehicle readily accessible and usable by individuals with disabilities alters the historical character of the vehicle.

For commuter rail services, the ADA requires that the public entity provide at least one passenger car per train that is accessible to and usable by individuals with disabilities. Commuter rail services should comply with this requirement as soon as practicable but in no event later than July 26, 1995. Intercity rail systems must comply with the requirements of the ADA by July 26, 2010. Commuter rail stations with a large number of riders or serving as feeder stations for other transportation systems must be made readily accessible and usable by individuals with disabilities by July 26, 1993, although if "extraordinarily expensive structural changes" are required, the Secretary of Transportation may extend the compliance date to July 26, 2020.

For public entities who operate fixed-route public transportation systems that are currently not accessible to individuals with disabilities, the public entity is required to provide paratransit or other special transportation to individuals with disabilities. The paratransit system must provide a comparable level of service and comparable response time to individuals with disabilities. If the paratransit system or other special transportation service imposes an undue hardship on the public entity, the public entity may be required to provide this service to the fullest extent possible without causing an undue hardship on the public entity.

Compliance with Title II

The U.S. Department of Justice is the enforcing agency for Title II of the ADA. The Department of Justice has issued regulations prohibiting the aforementioned discriminatory practices and has instituted administrative procedures for initiating complaints and resolving disputes in an administrative setting. The Department of Justice regulations require that any public entity with fifty or more employees designate at least one employee to coordinate efforts to comply with Title II. Additionally, the Department of Justice provides a procedure for self-evaluation to assist public entities in achieving compliance.

In summarizing the Department of Justice's regulations, a covered public entity is prohibited by the ADA from:

- Denying a disabled individual an equal opportunity to participate in its activities, services, or programs.
- Requiring that disabled individuals participate in separate but equal programs.
- Indirectly discriminating against individuals with disabilities by entering into contractual relationships with others who then discriminate against the individual with a disability.
- Requiring the individual with a disability to be treated separately or differently from nondisabled individuals unless necessary to provide an equal level of service or benefits.
- Providing assistance to or aiding an organization that discriminates against disabled individuals.
- Prohibiting a qualified individual with a disability from applying or holding a position on the planning or advisory board.
- Adopting and using criteria, policies, or methods of administration that have the effect of discriminating against individuals with disabilities.

To achieve compliance, covered public entities are encouraged to evaluate their particular situation and put into effect the procedures necessary to achieve compliance with Title II and all regulations promulgated by the U.S. Department of Justice. Covered public entities may want to use the Department of Justice self-evaluation program to identify potential deficiencies and required modifications. All public transportation systems should be closely scrutinized and all related facilities evaluated to insure compliance. The public entity should, as part and parcel of this evaluation, address the undue financial hardship exceptions and their applicability to their given circumstances.

TITLE III: PUBLIC ACCOMMODATIONS

Title III builds upon the foundation established by Congress under the Architectural Barriers Act and the Rehabilitation Act. Title III basically extends the prohibition against discrimination that existed for facilities constructed or financed by the federal government to all private-sector public facilities. Title III requires all goods, services, privileges, advantages, or facilities of any public place to be offered "in the most integrated setting appropriate to the needs of the [disabled] individual," except when the individual poses a direct threat the the safety or health of others. Title III additionally prohibits discrimination against individuals with disabilities in the "full and equal enjoyment" of all goods, services, facilities, and so on.

Title III covers public transportation offered by private-sector entities in addition to all places of public accommodation without regard to size. To enable small businesses to have time to comply with this mandatory change without fear of civil action, Congress provided that no civil action could be brought against businesses between January 26, 1992, and July 26, 1992, that employ twenty-five or fewer employees and have annual gross receipts of $1 million or less. In addition, businesses with fewer than ten employees and with gross annual receipts of $500,000 or less were provided a grace period from January 26, 1992, to January 26, 1993 to achieve compliance. Residential accommodations, religious organizations, and private clubs were made exempt from these requirements.

Title III provides twelve categories and examples of places requiring public accommodations:

- Places of lodging, such as inns, hotels, and motels, except for those establishments located in the proprietor's residence and not more than 5 rooms are for rent.
- Restaurants, bars, or other establishments serving food or drink.
- Motion picture house, theater, concert hall, stadium, or other place of exhibition or entertainment.
- A bakery, grocery store, clothing store, hardware store, shopping center, or other sales or rental establishments.
- A laundromat, dry cleaner, bank, barber shop, beauty shop, travel service, funeral parlor, gas station, office of an accountant or lawyer, pharmacy, insurance office, professional office of a health care provider, hospital, or other service establishment.
- A terminal depot, or other station used for specified public transportation.
- A park, zoo, amusement park, or other place of entertainment.
- A nursery, elementary, secondary, undergraduate, or post-graduate private school, or other place of education.
- A day-care center, senior citizen center, homeless shelter, food bank, adoption agency, or other social service center establishment.
- A gymnasium, health spa, bowling alley, golf course, or other place of exercise or recreation.[123]

It is considered discriminatory under Title III for a covered entity to fail to remove structural, architectural, and communication barriers from existing facilities when the removal is "readily achievable," easily accomplished, and can be performed with little difficulty or expense. As discussed in detail in the Facility Modification section of this chapter, the covered entity is required to determine whether removal of a structural barrier or other barrier to individuals with disabilities is "readily achievable." Factors to be considered include the nature and cost of the modification, the size and type of the business, and the financial resources of the business. If the removal of a barrier is not "readily achievable," the covered entity may make goods and services readily available and achievable to individuals with disabilities through alternative methods.

Title III requires that all new facilities be "readily accessible and usable" by individuals with disabilities except where "structurally impracticable." (See

Facility Modification in Chapter 5.) In addition, Title III requires that covered employers running private fixed-route transportation systems who purchase or lease new vehicles with a seating capacity of sixteen or more ensure that all new vehicles are readily accessible and usable by individuals with disabilities, or provide equivalent services that are accessible to individuals with disabilities. Demand transportation systems with a seating capacity of eight or more must also comply with Title III.

Effective July 26, 1997, all new over-the-road buses purchased or leased by "small providers" must be accessible to and usable by individuals with disabilities and by July 26, 1996, all "other providers" must comply with this requirement. New rail-passenger cars must comply with this requirement and all remanufactured cars with a usable life of ten years or more that are purchased or leased to a covered entity must also comply. Historical rail passenger cars are exempt from this requirement.

Covered private sector employers may not use application or other eligibility criteria that screen out or tend to screen out individuals with disabilities unless they can prove that doing so is necessary to providing the goods or services they provide to the public. Title III additionally makes discriminatory the failure to make reasonable accommodations in policies, business practices, and other procedures that afford access to and use of public accommodations to individuals with disabilities.

Title III additionally prohibits covered employers from denying access to goods and services because of the absence of "auxiliary aids" unless the providing of such auxiliary aids would fundamentally alter the nature of the goods or services or would impose an undue hardship. The ADA defines "auxiliary aids and services" as

- qualified interpreters or other effective methods of making aurally delivered materials available to individuals with hearing impairments;
- qualified readers, taped texts, or other effective methods of making visually delivered materials available to individuals with visual impairments;
- acquisition or modification of equipment or devices; and
- other similar services or actions.[124]

Title III does not specify the type of auxiliary aid that must be provided, but requires that individuals with disabilities be provided equal opportunity to obtain the same result as individuals without disabilities. For example, a restaurant does not have to provide a braille menu for sight-impaired customers but can instead provide an employee to read the menu aloud to the individual.

The general effective date for Title III is January 26, 1992, although certain provisions went into effect immediately upon the signing of the ADA on July 26, 1990:

- Provisions that deal with discrimination in the transportation areas by private

entities not primarily in the business of providing fixed route or demand transportation for individuals.
- Provisions that deal with discrimination in the transportation area by private entities whose business primarily involves the purchase or lease of new vehicles or who otherwise provide transportation to people (with the exception of automobiles, vans with less than eight seats, or over-the-road buses).

Unlike other provisions of the ADA, the remedies under Title III are enforced by the Attorney General or by private lawsuit. Remedies can include ordering alteration of a facility to make the facility accessible, ordering the business to provide auxiliary aids to individuals with disabilities, ordering the business to pay monetary damages to the aggrieved individual, and may assess civil penalties up to $50,000 for the first offense and $100,000 for subsequent violations. Punitive damages do not appear to be available under this title.

Compliance with Title III

The most dramatic and arguably the most costly change in the business practices of most employers will result from Title III of the ADA. Employers are required to ensure that their facilities and operations comply with the provisions of this section and may be required to invest in modifications to their facilities to insure compliance. Employers should be aware, however, that an investment in a barrier-free business environment may pay unseen dividends in such areas as increased patronage by the estimated 43 million to 45 million disabled individuals, and increased productivity and quality by disabled employees, as well as in other areas.

Title III prohibits discrimination that deprives individuals with disabilities the full and equal enjoyment of the goods, services, facilities, and accommodation by retail or service establishments that serve the general public; these businesses are required to provide individuals with disabilities an equal opportunity to obtain the same result as nondisabled individuals. Individuals with disabilities must be integrated, to the greatest extent possible, into the usual customer group and cannot be provided different services unless absolutely necessary. Employers should note, however, that the entire operation may not require modification. Only the areas that are open to the public or are common-use areas may require accessibility to individuals with disabilities.

STEP 1: Facility Evaluation

The initial step in achieving compliance with Title III is to evaluate your facility and operations. All areas of the facility should be examined and evaluated in terms of accessibility, including such outside areas as parking lots and outside walkways. Below is an accessibility evaluation checklist that may assist in such evaluation:

A. Parking Areas (Fig. 1)

- Does your facility have parking accommodations?
- Are international symbols designating parking spaces for individuals with disabilities clearly marked at the lot entrance?
- Is there an international symbol of accessibility above grade to identify reserved parking spaces?
- Does the designated reserved parking space not adjacent to accessible entrances have directional signage to accessible entrance or walkway?

B. Walks, Curbs, and Ramps (Fig. 2)

- Is there at least one marked accessible route from the parking area to the facility entrance?
- Is the international symbol for accessibility clearly displayed at entrances?
- Are primary entrances unlocked or are provisions made for a signaling device if the entrance must be locked for security purposes?
- Is the primary entrance accessible with a clear 32-inch opening?
- Is the curb area from the parking lot accessible?

C. Entrances, Corridors, and Stairs (Fig. 3)

- Is there a clear space of 12 inches on the pull side of the door for maneuvering?
- Is there a minimum of 60 x 60 inches of level space in front of the entrance for access?
- Are doors relatively easy to open (requiring no more than 8.5 lbs. of pressure for push or pull and 5 lbs. of pressure for sliding doors and interior doors)? Fire doors require a minimum of 15 lbs. of pressure.
- Are doormats stationary, flat or recessed, and less than one-half-inch high?
- Are handles, pulls, latches, locks, and other operating devices on accessible

Figure 1

Figure 2

Figure 3

doors easily grasped with one hand, and require no tight grasping, pinching, or twisting of the wrist to operate?

- Does approximately 48 inches, in addition to the width of inswinging door(s) space, exist between two doors in a series to allow backing and turning for a wheelchair to clear the inswinging door?
- Do automatic and/or power-assisted doors operate in a manner that does not present a hazard?
- Is there an accessible door adjacent to all revolving doors?
- Are thresholds at exterior doors flush with the floor or is there a maximum edge height of one-half inch?
- If a framed glass door is used, is the bottom at least 7.5 inches in height?
- Do all steps and stairs have

  1. Closed risers with uniform height (maximum 7 inches, minimum 4 inches)?
  2. Treads no less than 11 inches?
  3. Nosing that is not abrupt and does not project more than 1.5 inches?
  4. Treads with nonslip surface?

- Do handrails on side of all stairs extend at least 12 inches beyond the top riser and 12 inches plus the width of one tread beyond the bottom tread?
- Is handrail height 34–38 inches above the tread?
- Are grab bars 1¼ to 1½ inches in diameter and easy to grasp, and 1½ inches from the wall?
- Are all suspended stairs provided with sufficient warning devices?
- Do protruding and hanging objects (such as telephones, water fountains, and so on), with their leading edge 27 inches to 80 inches above the floor, protrude not more than 4 inches into the path of travel?
- Are there tactile designations at the top and bottom of stair runs?
- Are all interior floors nonslip? Is carpeting high-density, low-pile, and nonabsorbent?

Figure 4

D. Public Restrooms (Fig. 4)

- Is there an accessible restroom for each sex clearly marked with an international symbol?
- Is the restroom identified in braille or raised/incised characters located on the door or alongside of the door on the latch side no higher than 5'6" above the finished floor?
- Do restroom entrances have a clear opening of 32 inches?
- Is mirror mounted within 40 inches from the floor?
- Is the lavatory mounted at least 29 inches from the floor (measured from the bottom of the apron) for wheelchair clearance, the top of the rim being no greater than 34 inches maximum?
- Is the drain pipe at least 9 inches from the floor for toe clearance?
- Is insulation or protective covering used on bathroom hot-water pipes under lavatory to prevent burns to persons in wheelchairs?
- Is there clear floor space (30 x 48 inches) provided in front of the lavatory to allow the forward approach of a wheelchair?
- Are faucet controls of a push or lever type?
- Are restroom dispensers and accessories no higher than 40 inches from the floor to bottom of dispensers, within reach of a person seated in a wheelchair?
- Is at least one restroom stall available with a clear opening of 32 inches?
- Does the stall door swing out?
- Is the accessible toilet stall of the design to provide a handrail easily accessible to the bowl?
- Is the side approach a minimum depth of 56 inches and a width of 60 inches from wall-mount water closet? (Add 3 inches to the depth if the commode is floor-mounted).
- Is the front approach a minimum depth of 66 inches and a width of 36 to 48 inches for wall-mounted water closets? (Add 3 inches to length if commode is floor-mounted).

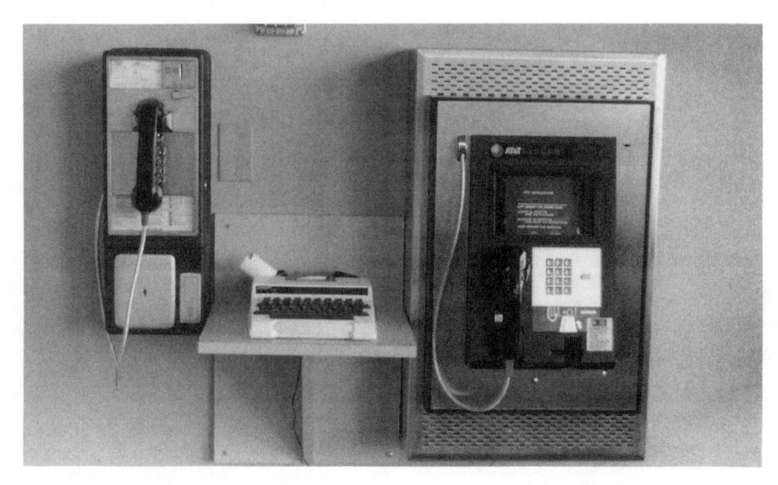

Figure 5

- Are toilet paper and seat cover dispensers located within easy reach of a person using the commode?
- Do toilet paper dispensers permit delivery of a continuous paper flow?
- Does the men's restroom have at least one stall-type or wall-hung urinal with elongated rim at a maximum of 17 inches above the floor?
- Is top of commode seat between 17 inches and 19 inches from the floor?
- Are there two grab bars (a 42-inch bar to the side and a 36-inch bar to the back) when stall is 60 inches wide and side transfer is necessary?
- Are grab bars 42 inches in length and located on both sides of the stall and 33 to 36 inches from floor? Are they capable of supporting a 250-lb. load?
- Are the flush controls hand-operated and mounted no more than 40 inches above the floor?
- Are flush controls operable with one hand and not requiring tight grasping, pinching, or twisting of the wrist?
- Does the stall door swing out with 32 inches clearance?
- When there is a privacy wall at the entrance, is there a minimum of 60 inches to allow clear floor space to allow for turning within the restroom (60 x 60 inches minimum)?

E. Public Telephones and Water Fountains (Fig. 5)

- If public telephones are provided, are phone dial and coin receiver accessible (48 inches high for forward approach or 54 inches high for parallel approach)?
- Is the phone cord at least 29 inches long?
- Does the telephone enclosure have a clear path width of at least 30 inches?
- Are phone directories usable at wheelchair level?
- Are operation directions available in braille and/or large print (recommended option)?

Figure 6

Figure 7

- Are telephones equipped with an amplifier available for the hearing impaired?
- In an alcove, is there clear floor space of 30 x 40 inches for parallel approach plus space for maneuvering?
- Is there a water fountain available a minimum of 27 inches high and 17 to 19 inches deep that can be utilized by a person in a wheelchair?
- Is the fountain controlled by an easily operated hand lever or push button?
- Are drinking cups provided when water fountain exceeds recommended height?

F. Meeting Rooms (Fig. 6)

- Are accessible meeting rooms available?
- Is the meeting room centrally located to prevent undue problem to the mobility impaired?
- Do hallways and corridors have a clearance of 36 inches with an occasional space allowance for turning and passing at intervals not exceeding 200 feet?
- Do the doors to meeting rooms have a clear opening of 32 inches?
- Do thresholds of interior doors have a maximum edge height of ½ inch?
- Are an amplifier and sound-system equipment available with individual or lavaliere microphones?

G. Restaurants (Fig. 7)

- Do entrances to food-service establishments have a door with a 32-inch clear opening, single-effort door pull, and negotiable thresholds (½ inch or less in height)?
- Are tables accessible with 30-inch width and 27-inch vertical clearance, and 19-inch depth under the table?

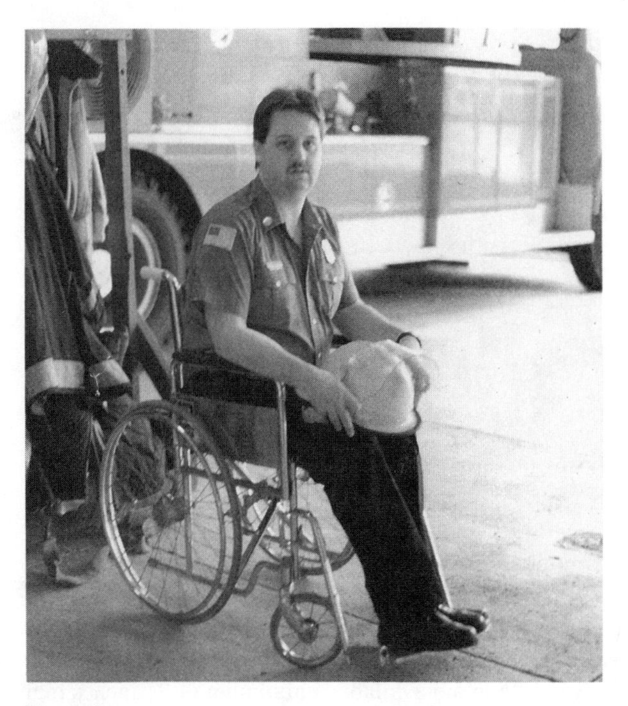

Figure 8

- Do tables have a 36-inch clearance between them?
- Are cafeteria/buffet lines accessible: at least 36 inches wide with adequate turning space at corners?
- Does the restaurant have menus in braille and large print?
- Is the restaurant staff able and willing to make reasonable accommodations (minor menu changes, reading menus, tray assistance)?
- Is the lounge accessible, including tables and aisles?

H. Guest Rooms

- Are guest rooms numbered in consecutive sequence (100, 102, 104, etc.), and are numbers raised for tactile identification?
- Are room keys available with a large fixed handle for easy handling?
- Do entry, bathroom, and closet doors have a clear opening of 32 inches with maximum threshold height of ½ inch?
- Is there a 36-inch minimum opening by at least one side of the bed?
- Are the telephones in rooms accessible from the bed?
- Are amplified telephones available in the guest rooms?
- Are rooms free of low-level wall-mounted protruding objects (such as televisions, hanging lamps, etc.)?
- Are light switches; heating, cooling, and drapery controls; and other similar

items accessible and placed so that they will allow forward or parallel approach?
- Are tactile directions available on controls?
- Are towel and closet racks located at a maximum height of 48 inches?
- Do guest rooms and bathrooms allow sufficient turning space for a wheelchair (preferable 60-inch diameter)?
- Are mirrors mounted within 40 inches of the floor?
- Is the lavatory mounted at least 29 inches from the floor (measured from the bottom of the apron), for wheelchair clearance, and is the drainpipe at least 9 inches high for toe clearance?
- Are televisions, telephone, and other appliances accessible?

I. Hazards and Emergency Procedures (Fig. 8)
- Has the hotel/motel staff received special instructions about the needs of persons with handicaps, particularly emergency procedures?
- Is the boundary between pedestrian and vehicle area marked with some type of tactile warning?
- Are standardized/textured surfaces for tactile warnings present for hazardous conditions (i.e., fountains, stairs, pools, floors, doors, and so on)?
- Are all glass panels in doors protected by a kick plate on the push side located within 7½ inches of the floor?
- Are all emergency exit doors clearly marked with a 32-inch clear opening and equipped with a crash (panic) bar?
- Are exit doors equipped with tactile symbols to designate location?
- Are doors leading to potentially dangerous areas identifiable to the touch by textured surface on the handle, knob, or pull?
- Are all audible alarms accompanied by simultaneous visual signals?

J. Elevators (Fig. 9)
- Does the facility have elevator(s)?
- Is an elevator required for accessibility to all levels of the facility?
- Is a visual as well as an audible signal used to identify direction of elevator travel (sound once for up and twice for down)?
- Are the accessible elevators on a normally used accessible route?
- Are call buttons in lobbies and halls located 42 inches above the floor with no obstructions?
- Are there raised, indented, or braille floor designations on both elevator jambs 60 inches from the floor?
- Does the elevator have inside dimensions of no less than 54 x 68 inches and a clear door opening of 32 inches, and can it accommodate a wheelchair?
- Does the elevator stop within ½ inch of floors on each level?
- Is the space between the floor and the elevator platform no greater than 1¼ inches?

Figure 9

- Are the elevator doors minimally equipped with an automatic bumper safety system (preferably electric eye)?
- Does the elevator interior have handrails mounted 34 to 36 inches above the floor?
- Are controls, call buttons, and alarm buttons 3/4 inch in diameter with braille and raised lettering to the left of the button?
- Is the elevator control panel located at a height no greater than 48 inches?[125]

In making the determination whether modification of an existing facility is "readily achievable," the covered employer should balance the overall size and type of the operation with the cost involved in making the modification. Some examples of architectural modifications to existing facilities that have been noted as not being required include such modifications as the addition of elevators, widening of entrance doors to smaller stores and offices where substantial structural changes would be required, and construction of new, wider walkways where the cost is great compared to the type and number of individuals with disabilities who may use the sidewalk. Covered employers are, however, encouraged to make a good faith effort in conducting the facility evaluation and making necessary modifications.

Covered employers should bear in mind that various requirements for new construction, partial renovations, and other types of construction are required under the ADA. These requirements are provided later in the Facility Modification section.

STEP 2: Evaluate Policies, Procedures, and Practices

A form of discrimination under Title III is the failure to make reasonable modifications in policies, procedures, and practices when modification is required to afford individuals with disabilities the same access to and the ability to use goods, services, facilities, privileges, and advantages provided to nondisabled individuals. Covered employers should evaluate all policies, practices, and procedures that may directly or indirectly affect individuals with disabilities in the acquisition of services to ensure compliance. Modification of current policies, procedures, or practices is not required if the employer can prove that the modification would be unreasonable or if the fundamental nature of what is being offered would be altered by the modification. For example, if a seeing-eye dog communicated with a blind individual by barking, a public accommodation at which complete silence was essential would not be discriminating if it failed to modify its no-dog policies to admit the seeing-eye dog.

The following are business practices that will be considered discriminatory under ADA:

- A retail grocery store refusing to serve customers who are blind or deaf.
- A restaurant requiring an individual with Down's syndrome to be seated at the counter, rather than at a table in the main dining area.
- A drug store refusing to accept personal checks without the customer showing a driver's license (an item that many individuals with disabilities do not possess).
- A movie theater not allowing people in wheelchairs to attend without an attendant or other person accompanying them.[126]

Step 3: Auxiliary Aids

If requested, covered employers are required to provide auxiliary aids needed by the individual with a disability. There is no requirement that the covered employer offer auxiliary aids to customers, clients, or other members of the public. Auxiliary aids can include a wide variety of equipment or services, such as interpreters for hearing-impaired individuals, taped text for visually impaired individuals, among other items.

Specifically addressed in Title III is the requirement for employers to provide auxiliary aids for any examinations or courses relating to applications, licensing, certification, or credentialing for secondary or postsecondary education, or professional or trade purposes. Additionally, these examinations or courses are required to be accessible to disabled individuals or alternative arrangements must be made for individuals with disabilities. Auxiliary aids need not be offered if they would create an undue burden or would fundamentally alter the particular examination or course.

The covered employer should prepare beforehand to anticipate the various types of auxiliary aids that could be requested. A prudent employer may wish to assemble a list of auxiliary aids—particularly specialized equipment—that are available within the local areas. Some potential sources include disabled individual organizations, state and local governmental agencies, and universities. Another exceptional source is the Resource Directory prepared by the EEOC, which includes the names, addresses, and telephone numbers of ADA Technical Assistance Centers in your state that could assist in the assembly of your auxiliary aids information.

Step 4: Alternative Methods of Accommodation

The ADA does not specify which auxiliary aids need to be provided in a given circumstance. It is the covered employer's choice to select the least expensive alternative so long as the accommodation is effective in meeting the needs of the disabled individual.

Again, preplanning and preparation will assist the employer in identifying alternative methods of accommodation that are less expensive while still meeting the needs of the disabled individual. Employers are encouraged to communicate with the disabled individual requesting an accommodation to ascertain the extent of the needed accommodation. Remember, the disabled individual is the expert in this area. Employers should discuss all potential accommodations with the disabled individuals and use their expertise in this area before making an accommodation.

Examples of alternative accommodations include the following:

- Restaurants are not required to furnish menus in braille for blind customers but may instead provide menus read aloud.
- Bookstores need not place all books on lower shelves so that they can be reached by individuals in wheelchairs, if bookstore personnel will retrieve books that are out of the customer's reach.[127]

Step 5: Evaluate Accommodation for Undue-Burden Exception

Covered employers may decline to provide auxiliary aids if it should cause an undue burden to the employer. An "undue burden" is defined as an accommodation causing "significant difficulty or expense."[128] Employers should be aware that this exception is very narrow and the burden of proof is on the employer. An undue burden is determined by examining and balancing four factors: the nature and cost of the auxiliary aid; the overall financial resources of the particular operation, including the size of the budget; the type and size of the particular operation; and the overall financial resources of the covered entity (i.e., the parent company).

Covered employers would be advised to analyze this exception closely before pursuing this exception. Many corporations do not wish to have their "books" examined in a public forum as would be the case if a covered employer was requested to justify such exception.

Step 6: Evaluate Accommodation for Safety and Health Threat

An employer may require that an individual not pose a direct threat to his or her own safety or health, as well as to the safety and health of others. This determination must be based on valid medical analysis or other objective evidence and cannot be based on stereotypes, assumptions, or conjecture. If the individual poses a direct threat to the safety or health of others and the employer cannot safeguard the other individuals through reasonable accommodation, the employer may be excused from accommodating the individual with a disability.

In determining whether an individual poses a direct threat to the health or safety of others, an assessment must be made as to the nature, duration, and severity of the risk of harm in addition to the probability that the potential injury or illness will occur. Additionally, an assessment is required to ascertain whether a reasonable modification of policies, practices, procedures, or other accommodations would mitigate the risk of harm. This assessment must be made using reasonable judgement based upon the most current medical knowledge or on the best available objective evidence.

For employers in the food related industries, the employer must consider whether there is a reasonable accommodation that will eliminate the risk of transmitting the disease through the handling of food. The diseases that fall within this category are summarized on the Department of Human Services list of contagious and infectious diseases. If the employer can accommodate the individual without posing an undue hardship, the employer must provide the accommodation. If the employer cannot accommodate the individual, the employer may refuse to hire the individual. For current employees, the employer may reassign the individual to a non-food handling position.

Employers will encounter this situation when confronted by infectious or contagious diseases. Any analysis in this area should start with the Center for Disease Control's list of infectious diseases. The employer must acquire the best and most current data available regarding the disease or illness and make a reasonable determination as to whether the disease or illness can be accommodated. The employer must assess the nature, duration, severity, and probability factors involved in the risk of harm and direct threat to others in making this assessment. Employers are encouraged whenever making such a determination to document each and every step in this analysis in preparation for potential litigation in the future.

Step 7: Evaluate Contracts and Leases

Covered employers should evaluate any and all rental agreements, leases, or other contractual arrangements to insure the facility meets the requirements of the ADA. Legal counsel should review all contract documents to insure that the appropriate party is informed of and bound to make the necessary facility modifications and accommodations.

Step 8: Evaluate for Tax Benefits

Last but not least, sources of funding to assist in the cost of modifying a workplace to achieve compliance should be explored. Several tax credit programs are available and many accommodations qualify for tax deductions.

TITLE IV: TELECOMMUNICATIONS

Title IV amends Title II of the Communication Act of 1934[129] mandate that telephone companies provide "telecommunication relay services in their service areas by July 26, 1993." Telecommunication relay services provide individuals with speech-related disabilities the ability to communicate with hearing individuals through the use of telecommunication devices like TDD systems or other nonvoice transmission devices.

Regulations governing the implementation of Title IV are to be issued by the Federal Communication Commission (known as the FCC) no later than July 26, 1992. These regulations are to establish the minimum standards, guidelines, and other requirements mandated under Title IV, in addition to establishing regulations requiring round-the-clock relay service operations, operator-maintained confidentiality of all messages, and rates for the use of the telecommunication relay systems that are equivalent to current voice-communication services.

Title IV requires that public service television announcements produced or funded in whole or part with federal funding include close captioning.

Compliance with Title IV

Given the narrow focus of Title IV on the telephone and television industries, these affected industries are advised to review the requirements with legal counsel or other knowledgeable sources.

The basic perimeters of any evaluation under Title IV should include

- Identifying whether your organization is covered and thus required to comply with Title IV and other provisions of the ADA;
- Identifying sources of assistance in acquiring the necessary equipment and expertise to comply with the requirements of Title IV;
- Establishing a plan of action for implementation in order to achieve compliance by the effective date;
- Managing and directing the compliance effort to achieve compliance by the effective date;
- Evaluating and auditing your program after compliance is achieved to insure ongoing compliance with this requirement.

TITLE V: MISCELLANEOUS PROVISIONS

Title V is a myriad of provisions addressing a wide assortment of related coverage under the ADA. First, Title V permits insurance providers to continue to underwrite insurance, to continue to use preexisting condition clauses, and to classify risks as long as consistent with state enacted laws. Title V also permits insurance carriers to provide bona-fide benefit plans based upon risk classifications but prohibits denial of health insurance coverage to an individual with a disability based solely on that person's disability.

Title V does not require special treatment in the area of health or other insurance for individuals with disabilities. An employer is permitted to offer insurance policies that limit coverage for a certain procedure or treatment even though this might have an adverse impact on the individual with a disability.[130] The employer or insurance provider may not, however, establish benefit plans as a subterfuge to evade the purposes of the ADA.[131]

Second, Title V provides that the ADA will not limit or invalidate other federal or state laws that provide equal or greater protections to individuals with disabilities. Additionally, the ADA does not preempt medical or safety standards established by Federal law or regulation, nor does it preempt state, county, or local public health laws. However, state and local governments and their agencies are subject to the provisions of the ADA, and courts may provide the same remedies (except punitive damages at this time) against state or local governments as any other public or private covered entity.

Third, Title V prohibits members, officers, and employees of Congress and its agencies from terminating, refusing to hire, or otherwise discriminating against individuals with disabilities. Congress did, however, enact special rules for the enforcement of the ADA provisions against itself. An individual with a disability who alleges discrimination against Congress or its agencies is limited to administrative relief and may not file a civil action against either the House or Senate. In the Senate, claims under the ADA are to be adjudicated before the Senate Select Committee on Ethics, and in the House the procedures established under the Fair Employment Practices Resolution are to be used.[132] Agencies such as the Architect of the Capitol are required to establish remedies and procedures for enforcement under the ADA. Nothing under Title V alters the enforcement procedures established by the General Accounting Office Personnel Act of 1980 or related regulations.

In an effort to minimize litigation under the ADA, Title V promotes the use of alternate dispute-resolution procedures to resolve conflicts under the ADA. As stated in Section 513: "Where appropriate and to the extent authorized by law, the use of alternate dispute resolution, including settlement negotiations, conciliation, fact-finding, mini-trials, and arbitration, is encouraged to resolve disputes under the ADA."[133] It is worth noting, however, that the use of alternate dispute resolution is voluntary and, if used, the same remedies must be available as provided under the Act. Typical arbitration clauses in collective-bargaining agreements and individual employment contracts calling for arbitration of disputes do not prevent individuals from pursuing their rights as provided under the ADA.

Last, but not least, Title V does not preclude or restrict the imposition of restrictions on smoking in places of employment.[134] Employers are free to impose or to refrain from imposing rules and regulations governing smoking in their workplaces.

Compliance with Title V

For virtually all employers, Title V does not mandate modification of current procedures, policies, and facilities as under Title I and other provisions of the ADA. Title V is titled appropriately in that this provision is a number of miscellaneous provisions to define the scope of coverage and to insure that the ADA did not preempt other laws and regulations already enacted to provide protections to individuals with disabilities.

Two provisions of which covered employers should take note is the use of alternate dispute resolution and the possibility of the existence of other laws and regulations in their state or city that may provide protections to individual with disabilities.

Employers are encouraged to use alternate dispute-resolution methods and procedures to resolve claims under the ADA. Use of alternate dispute-resolution procedures tend to be a more cost-effective alternative to litigation, normally reduce the potential of adverse publicity, and tend to be less stressful on the parties. Employers should also bear in mind that if the claimant is successful in an ADA action, the employer may be required to pay the cost of the claimant's attorney fees and other costs related to this litigation.

With the ADA's deferment to state and local laws that offer protections equal to or greater than the ADA to individuals with disabilities, a prudent employer should evaluate the state and local laws, regulations, and ordinances to insure compliance. The ADA has propelled the issue of disabled individual's rights and protections to the forefront, but many state and local governments have previously addressed these issues and enacted laws governing their particular jurisdictions. Employers should acquire these related laws and insure compliance in affected operations.

5

Employment Selection

QUALIFICATION STANDARDS

The ADA does not prohibit an employer from establishing job-related qualification standards, including such criteria as education, skills, work experience, and mental and physical standards necessary for job performance and health and safety. However, a disabled individual cannot be denied employment because of a failure to meet a particular "standard, test, or selection criteria," unless the employer can prove that the standard, test, or selection criteria

- is job-related for the position in question
- is consistent with business necessity
- cannot be modified to reasonably accommodate the disability in question.[135]

The ADA does not interfere with an employer's right to establish appropriate job qualifications to hire employees who can perform jobs effectively and safely. The ADA additionally does not interfere with the employer's ability to hire the most qualified individual for a particular job. The purpose of the ADA is to assure that individuals with disabilities are placed on the same level as other individuals and are not excluded simply because of their disability.

Qualification standards or selection criteria that screen out or tend to screen out an individual with a disability on the basis of disability, including such standards and procedures as education and work-experience requirements, physical and mental requirements, safety requirements, paper-and-pencil tests, physical or psychological tests, interview questions, and rating systems, must be job-related and consistent with business necessity.

An employer is not required to lower existing production or quality standards if the standard is uniformly applied to all applicants or employees. An employer must, however, consider whether the individual with a disability could meet the job-related standard or selection criteria with a reasonable accommodation. All hiring decisions must be based upon the individual with a disability's ability to perform only the essential functions of the job, with or without a reasonable accommodation.

The burden of proof to show that a particular standard or criteria is job-related and consistent with business necessity is placed upon the employer. If a qualification standard, test, or other selection criterion is used to screen out an individual with a disability, the standard, test, or criterion must be a legitimate measure of qualification for the specific job and not for a general class of jobs.

The ADA does not require that a qualification standard or selection criterion apply only to the essential functions of a job. A job related standard may evaluate or measure all functions of a particular job and the employer may continue to select and hire individuals who can perform all the functions of the job. It is only when an individual's disability prevents or impedes performance of marginal job functions that the ADA requires the employer to evaluate this individual's qualifications solely on his/her ability to perform the essential functions of the job, with or without reasonable accommodations.

Under the ADA, "if a test or other selection criterion excludes an individual with a disability because of the disability and does not relate to the essential functions of a job, it is not considered with business necessity."[136] This definition is to be interpreted the same under the ADA as under Section 504 of the Rehabilitation Act. However, the ADA standard may apply to an individual who is screened out by a selection procedure because of a disability, as well as to a class of persons. It is not necessary to make statistical comparisons between a group of individuals with disabilities and individuals who are not disabled in order to show that a person with a disability is screened out by a discriminatory selection standard.

PREPARING TO ACCOMMODATE

Although many accommodations can be accomplished with little or no cost, the decision as to which accommodation is best for the individual with a disability and is best for the operation is often difficult. Planning is the key to accomplishing the accommodation duty in the most effective and cost-effective manner. Below is a preplanning strategy to address the reasonable accommodation requirements.

Step 1: Education

Your entire management team should be educated in the requirements of the ADA. Specialized training should be offered in the particular areas that directly affect specific levels of your management team. Line supervisors, for example, should be educated in the procedures to follow when a current employee requests an accommodation.

Step 2 : Communications

In addition to the required posting, employers should encourage individuals with disabilities to discuss possible accommodations in confidence. A designated person or team can be formed to field requests for accommodation from current employees. Individuals requesting accommodations should be involved in every phase of the accommodation evaluation in order to draw upon their experience and expertise regarding accommodation of particular disabilities.

Step 3: Analyze the Job Task

The employer should determine the essential and nonessential function of the job in question and any barriers that exist in the work environment. A written job description is the recommended method of documenting this assessment of essential and nonessential functions. An analysis should be performed of the individual's abilities and limitations. The employer should identify the job tasks or work environment that limit the individual's effectiveness or prevent performance.

Step 5: Evaluate Current Technology

Because of significant advancements in technology, employers should investigate and assess new methods of accommodating individuals with disabilities. Additionally, with changing technology, the cost of many accommodating devices is significantly lower now than a few years ago. Employers should also explore the acquisition older models of accommodating devices that would serve the purpose of the accommodation but can be acquired at a lower price.

Step 6: Outside Assistance

Employers may want to contact applicable agencies and organizations who may offer ideas for providing reasonable accommodations. Employers may also explore the numerous publications that provide examples and ideas for accommodations. One exceptional publication is the Resource Directory published by the EEOC, there are also other governmental publications that can be acquired at little or no cost.

Step 7: Team Approach

A team approach to evaluating possible accommodations provides additional areas of expertise and experience to assess the situation. Particular team members who should be part of the evaluation team include the individual requesting the accommodation, the supervisor or area manager where the accommodation may be required, the personnel manager or human resource manager, and others with particular expertise or experience in related specialty areas.

Step 8: Determine the Cost

In determining the cost of a particular accommodation, the employer should explore all possible accommodations and assess the cost of each accommodation. All cost estimates should be documented and evaluated.

Step 9: Evaluate Exceptions

The undue burden or hardship exception should be evaluated. A cost/benefit analysis should be conducted to assess the cost of the accommodation. The cost of the accommodation should be assessed in relationship to the overall financial resources of the facility, the type of operation, overall resources of the covered entity, and other factors. All evaluations for this exception should be documented.

Step 10: Implement Accommodation

Upon agreement as to the type of accommodation and evaluation of the exception areas, the employer should implement the accommodation recommended by the evaluation team. Periodic evaluations of the accommodation should be conducted to ensure the effectiveness of the accommodation.

Step 11: Complaint Mechanism

To minimize the potential of ADA-related claims, the employer should establish a mechanism through which job applicants or employees who have been denied an accommodation, a job position, a promotion, or otherwise denied a potential benefit under the ADA will be given a reason, in writing, why the accommodation was not provided. Additionally, the employer may want to provide access to a knowledgeable team member where the individual could discuss the reasons for the denial of the accommodation.

In summation, documentation is essential in proving the employer's good faith in making or denying a reasonable accommodation. All phases of this evaluation process should be properly documented and such documentation maintained in a confidential and secure manner.

WORKERS' COMPENSATION CONSIDERATIONS

Employers should be aware that many employees injured on the job may be afforded protection under the ADA if the injury or illness meets the definition of a "qualified individual with a disability." The fact that an employee is awarded workers' compensation benefits does not automatically establish that the person is protected under the ADA. However, if the injured employee possesses a permanent mental or physical disability that substantially affects one or more life functions or is perceived as possessing a disability that affects a major life function, the employee may be afforded protection under the ADA in addition to receiving workers' compensation coverage.

The ADA allows an employer to take reasonable steps to avoid increased workers' compensation liability while protecting persons with disabilities against exclusion from jobs they can safely perform.

After making a conditional offer of employment, an employer may inquire about a person's workers' compensation history in a medical inquiry or medical examination that is required of all applicants in the same job category. However, an employer may not require an applicant to have a medical examination because a response to a medical inquiry (as opposed to results from a medical examination) discloses a previous on-the-job injury, unless all applicants in the same job category are required to take the physical examination.

The employer may use information from medical inquiries and examinations to

- verify employment history
- screen out applicants with a history of fraudulent workers' compensation claims
- provide information to state officials as required by state law regulating workers' compensation and "second injury" funds
- screen out individuals who would pose a "direct threat" to the health or safety of themselves or others, which could not be reduced to an acceptable level or eliminated by reasonable accommodation.

An employer may not base an employment decision on the speculation that an applicant may cause increased workers' compensation costs in the future. However, an employer may refuse to hire, or may discharge an individual who is not currently able to perform a job without posing a significant risk of substantial harm to the health or safety of the individual or others, if the risk cannot be eliminated or reduced by reasonable accommodation.

Employers should be aware that most injured employees who have received some percentage of disability rating should be able to qualify for protection under the ADA. Employees who return to work after a work related injury or illness with some percentage of permanency may require an accommodation to be able to perform their jobs. The ADA possesses no requirements that an employer establish a "light duty" or "restricted duty" program. Employers should be prepared to address accommodation requests by these employees.

For applicants, the employer must make the conditional offer of employment before conducting any medical examinations or inquiring as to the applicant's workers' compensation history. A prudent employer may wish to document the conditional offer of employment in order to safeguard against any questions of impropriety in this area.

QUALIFIED INDIVIDUALS WITH A DISABILITY

In assessing whether an individual is qualified for protection under the ADA, the employer must determine if the individual meets the exact definition of a "qualified individual with a disability." The following assessment can be used by employers to ascertain whether an individual qualifies for protection under the ADA:

Step 1: Does the individual possess a permanent mental or physical disability?

A "physical impairment" is defined by the ADA as "[a]ny physiological disorder, or condition, cosmetic disfigurement, or anatomical loss affecting one or more of the following body systems: neurological, musculoskeletal, special sense organs, respiratory (including speech organs), cardiovascular, reproductive, digestive, genito-urinary, hemic and lymphatic, skin, and endocrine."

A "mental impairment" is defined by the ADA as "[a]ny mental or psychological disorder, such as mental retardation, organic brain syndrome, emotional or mental illness, and specific learning disabilities."

Note: HIV and AIDS are considered physical impairments. Stress and depression may or may not be considered impairments, depending on whether these conditions result from a documented physiological or mental disorder.

Step 2: Does the physical or mental impairment substantially limit one or more major life activities?

Substantially limiting one or more life activities means an individual must be unable to perform, or be significantly limited in the ability to perform, an activity compared to an average person in the general population.

A major life activity is any activity that an average person can perform with little or no difficulty. Major life activities include such activities as walking, talking, seeing, and hearing, as well as a multitude of other activities.

Step 3: Does the individual possess a record of such impairment?

A record of impairment is any medical or other documentation reflecting the impairment.

Step 4: Did the employer or any representative or agent of the employer regard the individual as having an impairment?

If the employer treats the individual as having an impairment and the individual does not have an impairment or has an impairment that does not qualify for protection according to the above, the individual is qualified for protection because of the employer's attitude, perception, or treatment. Employers must show legitimate, nondiscriminatory reasons for their actions or their beliefs or fears may permit the individual to qualify for protection.

Step 5: Is the individual "associated with" an individual with a disability?

Employers should be aware that protection under the ADA is provided to individuals associated with individuals with disabilities. This "association" protection is extremely wide and extends to family members, individuals living together, and other associations.

In making this determination, the employer must be cautious about when in the employment process the evaluation is made and about the framing of the questions asked of the individual. The vast majority of the needed information in making the determination as to whether an individual is a "qualified individual with a disability" must be acquired from the individual him/herself.

FACILITY MODIFICATIONS

In evaluating reasonable accommodations of facilities, transportation, and other areas, several concepts and terms should be considered.

1. Readily Accessible and Usable

The term "readily accessible to and usable by" a qualified individual with a disability is intended to enable people with disabilities (including mobility, sensory, and cognitive impairments) to get to, enter, and use a facility. While the term does not necessarily require the accessibility to every part of every area of the facility, the term contemplates a high degree of convenient accessibility, entailing accessible entrances, usable bathrooms and water fountains, accessibility to public and common use areas, and access to the goods, services, programs, facilities, accommodations, and work areas available at the facility.[137]

2. Readily Achievable

Title III makes it unlawful for a covered entity not to make a public accommodation involving the removal of architectural and communication barriers from existing facilities and transportation systems "where such removal is readily achievable."[138] In determining whether an action is "readily achievable," the factors Title III considers include the following

(A) the nature and cost of the action needed under this Act;
(B) the overall financial resources of the facility or facilities involved in the action; the

number of persons employed at such facility; the effect on expenses and resources, or the impact otherwise of such action upon the operation of the facility;

(C) the overall financial resources of the covered entity; the overall size of the business of the covered entity with respect to the number of its employees; the number, type, and location of its facilities; and

(D) the type of operation or operations of the covered entity, including the composition, structure, and functions of the workforce of such entity; the geographic separateness, administrative or fiscal relationship of the facility or facilities in question to the covered entity.[139]

Employers should be aware that the burden of proving or disproving that an accommodation is readily achievable is on the employer and each situation is to be evaluated on a case-by-case basis. If removal of the barrier is not readily achievable, the ADA still requires the employer to make its goods, services, facilities, privileges, advantages, or accommodations available to the disabled through alternative methods as long as the alternative methods are readily achievable.

"Readily achievable" is different from "readily accessible" in that "readily achievable" is used in connection with accessibility requirements and the ease by which the individual with a disability can enter and use a facility. "Readily achievable" focuses on the operation of the business and the degree of difficulty or ease the employer would have in removing a barrier or obstacle.[140]

Disproportionality

If the cost of an alteration to a facility in order to achieve an accommodation, provide an auxiliary aid, create an accessible path of travel, or other modification is disproportionate in terms of the scope of operation or facility, the employer may not be required to make the accommodation. The burden of proving the disproportionality of the circumstances is on the employer. The key comparison to be made is between the cost and scope of the alteration and the cost and scope of the entire modification or alteration the employer is performing at the facility.

The Justice Department's regulations define disproportionality by providing that alterations made to provide an accessible path of travel to the altered area are presumed to be disproportionate to the overall alteration when the cost exceeds 20 percent of the cost of the alteration to the primary function area.[141]

Employers should evaluate the Justice Department's regulations disproportionate criteria prior to initiating construction when making any modifications to accessways, paths of travel, or other accommodations. Additionally, this criteria should be discussed with the architect or builder before initiating any major facility construction projects.

STRUCTURALLY IMPRACTICABLE

An exception to the requirement to make all new public accommodations and commercial facilities readily accessible and usable by individuals with disabilities is when it is "structurally impracticable" to perform such accommodation. This is a very narrow exception limited to such cases when a structure must be built on stilts because of the location in marshlands or over water.

If it is structurally impracticable to construct a facility accessible to individuals with disabilities, the employer should make the facility as accessible as possible. Failure to make a structure as accessible as possible when it is structurally impossible to accommodate individuals with disabilities would constitute discrimination.[142]

TAX CONSIDERATIONS

Compliance with the requirements of the ADA will typically cause the employer to incur some expense in modifying facilities, procedures, policies, and the like. In most circumstances, the cost of such compliance can be used to reduce taxes either as a deduction from gross income in the year of the cost or as a capital expenditure requiring depreciation over a number of tax years. The Internal Revenue Code provides that individuals, corporations, and other taxpayers can deduct ordinary and necessary expenses paid or incurred during the tax year in carrying on any trade or business.[143]

A special provision for the tax treatment of expenditures to remove architectural barriers under the ADA has been provided under Section 190 of the Internal Revenue Code. This section allows qualified expenditures to be deducted (up to a maximum of $15,000), rather than capitalized, for architectural or transportation barrier removal. Amounts in excess of $15,000 are considered capital expenses and constitute an adjustment under Internal Revenue Code Section 1016(A).[144]

Under Internal Revenue Code Section 44, tax credits are provided for certain costs related to making businesses accessible for disabled individuals. Under this section, an eligible small business (gross receipts under $1 million and fewer than thirty employees) may elect application of credit and will be allowed a non-refundable income tax credit equal to 50 percent of the amount of the cost of the accommodation for any taxable year that exceeds $250 and is less than $10,250. To qualify, the expenditure for the accommodation must be reasonable and necessary and result in the removal of a barrier, modification of service, purchase of necessary equipment, or other accommodation.

The Targeted Job Tax Credit program (known as "TJTC") provides credit to employers who hire members of certain target groups.[145] Among the target groups are those individuals who possess physical or mental disabilities that constitute a substantial handicap to employment and who are referred to the employer while receiving, or completing, vocational rehabilitation services. Under this program, the employer may elect credit against income tax of 40 percent of the first-year wages of the disabled individual up to $6,000. Employers should be aware that this program requires some paperwork and there are several specific procedures that must be followed. In most states, additional information regarding the TJTC program can be acquired through the state office of unemployment benefits or Job Service.

This review of possible tax benefits and credits to assist employers in making the necessary modifications in their operations and facilities is not all-inclusive. Employers are advised to discuss possible tax benefits and deductions with their accountant or other qualified individuals.

CLAIMS PROCEDURES

The most significant number of anticipated claims to be filed appear under Title I of the ADA. Title I is enforced by the EEOC under the same procedures used to enforce Title VII of the Civil Rights Act of 1964. Any job applicant or employee who believes he/she has been discriminated against by a covered employee on the basis of a disability has the right to file a charge with the EEOC.

The EEOC receives and investigates the charges of discrimination and seeks to resolve any discrimination found and/or obtain relief for the affected individual. If the negotiations or conciliation efforts are unsuccessful, the EEOC may file suit or issue a "right to sue" letter to the individual who filed the charge to permit the individual to pursue a private course of action.

The ADA encourages the use of alternate dispute-resolution methods in settling ADA-related claims. Accordingly, the EEOC encourages the use of informal negotiation or mediation efforts to settle claims against an employer. Such informal dispute resolution methods can be used provided that this methodology does not deprive the individual of any legal rights granted under the ADA.

An individual who feels he/she has been discriminated against can file a claim at the nearest EEOC office, or call 1-800-669-4000 (TDD) or 1-800-800-3302 (voice), or initiate a claim by mail. The employer or covered entity should receive notification of the claim within 10 days of the filing. The EEOC is provided 180 days to investigate the claim and initiate any negotiations or conciliation efforts if the charges are valid. If conciliation or negotiation is unsuccessful, the EEOC may file suit on behalf of the individual with a disability or grant a "right to sue" letter, which permits the individual to acquire private legal counsel and pursue the action in a court of law within 90 days from the issuance of this notice.

The time limit for filing a claim with the EEOC is 180 days from the date of the alleged discriminatory act. If there is a state or local fair-employment-practices agency, the time limit may be extended up to 300 days after the alleged discriminatory act.

When investigating a charge of discrimination, the EEOC will begin by notifying the employer of the charge within 10 days of the filing. The EEOC will review information provided by the individual with a disability (called the "charging party") and may request information from the employer. Some of the information that may be requested includes:

- specific information on the issues raised in the charge
- the identity of witnesses who can provide evidence about issues in the charge
- information about the business operations, employment process, and work-place
- payroll and personnel records.

The employer is permitted to submit additional oral or written information on its own behalf.

The EEOC will then review the information and may interview witnesses. The EEOC may request additional information at any time during the investigation and may request conference to gather additional information or to promote negotiations. The EEOC may dismiss the charge at any time during the investigation for specified reasons such as an untimely filing or lack or evidence.

Upon completion of the investigation, the EEOC will inform the parties of the preliminary findings and the parties are permitted to submit additional information if necessary. After the review of all additional information, the EEOC will send an official "Letter of Determination" to the parties stating whether or not reasonable cause has been found to believe discrimination has occurred. If the EEOC investigation finds no cause to believe discrimination has occurred, the EEOC will take no further action but will issue a "right to sue" notice to the individual to permit initiation of a private suit.

REMEDIES

With the passage of the Civil Rights Act of 1991, the original remedies initially provided under the ADA were modified. Damages for employment discrimination, whether intentional or by practice which has a discriminatory effect, may include hiring, reinstatement, promotion, back pay, front pay, reasonable accommodation, or other action that will make an individual "whole." Payment of attorneys' fees, expert witness fees, and court fees were still permitted and jury trials were allowed.

Compensatory and punitive damages were also made available where intentional discrimination is found. Damages may be available to compensate for actual monetary losses, for future monetary losses, for mental anguish, and for inconvenience. Punitive damages are also available if an employer acted with malice or reckless indifference. The total amount of punitive damages and compensatory damages for future monetary loss and emotional injury for each individual is limited, based upon the size of the employer.

NUMBER OF EMPLOYEES	DAMAGES WILL NOT EXCEED
15–100	$ 50,000
101–200	100,000
201–500	200,000
500 or more	300,000

Punitive damages are not available against state or local governments.

In situations involving reasonable accommodation, compensatory or punitive damages may not be awarded if the employer can demonstrate that "good faith" efforts were made to accommodate the individual with a disability.

Employers should be aware that there are no recordkeeping requirements mandated under the ADA as with other compliance-type programs. The first notice that the employer will have that allegations of discrimination have been made against his/her organization is when a claim is filed with the EEOC or other charges are brought as prescribed under the Act. As discusses further in the recommendations to achieve compliance in Chapter 6, employers are advised to document all aspects of their efforts to achieve compliance in order to prepare for any and all charges against their organization.

The ADA recommends alternate dispute-resolution procedures be utilized, where feasible, to minimize the litigation costs for disputed claims. Employers should be aware that the use of alternate dispute-resolution procedures, such as negotiations, conciliation, and mediation, does not reduce the duties required, nor does use of alternate dispute-resolution procedures reduce the potential penalties provided under the Act. Alternate dispute resolution does provide another forum through which to settle disputes outside of litigation and tends to be less formal and is far less costly.

The best defense for an employer is to comply with all applicable provisions under the ADA. By insuring that your organization does not discriminate in any way against individuals with disabilities you will thus avoid all claims of discrimination. Given the fact that claims under the ADA will be evaluated on a case-by-case basis, employers should be aware of the potential direct monetary penalties, indirect monetary costs such as attorney fees and costs, and efficacy losses that could result due to noncompliance.

6

Program Development to Insure Compliance

Employers are advised to preplan and prepare their organizations to achieve compliance with the ADA by the effective dates. Although there are no recordkeeping requirements mandated by the ADA, the following program recommends a substantial amount of documentation in order to prepare the employer to mount an appropriate and formidable defense if and when a claim of discrimination should ever be filed by an individual with a disability. Preparation and documentation will enable you to comply with the spirit and letter of the law under the ADA while also safeguarding your organization against the potential of penalties or other losses and costs that could arise for noncompliance with the ADA.

MANAGEMENT THEORY

The basic idea is to manage your ADA program in the same fashion as you would manage the other functions in your business, such as safety, quality control, and production. The first step is to plan your activities to achieve compliance. The second step is to organize your activities to achieve compliance in the most efficient and cost-effective manner. The third step is to direct the ADA activities in order to achieve compliance. And the last step is to control your ADA compliance program to insure that it is functioning appropriately, not only immediately after installation but for the long run.

A prudent employer should view the ADA compliance program as a long-term investment in the business. The requirements proscribed under the ADA are law and will not disappear if an employer "sticks his/her head in the sand" and disregards the requirements. Employers should marshall the resources, expertise, and experience within and outside their organization to design a functional and cost-effective program that meets the requirements of the ADA and can be incorporated into the current management system in an efficient manner. Employers should use the basic management principles that have been successful in the past for solving problems of production, personnel, and related opportunities to address and solve internal opportunities in achieving compliance with the ADA.

PROGRAM STRATEGY

The strategy behind the development of the following ADA compliance program is two-fold: first, to achieve compliance with all phases and requirements mandated by the ADA, and second, to prepare the employer successfully to face a challenge or claim brought against the employer under the ADA.

The ADA does not require an affirmative action program nor does it mandate recordkeeping requirements of any kind. Thus, an employer may be provided no notice of potential liabilities that exist in the workplace until after a claim or charge has been filed against the organization. Upon the filing of a claim or charge, the employer is immediately placed on the defensive with minimal knowledge of the alleged incident and shouldering the burden of disproving the charge of discrimination. Additionally, employers may be called upon to attempt to justify actions taken up to six months in the past or to justify decisions for such inactions as failure to provide an accommodation. Without documentation and exact knowledge of circumstances, decision-making processes, and other facts, the development of any defense is tenuous at best. This program should enable an employer to prepare his/her organization to comply and, if a claim or charge should arise, to mount a formidable defense accurately and cost-effectively.

PROGRAM DEVELOPMENT

All covered employers should begin immediately to insure compliance with the Americans with Disabilities Act by the target dates. A general outline of the key areas to be considered when developing your plan of action are as follows:

1. Acquire and read the entire Americans with Disabilities Act. Acquire and review the rules and interpretations provided by the EEOC, the Department of Labor, and the Department of Federal Contract Compliance. Acquire the Health and Human Services List of Communicable Diseases. Keep abreast with governmental publications and case law as published. It may be prudent to have your organization's counsel or designated agency representative review and identify pertinent issues.
2. Educate and prepare your organizational hierarchy. Explain in detail the requirements of the ADA and the limited perimeters of the "undue hardship" and "safety or health" exceptions. Ensure complete and total under-

standing regarding the ADA. Communicate the philosophy and express the organization's commitment to achievement of the goals and objectives of the ADA.

3. Acquire needed funding to make the necessary accommodations and acquire the auxiliary aids. If necessary, search for outside agency funding and assistance. Review possible tax incentives available with appropriate department or agency.
4. Designate individual(s) (either an employee or consultant) well versed on the requirements of the ADA or establish an advisory group to serve as the ADA "expert" within your organization.
5. Establish a relationship with organizations serving individuals with disabilities for recruiting, advice, or other purposes.
6. Analyze your operations and identify applicable areas, practices, policies, procedures, and the like, requiring modification. Remember to include all public areas, parking lots, access ways, and all equipment. Document this analysis in detail.
7. Develop a written plan of action for each required area under the ADA. Set completion dates for each phase of your compliance plan in accordance with the mandated target date.
8. Develop and publish a written organizational policy incorporating all of the provisions of the ADA.
9. Review and, where applicable, renegotiate collective bargaining agreements, employment agency contracts, referral contracts, and other applicable contractual arrangements. Document any and all modifications.
10. Acquire the posting information and make certain this document is appropriately posted within your facility. Develop and place notices of ADA compliance on all applications, medical reports, and other appropriate documents.
11. Develop an employee and applicant self-identification program and communication system to permit employees and applicants to identify themselves as qualified individuals with disabilities and communicate the limitations of their disability. This program should be in writing and available for review by employees.
12. Implement your plan of action.
13. Review and modify selection policies and procedures including, but not limited to, the following:

    - interviewing procedures
    - selection criteria
    - physical and psychological testing procedures
    - alcohol and controlled substance testing programs
    - application forms
    - medical forms

- filing procedures
- disability and retirement plans
- medical examination policies and procedures
- physical and agility testing
- other applicable policies and procedures.

Develop procedures to ensure confidentiality of medical records. All new procedures or modifications should be documented.

14. Develop a written offer of employment form that conditions the offer of employment upon appropriate nondiscretion evaluations. This conditional offer of employment must be provided prior to all procedures except drug testing.
15. Review all current job descriptions and identify the essential functions for each position. Develop a *written job description* for each and every job in your organization. Remember, the *written job description* is evidence of the "essential functions" of your jobs and is your first line of defense.
16. Review and modify your personnel and medical procedures and policies. Maintain all medical files separately and confidentially. Address the option of a separate entity to conduct medical review.
17. Develop a list of approved questions to be catalyzed by individuals who will be conducting interviews or other evaluations. Insure all possible discriminations statements or questions are evaluated.
18. Plan and complete all physical accommodations to your workplace. Remember to analyze your complete work environment and the entire surrounding areas including parking lots, access ways, doors, water fountains, restrooms, and the like. Document all physical accommodations made to the workplace. Provide documentation of all bids, reviews, and so on for any accommodation not made due to undue hardship.
19. Document all accommodations requested by job applicants or current employees. Document the accommodation provided or, if unable to accommodate, the reason for the failure to accommodate.
20. Analyze your workplace for the need for possible "auxiliary aids" and other accommodation devices. Prepare a list of vendors and services to be able to acquire all possible "auxiliary aid" within a reasonable time. Maintain documentation of all auxiliary aids requested and provided.
21. If the health or safety exception is relied upon for employment decisions or other situations, the safety director or other individual making this determination should document all reasonable accommodations explored and all other information used to make this determination.
22. If the undue hardship or burden exceptions are to be used, all financial records, workforce analyses, and other information used to make this decision should be documented and secured for later viewing.
23. Educate and train all levels of management within your organizational

structure. Remember, if members of your organizational team discriminate against a qualified individual with a disability, your organization will be responsible for their actions. Develop oversight mechanisms to ensure compliance.

24. Develop mechanism to encourage employees to come forward in confidence and discuss their disabilities.
25. Evaluate and analyze your employee assistance programs, restricted duty or light duty programs, and other related programs. Organizations should address and plan for such situations as permanent light-duty positions in advance.
26. If necessary, enter into negotiations with any labor organizations to reopen or otherwise modify collective-bargaining agreements to insure compliance with the provisions of the ADA. Evaluate all insurance plans, retirement plans, contracts with employment agencies, or other contractual arrangements to insure compliance with the ADA. Documentation of any agreement should be included in the written contract.
27. Develop a written evaluation or audit instrument in order to properly gauge your compliance efforts. Designate specific individual(s) responsible for the audit and corrective actions. Establish a schedule for conducting your ADA audit. Document the results of your audit.

Prudent organizations should evaluate their program on at least a quarterly basis for the first two to three years to insure compliance.

PROGRAM TRAINING

Training and education of the entire management team, from the board of directors to the newest first line supervisor, is essential in insuring compliance with the ADA. The recommended methods of training are the specialized training programs providing an overview of the ADA and the areas that directly impact the particular management team members (i.e. specialized interview training for personnel).

Training and education programs should include classroom and hands-on training if possible. Management team members should be permitted to ask pertinent questions regarding their particular circumstances and a knowledgeable individual should be present to answer these questions. Audiovisual aids, role playing, and other mechanisms should be used to enhance training and education programs.

AUXILIARY AIDS

With the numerous possibilities of auxiliary aids and services that might be requested, it is often not cost-effective for an employer to purchase an equipment-type auxiliary aid for a single-use situation. Employers may want to conduct a survey of the organizations, agencies, and other sources who may possess equipment-related auxiliary aids beforehand and compile a list of the location, rental price (if any), and other information regarding the auxiliary aid. with this information source in hand, if a particular auxiliary aid is requested, the employer can readily acquire the auxiliary aid with minimal expenditure of time and effort.

Employers should also keep in mind that alternate methods of accommodating a request for an auxiliary aid may be utilized so long as the auxiliary aid is as effective as the requested aid. Employers are encouraged to discuss the requested auxiliary aid with the individual with a disability and acquire possible alternatives to a specific requested aid.

FACILITY MODIFICATIONS

A common myth that should be dispelled is that the employer is required to modify the entire facility to make all areas accessible to individuals with disabilities. Common-use areas, areas open to the public, and other related areas should be modified and other accommodations within the actual operations area must be accommodated only when an employee with a disability requests such accommodation.

When confronted with a modification situation, the employer should identify the barrier and identify all possible accommodations. (Discussions with the individual with a disability, the supervisor, and other competent personnel should provide the perimeters of the barrier and possible accommodations). The reasonableness, cost, effect on the workforce or process, and so on, of each possible accommodation should be explored and documented. The undue hardship and health or safety exceptions should be analyzed for applicability. The selection process for the accommodation should include the individual with a disability and other appropriate management team members. Upon selection of the accommodation, the modification should be implemented and monitored for effectiveness.

PROGRAM MANAGEMENT

In order to properly manage an effective ADA compliance program, the organization should designate an individual or individuals to be directly responsible for this program and these individuals should be held accountable for the implementation and maintenance of this program. The organization must be committed from the top down to achieving compliance with the ADA and all necessary resources should be provided in the achievement of this directive. A policy or directive should outline the management group's commitment to creating a nondiscriminatory workplace for individuals with disabilities.

The individual(s) selected to manage this program should be provided with all of the necessary "tools" and resources to implement and manage this program. The individual(s) should acquire all necessary education and training in order to manage this program adequately and should be held accountable to the management team for achieving the objectives of this program.

PROGRAM AUDIT

In order to evaluate the effectiveness of your program and to identify deficiencies for immediate corrective action, a written audit should be conducted at least quarterly during the initial implementation phase of the compliance program. This written audit should identify all goals or objectives of the program in addition to providing a detailed evaluation of each and every element of the compliance program. All written audits should be maintained for a period of at least ten years in a secure location.

The written audit evaluation should be conducted by a team of management team members, employees, and others, as applicable, to insure impartiality. All deficiencies should be identified and noted. All corrective actions should be discussed and the appropriate team member required to identify the necessary actions to be taken to make the correction and provide a target date for the completion of the appropriate action. The responsible team member should be held accountable for the achievement of the necessary corrective action within the specified time frame.

7

Questions and Answers

EMPLOYMENT

Q: What employers are covered by the Americans with Disabilities Act (ADA), and when is the coverage effective?

A: The employment provisions apply to private employers, state and local governments, employment agencies, and labor unions. Employers with 25 or more employees will be covered starting July 26, 1992, when the employment provisions go into effect. Employers with 15 or more employees will be covered two years later, beginning July 26, 1994.

Q: What practices and activities are covered by the employment nondiscrimination requirements?

A: The ADA prohibits discrimination in all employment practices, including job application procedures, hiring, firing, advancement, compensation, training, and other terms, conditions, and privileges of employment. It applies to recruitment, advertising, tenure, layoff, leave, fringe benefits, and all other employment-related activities.

Q: Who is protected against employment discrimination?

A: Employment discrimination is prohibited against "qualified individuals with disabilities." Persons discriminated against because they have a known association or relationship with a disabled individual are protected also. The ADA defines an "individual with a disability" as a person who has a physical or mental impairment that substantially limits one or more major life activities, who has a record of such an impairment, or who is regarded as having such an impairment.

The first part of the definition makes clear that the ADA applies to persons who have substantial, as distinct from minor, impairments, and that these must be impairments that limit major life activities such as seeing, hearing, speaking, walking, breathing, performing manual tasks, learning, caring for oneself, and working. An individual with epilepsy, paralysis, a substantial hearing or visual impairment, mental retardation, or a learning disability would be covered, but someone with a minor, nonchronic condition of short duration—a sprain, infection, or broken limb—generally would not.

The second part of the definition would include a person with a history of cancer currently in remission or a person with a history of mental illness.

The third part of the definition protects those who are regarded and treated as though they have a substantially limiting disability, even though they may not have such an impairment. For example, this provision would protect a severely disfigured qualified individual from being denied employment because an employer feared the "negative reactions" of others.

Q: Who is a "qualified individual with a disability"?

A: A qualified individual with a disability is a person who meets legitimate skill, experience, education, or other requirements of an employment position that he or she holds or seeks, and who can perform the "essential functions" of the position with or without reasonable accommodation. Requiring that he or she be able to perform "essential" functions assures that the individual will not be considered unqualified simply because of an inability to perform marginal or incidental job functions. If the person is qualified to perform essential job functions except for limitations caused by a disability, the employer must consider whether that person could perform these functions with a reasonable accommodation. A written job description that has been prepared in advance of advertising or interviewing applicants for a job will be considered as evidence, although not necessarily conclusive evidence, of the essential functions of the job.

Q: Does an employer have to give preference to a qualified applicant with a disability over other applicants?

A: No. An employer is free to select the most qualified applicant available and to make decisions based on reasons unrelated to the existence or consequence of a disability. For example, if two persons apply for a job as a typist, one a person with a disability who accurately types 50 words per minute, the other a person without a disability who accurately types 75 words per minute, the employer may hire the applicant with the higher typing speed, if typing speed is required for successful performance of the job.

Q: What is "reasonable accommodation"?

A: Reasonable accommodation is any modification or adjustment to a job or the work environment that will enable a qualified applicant or employee with a disability to perform essential job functions. Reasonable accommodation also includes adjustments to assure that a qualified individual with a disability has the same rights and privileges in employment as nondisabled employees.

Q: What kinds of actions are required to reasonably accommodate applicants and employees?

A: Examples of reasonable accommodation include making existing facilities used by employees readily accessible to and usable by an individual with a disability; restructuring a job; modifying work schedules; acquiring or modifying equipment; providing qualified readers or interpreters; or appropriately modifying examinations, training, or other programs. Reasonable accommodation also may include reassigning a current employee to a vacant position for which he or she is qualified, if that person becomes disabled and is unable to do the original job. However, there is no obligation to find a position for an applicant who is not qualified for the position sought. Employers are not required to lower quality or quantity standards in order to make an accommodation, nor are they obligated to provide personal use items such as glasses or hearing aids.

The decision as to the appropriate accommodation must be based on the particular facts of each case. In selecting the particular type of accommodation to provide, the principal test is the effectiveness, i.e., whether the accommodation will enable the person with a disability to do the job in question.

Q: Must employers be familiar with the many diverse types of disabilities to know whether or how to make a reasonable accommodation?

A: No. An employer is only required to accommodate a "known" disability in an applicant or employee. The requirement generally will be triggered by a request from an individual with a disability, who frequently can suggest an appropriate accommodation. Accommodations must be made on an individual basis, because the nature and extent of a disabling condition and the requirements of the job will very in each case. If the individual does not request an accommodation, the employer is not obligated to provide one. If a disabled person requests, but cannot suggest, an appropriate accommodation, the individual and employer should work together to identify one. In addition, many public and private resources can provide assistance without cost.

Q: What are the limitations on the obligation to make accommodation?

A: The disabled individual requiring the accommodation must be otherwise qualified, and the disability must be known to the employer. In addition, an employer is not required to make an accommodation if it would impose an "undue hardship" on the operation of the employer's business. "Undue hardship" is defined as "an action requiring significant difficulty or expense" when considered in light of a number of factors. These factors include the nature and cost of the accommodation in relation to the size, resources, nature, and structure of the employer's operation. Where the facility making the accommodation is part of a larger entity, the structure and overall resources of the larger organization and the financial and administrative relationship of the facility to the larger organization would be considered. In general, a larger employer would be expected to make accommodations requiring greater effort or expense than would be required of a smaller employer.

Q: Must an employer modify existing facilities to make them accessible?

A: An employer may be required to modify facilities to enable an individual to perform essential job functions and to have equal opportunity to participate in other employment-related activities. For example, if an employee lounge is in a location that is inaccessible to a person using a wheelchair, the place might be modified or relocated, or comparable facilities might be provided in a location that would enable the individual to take a break with coworkers.

Q: May an employer inquire as to whether a prospective employee is disabled?

A: An employer may not make a pre-employment inquiry on an application form or in an interview as to whether, or to what extent, an individual is disabled. The employer may ask a job applicant whether he or she can perform particular job functions. If the applicant has a disability known to the employer, the employer may ask how he or she can perform job functions that the employer considers difficult or impossible to perform because of the disability, and whether an accommodation would be needed. A job offer may be conditioned on the results of a medical examination, provided that the examination is required for all entering employees in the same job category regardless of disability, and that information obtained is handled according to confidentiality requirements specified in the Act. After an employee enters on duty, all medical examinations and inquiries must be job-related and necessary for the conduct of the employer's business. These provisions of the law are intended to prevent the employer from basing hiring and employment decisions on unfounded assumptions about the effects of a disability.

Q: Does the ADA take safety issues into account?

A: Yes. The ADA expressly permits employers to establish qualification standards that will exclude individuals who pose a direct threat—i.e., a significant risk—to the health and safety of others, if that risk cannot be lowered to an acceptable level by reasonable accommodation. However, an employer may not simply assume that a threat exists; the employer must establish through objective, medically supportable methods that there is genuine risk that substantial harm could occur in the workplace. By requiring employers to make individualized judgments based on reliable medical evidence rather than on generalizations, ignorance, fear, patronizing attitudes, or stereotypes, the ADA recognizes the need to balance the interests of people with disabilities against the legitimate interests of employers in maintaining a safe workplace.

Q: Can an employer refuse to hire an applicant or fire a current employee who is illegally using drugs?

A: Yes. Individuals who currently engage in the illegal use of drugs are specifically excluded from the definition of a "qualified individual with a disability" protected by the ADA when an action is taken on the basis of their drug use.

Q: Is testing for illegal drugs permissible under the ADA?

A: Yes. A test for illegal drugs is not considered a medical examination under the ADA; therefore, employers may conduct such testing of applicants or employees and make employment decisions based on the results. The ADA does not encourage, prohibit, or authorize drug tests.

Q: Are people with AIDS covered by the ADA?

A: Yes. The legislative history indicates that Congress intended the ADA to protect persons with AIDS and HIV disease from discrimination.

Q: How does the ADA recognize public health concerns?

A: No provision in the ADA is intended to supplant the role of public health authorities in protecting the community from legitimate health threats. The ADA recognizes the need to strike a balance between the right of a disabled person to be free from discrimination based on unfounded fear and the right of the public to be protected.

Q: What is discrimination based on "relationship or association"?

A: The ADA prohibits discrimination based on relationship or association in order to protect individuals from actions based on unfounded assumptions that their relationship to a person with a disability would affect their job performance, and from actions caused by bias or misinformation concerning certain disabilities. For example, this provision would protect a person with a disabled spouse from being denied employment because of an employer's unfounded assumption that the applicant would use excessive leave to care for the spouse. It also would protect an individual who does volunteer work for people with AIDS from a discriminatory employment action motivated by that relationship or association.

Q: Will the ADA increase litigation burdens on employers?

A: Some litigation is inevitable. However, employers who use the period prior to the effective date of employment coverage to adjust their policies and practices to conform to ADA requirements will be much less likely to have serious litigation concerns. In drafting the ADA, Congress relied heavily on the language of the Rehabilitation Act of 1973 and its implementing regulations. There is already an extensive body of law interpreting the requirements of that Act to which employers can turn for guidance on their ADA obligations. The Equal Employment Opportunity Commission will issue specific regulatory guidance one year before the ADA's employment provisions take effect, publish a technical assistance manual with guidance on how to comply, and provide other assistance to help employers meet ADA requirements. Equal employment opportunity for people with disabilities will be achieved most quickly and effectively through widespread voluntary compliance with the law, rather than through reliance on litigation to enforce compliance.

Q: How will the employment provisions be enforced?

A: The employment provisions of the ADA will be enforced under the same procedures now applicable to race, sex, national origin, and religious discrimination under Title VII of the Civil Rights Act of 1964. Complaints regarding actions that occur after July 26, 1992, may be filed with the Equal Employment Opportunity Commission or designated state human rights agencies. Available remedies will include hiring, reinstatement, back pay, and court orders to stop discrimination.

PUBLIC ACCOMMODATIONS

Q: What are public accommodations?

A: Public accommodations are private entities that affect commerce. The ADA public accommodations requirements extend, therefore, to a wide range of entities, such as restaurants, hotels, theaters, doctors' offices, pharmacies, retail stores, museums, libraries, parks, private schools, and day care centers. Private clubs and religious organizations are exempt from the ADA's requirements for public accommodations.

Q: Will the ADA have any effect on the eligibility criteria used by public accommodations to determine who may receive services?

A: Yes. If a criterion screens out or tends to screen out individuals with disabilities, it may only be used if necessary for the provision of the services. For instance, it would be a violation for a retail store to have a rule excluding all deaf persons from entering the premises, or for a movie theater to exclude all individuals with cerebral palsy. More subtle forms of discrimination are also prohibited. For example, requiring presentation of a driver's license as the sole acceptable means of identification for purposes of paying by check could constitute discrimination against individuals with vision impairments. This would be true if such individuals are ineligible to receive licenses and the use of an alternative means of identification is feasible.

Q: Does the ADA allow public accommodations to take safety factors into consideration in providing services to individuals with disabilities?

A: The ADA expressly provides that a public accommodation may exclude an individual, if that individual poses a direct threat to the health or safety of others that cannot be mitigated by appropriate modifications in the public accommodation's policies or procedures, or by the provision of auxiliary aids. A public accommodation will be permitted to establish objective safety criteria for the operation of its business; however, any safety standard must be based on objective requirements rather than stereotypes or generalizations about the ability of persons with disabilities to participate in an activity.

Q: Are there any limits on the kinds of modifications in policies, practices, and procedures required by the ADA?

A: Yes. The ADA does not require modifications that would fundamentally alter the nature of the services provided by the public accommodation. For example, it would not be discriminatory for a physician specialist who treats only burn patients to refer a deaf individual to another physician for treatment of a broken limb or respiratory ailment. To require a physician to accept patients outside of his or her specialty would fundamentally alter the nature of the medical practice.

Q: What kinds of auxiliary aids and services are required to ensure effective communication with individuals with hearing or vision impairments?

A: Appropriate auxiliary aids and services may include services and devices such as qualified interpreters, assistive listening devices, notetakers, and written materials for individuals with hearing impairments; and qualified readers, taped texts, and Braille or large-print materials for individuals with vision impairments.

Q: Are there any limitations on the ADA's auxiliary aids requirements?

A: Yes. The ADA does not require the provision of any auxiliary aid that would result in an undue burden or in a fundamental alteration in the nature of the goods or services provided by a public accommodation. However, the public accommodation is not relieved from the duty to furnish an alternative auxiliary aid, if available, that would not result in a fundamental alteration or undue burden. Both of these limitations are derived from existing regulations and case law under section 504 and are to be determined on a case-by-case basis.

Q: Will restaurants be required to have Braille menus?

A: No, not if waiters or other employees are made available to read the menu to a blind customer.

Q: Will a clothing store be required to have Braille price tags?

A: No. Sales personnel could provide price information orally upon request.

Q: Will a bookstore be required to maintain a sign language interpreter on its staff in order to communicate with deaf customers?

A: No, not if employees communicate by pen and notepad when necessary.

Q: Are there any limitations on the ADA's barrier removal requirements for existing facilities?

A: Yes. Barrier removal need only be accomplished when it is "readily achievable" to do so.

Q: What does the term "readily achievable" mean?

A: It means "easily accomplishable and able to be carried out without much difficulty or expense."

Q: What are examples of the types of modifications that would be readily achievable in most cases?

A: Examples include the simple ramping of a few steps, the installation of grab bars where only routine reinforcement of the wall is required, the lowering of telephones, and similar modest adjustments.

Q: Will businesses need to rearrange furniture and display racks?

A: Possibly. For example, restaurants may need to rearrange tables and department stores may need to adjust their layout of racks and shelves in order to permit wheelchair access.

Q: Will businesses need to install elevators?

A: Businesses are not required to retrofit their facilities to install elevators unless such installation is readily achievable, which is unlikely in most cases.

Q: When barrier removal is not readily achievable, what kinds of alternative steps are required by the ADA?

A: Alternatives may include such measures as in-store assistance for removing articles from high shelves, home delivery of groceries, or coming to the door to receive or return dry cleaning.

Q: Must alternative steps be taken without regard to cost?

A: No; only readily achievable alternative steps must be undertaken.

Q: How is "readily achievable" determined in a multi-site business?

A: In determining whether an action to make a public accommodation accessible would be "readily achievable," the overall size of the parent corporation or entity is only one factor to be considered. The ADA also permits consideration of the financial resources of the particular facility or facilities involved and the administrative or fiscal relationship of the facility or facilities to the parent entity.

Q: Who has responsibility for removing barriers in a shopping mall, the landlord who owns the mall or the tenant who leases the store?

A: Legal responsibility for removing barriers depends upon who has legal authority to make alterations, which is generally determined by the contractual agreement between the landlord and tenant. In most cases the landlord will have full control over common areas.

Q: What does the ADA require in new construction?

A: The ADA requires that all new construction of places of public accommodation, as well as of "commercial facilities" such as office buildings, be accessible. Elevators are generally not required in facilities under three stories or with fewer than 3,000 square feet per floor, unless the building is a shopping center, mall, or professional office of a health care provider.

Q: Is it expensive to make all newly constructed public accommodations and commercial facilities accessible?

A: The cost of incorporating accessibility features in new construction is less than one percent of construction costs. This is a small price in relation to future economic benefits to be derived from full accessibility, such as increased employment and consumer spending and decreased welfare dependency.

Q: Must every feature of a new facility be accessible?

A: No, only a reasonable number of elements such as parking spaces and bathrooms must be made accessible in order for a facility to be "readily accessible." Moreover, mechanical areas, such as catwalks and fan rooms, to which access is required only for purposes of maintenance and repairs, might not need to be physically accessible if the essential functions of the work performed in those areas require physical mobility.

Q: What are the ADA requirements for altering facilities?

A: All alterations that could affect the usability of a facility must be made in an accessible manner to the maximum extent feasible. For example, if during renovations a doorway is being relocated, the new doorway must be wide enough to meet the new construction standard for accessibility. When alterations are made to a primary function area, such as the lobby of a bank or the dining area of a cafeteria, an accessible path of travel to the altered area must also be provided. The bathrooms, telephones, and drinking fountains serving that area must also be made accessible. These additional accessibility alterations are only required to the extent that the added accessibility costs are not disproportionate to the overall cost of the alterations. Elevators are generally not required in facilities under three stories or with fewer than 3000 square feet per floor, unless the building is a shopping center, mall, or professional office of a health care provider.

Q: Does the ADA permit a disabled person to sue a business when that individual believes that discrimination is about to occur, or must the individual wait for the discrimination to occur?

A: The ADA public accommodations provisions permit an individual to allege discrimination based on a disabled person's reasonable belief that discrimination is about to occur. This provision allows a person who uses a wheelchair to challenge the planned construction of a new place of public accommodation, such as a shopping mall, that would not be accessible to wheelchair users. The resolution of such challenges prior to the construction of an inaccessible facility would enable any necessary remedial measures to be incorporated in the building at the planning stage, when such changes would be relatively inexpensive.

Q: How does the ADA affect existing state and local building codes?

A: Existing codes remain in effect. The ADA allows the Attorney General to certify that a state law, local building code, or similar ordinance that establishes accessibility requirements meets or exceeds the minimum accessibility requirements for public accommodations and commercial facilities. Any state or local government may apply for certification of its code or ordinance. The Attorney General can certify a code or ordinance only after prior notice and a public hearing at which interested people, including individuals with disabilities, are provided an opportunity to testify against the certification.

Q: What is the effect of certification of a state or local code or ordinance?

A: Certification can be advantageous if an entity has constructed or altered a facility according to a certified code or ordinance. If some one later brings an enforcement proceeding against the entity, the certification is considered "rebuttable evidence" that the state law or local ordinance meets or exceeds the minimum requirements of the ADA. In other words, the entity can argue that the construction or alteration met the requirements of the ADA because it was done in compliance with the state or local code that had been certified.

Q: When are the public accommodations provisions effective?

A: In general, they become effective on July 26,1992.

Q: How will the public accommodations provisions be enforced?

A: Private individuals may bring lawsuits in which they can obtain court orders to stop discrimination. Individuals may also file complaints with the Attorney General, who is authorized to bring lawsuits in cases of general public importance or where a "pattern or practice" of discrimination is alleged. In these cases, the Attorney General may seek monetary damages and civil penalties. Civil penalties may not exceed $50,000 for a first violation or $100,000 for any subsequent violation.

MISCELLANEOUS

Q: Is the Federal government covered by the ADA?

A: The ADA does not cover the executive branch of the Federal government. The executive branch continues to be covered by Title V of the Rehabilitation Act of 1973, which prohibits discrimination in services and employment on the basis of handicap, and which is a model for the requirements of the ADA. The ADA, however, does cover Congress and other entities in the legislative branch of the Federal government.

Q: What requirements, other than those mandating nondiscrimination in employment, does the ADA place on state and local governments?

A: All government facilities, services, and communications must be accessible consistent with the requirements of Section 504 of the Rehabilitation Act of 1973. Individuals may file complaints with Federal agencies to be designated by the Attorney General or bring private lawsuits.

Q: Does the ADA cover private apartments and private homes?

A: The ADA generally does not cover private residential facilities. These facilities are addressed in the Fair Housing Amendments Act of 1988, which prohibits discrimination on the basis of disability in selling or renting housing. If a building contains both residential and nonresidential portions, only the non-residential portions are covered by the ADA. For example, in a large hotel that has a residential apartment wing, the residential wing would be covered by the Fair Housing Act and the other rooms would be covered by the ADA.

Q: Does the ADA cover air transportation?

A: Discrimination by air carriers is not covered by the ADA but rather by the Air Carrier Access Act (49 U.S.C. 1374(c)).

Q: What are the ADA's requirements for public transit buses?

A: The ADA requires the Department of Transportation to issue regulations mandating accessible public transit vehicles and facilities. The regulations must include a requirement that all new fixed-route, public transit buses be accessible and that supplementary transit services be provided for those individuals with disabilities who cannot use fixed-route bus service.

Q: How will the ADA make telecommunications accessible?

A: The ADA requires the establishment of telephone relay services for individuals who use telecommunications devices for the deaf (TDDs) or similar devices. The Federal Communications Commission will issue regulations specifying standards for the operation of these services.

Q: Are businesses entitled to any tax benefit to help pay for compliance?

A: As amended in 1990, the Internal Revenue Code allows a deduction of up to $15,000 per year for expenses associated with the removal of qualified architectural and transportation barriers. The 1990 amendment also permits eligible small businesses to receive a tax credit for certain costs of compliance with the ADA. An eligible small business is one whose gross receipts do not exceed one million dollars or whose workforce does not consist of more than 30 full-time workers. Qualifying businesses may claim a credit of up to 50 percent of eligible access expenditures that exceed $250 but do not exceed $10,250. Examples of eligible access expenditures include the necessary and reasonable costs of removing architectural, physical, communications, and transportation barriers; providing readers, interpreters, and other auxiliary aids; and acquiring or modifying equipment or devices.

Appendix A

Addendum

PUBLIC LAW 101-336, JULY 26, 1990 104 STAT. 327

Public Law 101–336 101st Congress

AN ACT

To establish a clear and comprehensive prohibition of discrimination on the basis of disability.

Be it enacted by the Senate and House of Representatives of the United States of America in Congress assembled,

SECTION 1. SHORT Title: TABLE OF CONTENTS.

(a) SHORT TITLE.—This Act may be cited as the "Americans with Disabilities Act of 1990." 42 USC 12101 note.

(b) TABLE OF CONTENTS.—The table of contents is as follows: Sec. 1. Short title; table of contents.

Sec. 2. Findings and purposes.
Sec. 3. Definitions.

TITLE I—EMPLOYMENT

Sec. 101. Definitions.
Sec. 102. Discrimination.
Sec. 103. Defenses.
Sec. 104. Illegal use of drugs and alcohol.
Sec. 105. Posting notices.
Sec. 106. Regulations.
Sec. 107. Enforcement.
Sec. 108. Effective date.

TITLE II—PUBLIC SERVICES

Subtitle A—Prohibition Against Discrimination and Other Generally

Applicable Provisions

Sec. 201. Definition.
Sec. 202. Discrimination.
Sec. 203. Enforcement.
Sec. 204. Regulations.
Sec. 205. Effective date.

Subtitle B—Actions Applicable to Public Transportation Provided by Public

Entities Considered Discriminatory

PART I—PUBLIC TRANSPORTATION OTHER THAN BY AIRCRAFT OR CERTAIN RAIL OPERATIONS

Sec. 221. Definitions.
Sec. 222. Public entities operating fixed route systems.
Sec. 223. Paratransit as a complement to fixed route service.
Sec. 224. Public entity operating a demand responsive system.
Sec. 225. Temporary relief where lifts are unavailable.
Sec. 226. New facilities.
Sec. 227. Alterations of existing facilities.
Sec. 228. Public transportation programs and activities in existing facilities and one car per train rule.
Sec. 229. Regulations.
Sec. 230. Interim accessibility requirements.
Sec. 231. Effective date.

PART II—PUBLIC TRANSPORTATION BY INTERCITY AND COMMUTER RAIL

Sec. 241. Definitions.
Sec. 242. Intercity and commuter rail actions considered discriminatory.
Sec. 243. Conformance to accessibility standards.
Sec. 244. Regulations.
Sec. 245. Interim accessibility requirements.
Sec. 246. Effective date.

TITLE III—PUBLIC ACCOMMODATIONS AND SERVICES OPERATED BY PRIVATE ENTITIES

Sec. 301. Definitions.
Sec. 302. Prohibition of discrimination by public accommodations.

42 USC 12101. SEC. 2. FINDINGS AND PURPOSES.

(a) FINDINGS.—The Congress finds that—

(1) some 43,000,000 Americans have one or more physical or mental disabilities, and this number is increasing as the population as a whole is growing older;

(2) historically, society has tended to isolate and segregate individuals with disabilities, and, despite some improvements, such forms of discrimination against individuals with disabilities continue to be a serious and pervasive social problem;

(3) discrimination against individuals with disabilities persists in such critical areas as employment, housing, public accommodations, education, transportation, communication, recreation, institutionalization, health services, voting, and access to public services;

(4) unlike individuals who have experienced discrimination on the basis of race, color, sex, national origin, religion, or age, individuals who have experienced discrimination on the basis of failure to make modifications to existing facilities and practices, exclusionary qualification standards and criteria, segregation, and relegation to lesser services, programs, activities, benefits, jobs, or other opportunities;

(5) individuals with disabilities continually encounter various forms of discrimination, including outright intentional exclusion, the discriminatory effects of architectural, transportation, and communication barriers, overprotective rules and policies, failure to make modifications to existing facilities and practices, exclusionary qualification standards and criteria, segregation, and relegation to lesser services, programs, activities, benefits, jobs, or other opportunities;

(6) census data, national polls, and other studies have documented that people with disabilities, as a group, occupy an inferior status in our society, and are severely disadvantaged socially, vocationally, economically, and educationally;

(7) individuals with disabilities are a discrete and insular minority who have been faced with restrictions and limitations, subjected to a history of purposeful unequal treatment, and relegated to a position of political powerlessness in our society, based on characteristics that are beyond the control of such individuals and resulting from stereotypical assumptions not truly indicative of the individual ability of such individuals to participate in, and contribute to, society;

(8) the Nation's proper goals regarding individuals with disabilities are to assure equality of opportunity, full participation, independent living, and economic self-sufficiency for such individuals; and

(9) the continuing existence of unfair and unnecessary discrimination and prejudice denies people with disabilities the opportunity to compete on an equal basis and to pursue those opportunities for which our free society is justifiably famous, and costs the United States billions of dollars in unnecessary expenses resulting from dependency and nonproductivity.

(b) PURPOSE.—It is the purpose of this Act—

(1) to provide a clear and comprehensive national mandate for the elimination of discrimination against individuals with disabilities;

(2) to provide clear, strong, consistent, enforceable standards addressing discrimination against individuals with disabilities;

(3) to ensure that the Federal Government plays a central role in enforcing the standards established in this Act on behalf of individuals with disabilities; and

(4) to invoke the sweep of congressional authority, including the power to

enforce the fourteenth amendment and to regulate commerce, in order to address the major areas of discrimination faced day-to-day by people with disabilities.

SEC. 3. DEFINITIONS. 42 USC 12102.

As used in this Act:

(1) AUXILIARY AIDS AND SERVICES.—The term "auxiliary aids and services" includes—

(A) qualified interpreters or other effective methods of making aurally delivered materials available to individuals with hearing impairments;

(B) qualified readers, taped texts, or other effective methods of making visually delivered materials available to individuals with visual impairments;

(C) acquisition or modification of equipment or devices; and

(D) other similar services and actions.

(2) DISABILITY.—The term "disability" means, with respect to an individual—

(A) a physical or mental impairment that substantially limits one or more of the major life activities of such individual;

(B) a record of such an impairment; or

(C) being regarded as having such an impairment.

(3) STATE.—The term "State" means each of the several States, the District of Columbia, the Commonwealth of Puerto Rico, Guam, American Samoa, the Virgin Islands, the Trust Territory of the Pacific Islands, and the Commonwealth of the Northern Mariana Islands.

TITLE I—EMPLOYMENT

42 USC 12111.

SEC. 101. DEFINITIONS.

As used in this title:

(1) COMMISSION.—The term "Commission" means the Equal Employment Opportunity Commission established by section 705 of the Civil Rights Act of 1964 (42 U.S.C. 2000e-4).

(2) COVERED ENTITY.—The term "covered entity" means an employer, employment agency, labor organization, or joint labor-management committee.

(3) DIRECT THREAT.—The term "direct threat" means a significant risk to the health or safety of others that cannot be eliminated by reasonable accommodation.

(4) EMPLOYEE.—The term "employee" means an individual employed by an employer.

(5) EMPLOYER.—

(A) IN GENERAL.—The term "employer" means a person engaged in an industry affecting commerce who has 15 or more employees for each working day in each of 20 or more calendar weeks in the current or preceding calendar year, and any agent of such person, except that, for two years following the effective date of this title, an employer means a person engaged in an industry affecting commerce who has 25 or more employees for each working day in each of 20 or more calendar weeks in the current or preceding year, and any agent of such person.

(B) Exceptions.—The term "employer" does not include—

(i) the United States, a corporation wholly owned by the government of the United States, or an Indian tribe; or (ii) a bona fide private membership club (other than a labor organization) that is exempt from taxation under section 501(c) of the Internal Revenue Code of 1986.

(6) ILLEGAL USE OF DRUGS.—

(A) IN GENERAL.—The term "illegal use of drugs" means the use of drugs, the possession or distribution of which is unlawful under the Controlled Substances Act (21 U.S.C. 812). Such term does not include the use of a drug taken under supervision by a licensed health care professional, or other uses authorized by the Controlled Substances Act or other provisions of Federal law.

(B) Drugs.—The term "drug" means a controlled substance, as defined in schedules I through V of section 202 of the Controlled Substances Act.

(7) PERSON, ETC.-The terms "person", "labor organization", "employment agency", "commerce", and "industry affecting commerce", shall have the same meaning given such terms in Sections 701 of the Civil Rights Act of 1964 (42 U.S.C. 2000e).

(8) QUALIFIED INDIVIDUAL WITH A DISABILITY.—The term "qualified individual with a disability" means an individual with a disability who, with or without reasonable accommodation, can perform the essential functions of the employment position that such individual holds or desires. For the purposes of this title, consideration shall be given to the employer's judgement as to what functions of a job are essential, and if an employer has prepared a written description before advertising or interviewing applicants for the job, this description shall be considered evidence of the essential functions of the job.

(9) REASONABLE ACCOMMODATION.—The term "reasonable accommodation" may include—

(A) making existing facilities used by employees readily accessible to and usable by qualified individuals with disabilities; and

(B) job restructuring, part time or modified work schedules, reassignment to a vacant position, acquisition or modification of equipment or devices, appropriate adjustment or modifications of examinations, training materials or policies, the provision of qualified readers or interpreters, and other similar accommodations for individuals with disabilities.

(10) UNDUE HARDSHIP.—

(A) In general.-The term "undue hardship" means an action requiring significant difficulty or expense, when considered in light of the factors set forth in subparagraph (B).

(B) Factors to be considered.—In determining whether an accommodation would impose an undue hardship on a covered entity, factors to be considered include—

(i) the nature and cost of the accommodation needed under this Act;

(ii) the overall financial resources of the facility or facilities involved in the provision of the reasonable accommodation; the number of persons employed at such facility; the effect on expenses and resources, or the impact otherwise of such accommodation upon the operation of the facility;

(iii) the overall financial resources of the covered entity; the overall size of the business of a covered entity with respect to the number of its employees; the number, type, and location of its facilities; and

(iv) the type of operation or operations of the covered entity, including the composition, structure, and functions of the workforce of such entity; the geographic separateness, administrative, or fiscal relationship of the facility or facilities in question to the covered entity.

SEC. 102. DISCRIMINATION.

(a) General Rule- No covered entity shall discriminate against a qualified individual with a disability because of the disability of such individual in regard to job application procedures, the hiring, advancement, or discharge of employees, employee compensation, job training, and other terms, conditions, and privileges of employment.

(b) CONSTRUCTION.—As used in subsection (a), the term "discriminate" includes—

(1) limiting, segregating, or classifying a job applicant or employee in a way that adversely affects the opportunities or status of such applicant or employee because of the disability of such applicant or employee;

(2) participating in a contractual or other arrangement or relationship that has the effect of subjecting a covered entity's qualified applicant or employee with a disability to the discrimination prohibited by this title (such relationship

includes a relationship with an employment or referral agency, labor union, an organization providing fringe benefits to an employee of the covered entity, or an organization providing training and apprenticeship programs);

(3) utilizing standards, criteria, or methods of administration—

(A) that have the effect of discrimination on the basis of disability; or

(B) that perpetuate the discrimination of others who are subject to common administrative control;

(4) excluding or otherwise denying equal jobs or benefits to a qualified individual because of the known disability of an individual with whom the qualified individual is known to have a relationship or association;

(5)(A) not making reasonable accommodations to the known physical or mental limitations of an otherwise qualified individual with a disability who is an applicant or employee, unless such covered entity can demonstrate that the accommodation would impose an undue hardship on the operation of the business of such covered entity; or

(B) denying employment opportunities to a job applicant or employee who is an otherwise qualified individual with a disability, if such denial is based on the need of such covered entity to make reasonable accommodation to the physical or mental impairments of the employee or applicant;

(6) using qualification standards, employment tests or other selection criteria that screen out or tend to screen out an individual with a disability or a class of individuals with disabilities unless the standard, test or other selection criteria, as used by the covered entity, is shown to be job related for the position in question and is consistent with business necessity; and

(7) failing to select and administer tests concerning employment in the most effective manner to ensure that, when such test is administered to a job applicant or employee who has a disability that impairs sensory, manual, or speaking skills, such test results accurately reflect the skills, aptitude, or whatever other factor of such applicant or employee that such test purports to measure, rather than reflecting the impaired sensory, manual, or speaking skills of such employee or applicant (except where such skills are the factors that the test purports to measure).

(c) MEDICAL EXAMINATIONS AND INQUIRIES.—

(1) IN GENERAL.—The prohibition against discrimination as referred to in subsection (a) shall include medical examinations and inquiries.

(2) PREEMPLOYMENT.—

(A) PROHIBITED EXAMINATION OR INQUIRY.—Except as provided in paragraph (3), a covered entity shall not conduct a medical examination or make inquiries of a job applicant as to whether such applicant is an individual with a disability or as to the nature or severity of such disability.

(B) ACCEPTABLE INQUIRY.—A covered entity may make preemployment inquiries into the ability of an applicant to perform job-related functions.

(3) EMPLOYMENT ENTRANCE EXAMINATION.—A covered entity may require a medical examination after an offer of employment has been made to a job applicant and prior to the commencement of the employment duties of such applicant, and may condition an offer of employment on the results of such examination, if—

(A) all entering employees are subjected to such an examination regardless of disability;

(B) information obtained regarding the medical condition or history of the applicant is collected and maintained on separate forms and in separate medical files and is treated as a confidential medical record, except that—

(i) supervisors and managers may be informed regarding necessary restrictions on the work or duties of the employee and necessary accommodations;

(ii) first aid and safety personnel may be informed, when appropriate, if the disability might require emergency treatment; and

(iii) government officials investigating compliance with this Act shall be provided relevant information on request; and

(C) the results of such examination are used only in accordance with this title.

(4) EXAMINATION AND INQUIRY.—

(A) PROHIBITED EXAMINATIONS AND INQUIRIES.—A covered entity shall not require a medical examination and shall not make inquiries of an employee as to whether such employee is an individual with a disability or as to the nature or severity of the disability, unless such examination or inquiry is shown to be job-related and consistent with business necessity.

(B) ACCEPTABLE EXAMINATIONS AND INQUIRIES.—A covered entity may conduct voluntary medical examinations, including voluntary medical histories, which are part of an employee health program available to employees at that work site. A covered entity may make inquiries into the ability of an employee to perform job-related functions.

(C) REQUIREMENT—Information obtained under subparagraph (B) regarding the medical condition or history of any employee are subject to the requirements of subparagraphs (B) and (C) of paragraph (3).

SEC.103. DEFENSES.

(a) IN GENERAL.—It may be a defense to a charge of discrimination under this Act that an alleged application of qualification standards, tests, or selection criteria that screen out or tend to screen out or otherwise deny a job or benefit to an individual with a disability has been shown to be job-related and consistent with business necessity, and such performance cannot be accomplished by reasonable accommodation, as required under this title.

(b) QUALIFICATION STANDARDS.—The term "Qualified Standards" may include a requirement that an individual shall not pose a direct threat to the health or safety of other individuals in the workplace.

(c) RELIGIOUS ENTITIES.—

(1) IN GENERAL.—This title shall not prohibit a religious corporation, association, educational institution, or society from giving preference in employment to individuals of a particular religion to perform work connected with the carrying on by such corporation, association, educational institution, or society of its activities.

(2) RELIGIOUS TENETS REQUIREMENTS.—Under this title, a religious organization may require that all applicants and employees conform to the religious tenets of such organization.

(d) LIST OF INFECTIOUS AND COMMUNICABLE DISEASES.—

(1) IN GENERAL.—The Secretary of Health and Human Services, not later than 6 months after the date of enactment of this Act, Shall—

(A) review all infectious and communicable diseases which may be transmitted through handling the food supply;

(B) publish a list of infectious and communicable diseases which are transmitted through handling the food supply;

(C) publish methods by which such diseases are transmitted; and

(D) widely disseminate such information regarding the list of diseases and their modes of transmissibility to the general public.

Such lists shall be updated annually.

(2) APPLICATIONS.—In any case in which an individual has an infectious or communicable disease that is transmitted to others through the handling of food, that is included on the list developed by the Secretary of Health and Human Services under paragraph (1), and which cannot be eliminated by reasonable accommodations, a covered entity may refuse to assign or continue to assign to assign such individual to a job involving food handling.

(3) CONSTRUCTION.—Nothing in this Act shall be construed to preempt, modify, or amend any State, county, or local law, ordinance, or regulation applicable to food handling which is designed to protect the public health from individuals who pose a significant risk to the health or safety of others, which cannot be eliminated by reasonable accommodation, pursuant to the list of infectious or communicable diseases and modes of transmissibility published by the Secretary of Health and Human Services.

SEC. 104. ILLEGAL USE OF DRUGS AND ALCOHOL.

(a) QUALIFIED INDIVIDUAL WITH A DISABILITY.—For purposes of this title, the term "qualified individual with a disability" shall not include any employee or applicant who is currently engaging in the illegal use of drugs, when the covered entity acts on the basis of such use.

(b) RULES OF CONSTRUCTION—Nothing in subsection (a) shall be construed to exclude as a qualified individual with a disability an individual who—

(1) has successfully completed a supervised drug rehabilitation program and is no longer engaging in the illegal use of drugs, or has otherwise been rehabilitated successfully and is no longer engaging in such use;

(2) is participating in a supervised rehabilitation program and is no longer engaging in such use; or

(3) is erroneously regarded as engaging in such use, but is not engaging in such use; except that it shall not be a violation of this Act for a covered entity to adopt or administer reasonable policies or procedures, including but not limited to drug testing, designed to ensure that an individual described in paragraph (1) or (2) is no longer engaging in the illegal use of drugs.

(c) AUTHORITY OF COVERED ENTITY.—A covered entity—

(1) may prohibit the illegal use of drugs and the use of alcohol at the workplace by all employees;

(2) may require that employees shall not be under the influence of alcohol or be engaging in the illegal use of drugs at the workplace;

(3) may require that employees behave in conformance with the requirements established under the Drug-Free Workplace Act of 1988 (41 U.S.C. 701 et seq.);

(4) may hold an employee who engages in the illegal use of drugs or who is an alcoholic to the same qualification standards for employment or job performance and behavior that such entity holds other employees, even if any unsatisfactory performance or behavior is related to the drug use or alcoholism of such employee; and

(5) may, with respect to Federal regulations regarding alcohol and the illegal use of drugs, require that—

(A) employees comply with the standards established in such regulations of the Department of Defense, if the employees of the covered entity are employed in an industry subject to such regulations, including complying with regulations (if any) that apply to employment in sensitive positions in such an industry, in the case of employees of the covered entity who are employed in such positions (as defined in the regulations of the Department of Defense);

(B) employees comply with the standards established in such regulations of the Nuclear Regulatory Commission, if the employees of the covered entity are employed in an industry subject to such regulations, including complying with regulations (if any) that apply to employment in sensitive positions in such an industry, in the case of employees of the covered entity who are employed in such positions (as defined in the regulations of the Nuclear Regulatory Commission); and

(C) employees comply with the Standards established in such regulations of the Department of Transportation, if the employees of the covered entity are employed in a transportation industry subject to such regulations, including complying with such regulations (if any) that apply to employment in sensitive positions in such an industry, in the care of employees of the covered entity who are employed in such positions (as defined in the regulations of the Department of Transportation).

(d) DRUG TESTING.—

(1) In general—For purposes of this title, a test to determine the illegal use of drugs shall not be considered a medical examination.

(2) CONSTRUCTION.—Nothing in this title shall be construed to encourage, prohibit, or authorize the conducting of drug testing for the illegal use of drugs by job applicants or employed or making employment decisions based on such test results.

(e) TRANSPORTATION EMPLOYEES.—Nothing in this title shall be construed to encourage, prohibit, restrict, or authorize the otherwise lawful exercise by entities subject to the jurisdiction of the Department of Transportation of authority to

(1) test employees of such entities in, and applicants for, positions involving safety-sensitive duties for the illegal use of drugs and for on-duty impairment by alcohol; and

(2) remove such persons who test positive for illegal use of drugs and on-duty impairment by alcohol pursuant to paragraph (1) from safety-sensitive duties in implementing subsection (c).

SEC. 105. POSTING NOTICES.

Every employer, employment agency, labor organization, or joint labor-management committee covered under this title shall post notices in an accessible format to applicants, employees, and members describing the applicable provisions of this Act, in the manner prescribed by section 711 of the Civil Rights Act of 1964 (42 U.S.C. 2000e-10).

Not later than 1 year after the date of enactment of this Act, the Commission shall issue regulations in an accessible format to carry out this title in accordance with subchapter II of chapter 5 of title 5, United States Code.

Sec. 107. ENFORCEMENT.

(a) POWERS, REMEDIES, AND PROCEDURES.—The powers, remedies, and procedures set forth in actions 705, 706, 707, 709, and 710 of the Civil Rights Act of 1964 (42 U.S.C. 2000e-4, 2000e-5, 2000e-6, 2000e-8, and 2000e-9) shall be the powers, remedies, and procedures this title provides to the Commission, to the Attorney General, or to any person alleging discrimination on the basis of disability in violation of any provision of this Act, or regulations promulgated under section 106, concerning employment.

(b) COORDINATION.—The agencies with enforcement authority for actions which allege employment discrimination under this title and under the Rehabilitation Act of 1978 shall develop procedures to ensure that administrative complaints filed under this title and under the Rehabilitation Act of 1973 are dealt with in a manner that avoids duplication of effort and prevents imposition of inconsistent or conflicting standards for the same requirements under this title and the Rehabilitation Act of 1973. The Commission, the Attorney General, and the Office of Federal Contract Compliance Programs shall establish such coordinating mechanisms (similar to provisions contained in the joint regulations promulgated by the Commission and the Attorney General at Part 42 of Title 28 and Part 1691 of Title 29, Code of Federal Regulations, and the Memorandum of Understanding between the Commission and the Office of Federal Contract Compliance Programs dated January 16, 1981 (46 Fed. Reg. 7435, January 23,1981)) in regulations implementing this title and Rehabilitation Act of 1973 not later than 18 months after the date of enactment of this Act.

SEC. 108. EFFECTIVE DATE.

This Title shall become effective 24 months after the date of enactment.

TITLE II—PUBLIC SERVICES

SUBTITLE A—PROHIBITION AGAINST DISCRIMINATION AND OTHER GENERALLY APPLICABLE PROVISIONS

SEC. 201. DEFINITION.

As used in this title:

(1) PUBLIC ENTITY.—The term "public entity" means—

(A) any State or local government;

(B) any department, agency, special purpose district, or other instrumentality of a State or States or local government; and

(C) the National Railroad Passenger Corporation, and any commuter authority (as defined in section 103(8) of the Rail Passenger Service Act).

(2) QUALIFIED INDIVIDUAL WITH A DISABILITY.—The term "qualified individual with a disability" means an individual with a disability who, with or without reasonable modifications to rules, policies, or practices, the removal of architectural, communication, or transportation barriers, or the provision of auxiliary aids and services, meets the essential eligibility requirements for the receipt of services or the participation in programs or activities provided by a public entity.

SEC. 202. DISCRIMINATION.

Subject to the provisions of this title, no qualified individual with a disability shall, by reason of such disability, be excluded from participation in or be denied the benefits of the services, programs, or activities of a public entity, or be subjected to discrimination by any such entity.

SEC. 203. ENFORCEMENT.

The remedies, procedures, and rights set forth in section 505 of the Rehabilitation Act of 1973 (29 U.S.C. 794a) shall be the remedies, procedures, and rights this title provides to any person alleging discrimination on the basis of disability in violation of section 202.

SEC. 204. REGULATIONS.

(a) IN GENERAL.—Not later than 1 year after the date of enactment of this Act, the Attorney General shall promulgate regulations in an accessible format that implement this subtitle. Such regulations shall not include any matter within the scope of the authority of the Secretary of Transportation under section 223, 229, or 244.

(b) RELATIONSHIP TO OTHER REGULATIONS.—Except for "program accessibility, existing facilities", and "communications", regulations under subsection (a) shall be consistent with this Act and with the coordination regulations under part 41 of title 28, Code of Federal Regulations (as promulgated by the Department of Health, Education, and Welfare on January 13, 1978), applicable to recipients of Federal financial assistance under section 504 of the Rehabilitation Act of 1973 (29 U.S.C. 794). With respect to "program accessibility, existing facilities", and "communications", such regulations shall be consistent with regulations and analysis as in part 39 of title 28 of the Code of Federal Regulations, applicable to federally conducted activities under such section 504.

(c) STANDARDS.—Regulations under subsection (a) shall include standards applicable to facilities and vehicles covered by this subtitle, other than facilities, stations, rail passenger cars, and vehicles covered by subtitle B. Such standards shall be consistent with the minimum guidelines and requirements issued by the Architectural and Transportation Barriers Compliance Board in accordance with section 504(a) of this Act.

SEC. 205. EFFECTIVE DATE.

(a) GENERAL RULE.—Except as provided in subsection (b), this subtitle shall become effective 18 months after the date of enactment of this Act.

(b) EXCEPTION. Section 204 shall become effective on the date of enactment of this Act.

SUBTITLE B—ACTIONS APPLICABLE TO PUBLIC TRANSPORTATION PROVIDED BY PUBLIC ENTITIES CONSIDERED DISCRIMINATORY

PART I—PUBLIC TRANSPORTATION OTHER THAN BY AIRCRAFT OR CERTAIN RAIL OPERATIONS

SEC. 221. DEFINITIONS.

As used in this part:

(1) DEMAND RESPONSIVE SYSTEM.—The term "demand responsive system" means any system of providing designated public transportation which is not a fixed route system.

(2) DESIGNATED PUBLIC TRANSPORTATION.—The term "designated public transportation" means transportation (other than public school transportation) by bus, rail, or any other conveyance (other than transportation by aircraft or intercity or commuter rail transportation (as defined in section 241)) that provides the general public with general or special service (including charter service) on a regular and continuing basis.

(3) FIXED ROUTE SYSTEM.—The term "fixed route system" means a system of providing designated public transportation on which a vehicle is operated along a prescribed route according to a fixed schedule.

(4) OPERATES.—The term "operates", as used with respect to a fixed route system or demand responsive system, includes operation of such system by a person under a contractual or other arrangement or relationship with a public entity.

(5) PUBLIC SCHOOL TRANSPORTATION.—The term "public school transportation" means transportation by school bus vehicles of schoolchildren, personnel, and equipment to and from a public elementary or secondary school and school-related activities.

(6) SECRETARY.—The term "Secretary" means the Secretary of Transportation.

SEC. 222. PUBLIC ENTITIES OPERATING FIXED ROUTE SYSTEMS.

(a) PURCHASE AND ENTITIES OF NEW VEHICLES.—It shall be considered discrimination for purposes of section 202 of this Act and section 604 of the Rehabilitation Act of 1973 (29 U.S.C. 794) for a public entity which operates a fixed route system to purchase or lease a new bus, a new rapid rail vehicle, a new light rail vehicle, or any other new vehicle to be used on such system, if the solicitation for such purchase or lease is made after the 30th day following the effective date of this subsection and if such bus, rail vehicle, or other vehicle is not readily accessible to and usable by individuals with disabilities, including individuals who use wheelchairs.

(b) PURCHASE AND LEASE OF USED VEHICLES.—Subject to subsection (c)(1), it shall be considered discrimination for purposes of section 202 of this Act and section 504 of the Rehabilitation Act of 1973 (29 U.S.C. 794) for a public entity which operates a fixed route system to purchase to lease, after the 30th day following the effective date of this subsection, a used vehicle for use on such system unless such entity makes demonstrated good faith efforts to purchase or lease a used vehicle for use on such system that is readily accessible to and usable by individuals with disabilities, including individuals who use wheelchairs.

(c) REMANUFACTURED VEHICLES.—

(1) GENERAL RULE.—Except as provided in paragraph (2), it shall be considered discrimination for purposes of section 202 of this Act and section 504 of the Rehabilitation Act of 1973 (29 U.S.C. 794) for a public entity which operates a fixed route system—

(A) to remanufacture a vehicle for use on such system so as to extend its usable life for 5 years or more, which remanufacture begins (or for which the solicitation is made) after the 30th day following the effective date of this subsection; or

(B) to purchase or lease for use on such system a remanufactured vehicle which has been remanufactured so as to extend its usable life for 5 years or more, which purchase or lease occurs after such 30th day and during the period in which the usable life is extended; unless, after remanufacture, the vehicle is, to the maximum extent feasible, readily accessible to and usable by individuals with disabilities, including individuals who use wheelchairs.

(2) Exception for historic vehicles.—

(A) GENERAL RULE.—If a public entity operates a fixed route system any segment of which is included on the National Register of Historic Places and if making a vehicle of historic character to be used solely on such segment readily accessible to and usable by individuals with disabilities would significantly alter the historic character of such vehicle, the public entity only has to make (or to purchase or lease a remanufactured vehicle with) those modifications which are necessary to meet the requirements of paragraph (1) and which do not significantly alter the historic character of such vehicle.

(B) VEHICLES OF HISTORIC CHARACTER DEFINED BY REGULATIONS.—For purposes of this paragraph and section 228(b), a vehicle of historic character shall be defined by the regulations issued by the Secretary to carry out this subsection.

SEC. 223. PARATRANSIT AS A COMPLEMENT TO FIXED ROUTE SERVICE.

(a) GENERAL RULE.—It shall be considered discrimination for purposes of section 202 of the Act and section 504 of the Rehabilitation ACT of 1973 (29 U.S.C. 794) for a public entity which operates a fixed route system (other than a system which provides solely commuter bus service) to fail to provide with respect to the operations of its fixed route system, in accordance with this section, paratransit and other special transportation services to individuals with disabilities, including individuals who use wheelchairs, that are sufficient to provide to such individuals a level of service (1) which is comparable to the level of designated public transportation services provided to individuals without disabilities using such system; or (2) in the case of response time, which is comparable, to the extent practicable, to the level of designated public transportation services provided to individuals without disabilities using such system.

(b) ISSUANCE OF REGULATIONS.—Not later than 1 year after the effective date of this subsection, the Secretary shall issue final regulations to carry out this section.

(c) REQUIRED CONTENTS OF REGULATIONS.—

(1) ELIGIBLE RECIPIENTS OF SERVICE.—The regulations issued under this section shall require each public entity which operates a fixed route system to provide the paratransit and other special transportation services required under this section—

(A)(i) to any individual with a disability who is unable, as a result of a physical or mental impairment (including a vision impairment) and without the assistance of another individual (except an operator of a wheelchair lift or other boarding assistance device), to board, ride, or disembark from any vehicle on the system which is readily accessible to and usable by individuals with disabilities;

(ii) to any individual with a disability who needs the assistance of a wheelchair lift or other boarding assistance device (and is able with such assistance) to board, ride, and disembark from any vehicle which is readily accessible to and usable by individuals with disabilities if the individual wants to travel on a route on the system during the hours of operation of the system at a time (or within a reasonable period of such time) when such a vehicle is not being used to provide designated public transportation on the route; and

(iii) to any individual with a disability who has a specific impairment-related condition which prevents such individual from traveling to a boarding location or from a disembarking location on such system;

(B) to one other individual accompanying the individual with the disability; and

(C) to other individuals, in addition to the one individual described in subparagraph (B), accompanying the individual with a disability provided that space for these additional individuals is available on the paratransit vehicle carrying the individual with a disability and that the transportation of such additional individuals will not result in a denial of service to individuals with disabilities. For purposes of clauses (i) and (ii) of subparagraph (A), boarding or disembarking from a vehicle does not include travel to the boarding location or from the disembarking location.

(2) SERVICE AREA.—The regulations issued under this section shall require the provision of paratransit and special transportation services required under this section in the service area of each public entity which operates a fixed route system, other than any portion of the service area in which the public entity solely provides commuter bus service.

(3) SERVICE CRITERIA.—Subject to paragraphs (1) and (2), the regulations issued under this section shall establish minimum service criteria for determining the level of services to be required under this section.

(4) UNDUE FINANCIAL BURDEN LIMITATION.—The regulations issued under this section shall provide that, if the public entity is able to demonstrate to the satisfaction of the Secretary that the provision of paratransit and other special transportation services otherwise required under this section would impose an undue financial burden on the public entity, the public entity, notwithstanding any other provision of this section (other than paragraph (6)), shall only be required to provide such services to the extent that providing such services would not impose such a burden.

(5) ADDITIONAL SERVICES.—The regulations issued under this section shall establish circumstances under which the Secretary may require a public entity to provide, notwithstanding paragraph (4), paratransit and other special transportation services under this section beyond the level of paratransit and other special transportation services which would otherwise be required under paragraph (4).

(6) PUBLIC PARTICIPATION.—The regulations issued under this section shall require that each public entity which operates a fixed route system hold a public hearing, provide an opportunity for public comment, and consult with individuals with disabilities in preparing a plan under paragraph (7).

(7) PLANS.—The regulations issued under this section shall require that each public entity which operates a fixed route system—

(A) within 18 months after the effective date of this subsection, submit to the

Secretary, and commence implementation of, a plan for providing paratransit and other special transportation services which meets the requirements of this section; and

(B) on an annual basis thereafter, submit to the Secretary, and commence implementation of, a plan for providing such services.

(8) PROVISION OF SERVICES BY OTHERS.—The regulations issued under this section shall—

(A) require that a public entity submitting a plan to the Secretary under this section identify in the plan any person or other public entity which is providing a paratransit or other special transportation service for individuals with disabilities in the service area to which the plan applies; and by individuals with disabilities, including individuals who use wheelchairs, unless such system, when viewed in its entirety, provides a level of service to such individuals equivalent to the level of service such system provides to individuals without disabilities.

SEC. 224. PUBLIC ENTITY OPERATING A DEMAND RESPONSIVE SYSTEM.

If a public entity operates a demand response system, it shall be considered discrimination, for purposes of section 202 of this Act and section 504 of the Rehabilitation Act of 1973 (29 U.S.C. 794), for such entity to purchase or lease a new vehicle for use on such system, for which a solicitation is made after the 30th day following the effective date of this section, that is not readily accessible and usable by individuals with disabilities, including individuals who use wheelchairs, unless such system, when viewed in its entirety, provides a level of service to such individuals equivalent to the level of service such system provides to individuals without disabilities.

SEC. 225. TEMPORARY RELIEF WHERE LIFTS ARE UNAVAILABLE.

(a) GRANTING.—With respect to the purchase of new buses, a public entity may apply for, and the Secretary may temporarily relieve such public entity from the obligation under section 222(a) or 224 to purchase new buses that are readily accessible to and usable by individuals with disabilities if such public entity demonstrates to the satisfaction of the Secretary—

(1) that the initial solicitation for new buses made by the public entity specified that all new buses were to be lift equipped and were to be otherwise accessible to and usable by individuals with disabilities;

(2) the unavailability from any qualified manufacturer of hydraulic, electromechanical, or other lifts for such new buses;

(3) that the public entity seeking temporary relief has made good faith efforts to locate a qualified manufacturer to supply the lifts to the manufacturer of such buses in sufficient time to comply with such solicitation; and

(4) that any further delay in purchasing new buses necessary to obtain such lifts would significantly impair transportation services in the community served by the public entity.

(b) DURATION AND NOTICE TO CONGRESS.—Any relief granted under subsection (a) shall be limited in duration by a specified date, and the appropriate committees of Congress shall be notified of any such relief granted.

(c) FRAUDULENT APPLICATION.—If, at any time, the Secretary has reasonable cause to believe that any relief granted under subsection (a) was fraudulently applied for, the Secretary shall—

(1) cancel such relief if such relief is still in effect; and

(2) take such other action as the Secretary considers appropriate.

SEC. 226. NEW FACILITIES.

For purposes of Section 202 of this Act and Section 504 of the Rehabilitation Act of 1973 (29 U.S.C. 794), it shall be considered discrimination for a public entity to construct a new facility to be used in the provision of designated public transportation services unless such facility is readily accessible to and usable by individuals with disabilities, including individuals who use wheelchairs.

SEC. 227. ALTERATIONS OF EXISTING FACILITIES.

GENERAL RULE.—With respect to alterations of an existing facility or part thereof used in the provision of designated public transportation services that affect or could affect the usability of the facility or part thereof, it shall be considered discrimination, for purposes of Section 202 of this Act and Section 504 of the Rehabilitation Act of 1973 (29 U.S.C. 794), for a public entity to fail to make such alterations (or to ensure that the alterations are made) in such a manner that, to the maximum extent feasible, the altered portions of the facility are readily accessible to and usable by individuals with disabilities, including individuals who use wheelchairs, upon the completion of such alterations. Where the public entity is undertaking an alteration that affects or could affect usability of or access to an area of the facility containing a primary function, the entity shall also make the alterations in such a manner that, to the maximum extent feasible, the path of travel to the altered area and the bathrooms, telephones, and drinking fountains serving the altered area, are readily accessible to and usable by individuals with disabilities, including individuals who use wheelchairs, upon completion of such alterations, where such alterations to the path of travel or the bathrooms, telephones, and drinking fountains serving the altered area are not disproportionate to the overall alterations in terms of cost and scope (as determined under criteria established by the Attorney General).

(b) SPECIAL RULE FOR STATIONS.—

(1) GENERAL RULE.—For purposes of Section 202 of this Act and Section 504 of the Rehabilitation Act of 1973 (29 U.S.C. 79g), it shall be considered discrimination for a public entity that provides designated public transportation to fail, in accordance with the provisions of this subsection, to make key stations (as determined under criteria established by the Secretary by regulation) in rapid rail and light rail systems readily accessible to and usable by individuals with disabilities, including individuals who use wheelchairs.

(2) RAPID RAIL AND LIGHT RAIL KEY STATIONS.—

(A) ACCESSIBILITY.—Except as otherwise provided in this paragraph, all key stations (as determined under criteria established by the Secretary by regulation) in rapid rail and light rail systems shall be made readily accessible to and usable by individuals with disabilities, including individuals who use wheelchairs, as soon as practicable but in no event later than the last day of the 3-year period beginning on the effective date of this paragraph.

(B) EXTENSION FOR EXTRAORDINARILY EXPENSIVE STRUCTURAL CHANGES—The Secretary may extend the 3-year period under subparagraph (A) up to a 30-year period for key stations in a rapid rail or light rail system which stations need extraordinarily expensive structural changes to, or replacement of, existing facilities; except that by the last day of the 20th year following the date of the enactment of this Act at least ⅔ of such key stations must be readily accessible to and usable by individuals with disabilities.

(3) PLANS AND MILESTONES.—The Secretary shall require the appropriate public entity to develop and submit to the Secretary a plan for compliance with this subsection—

(A) that reflects consultation with individuals with disabilities affected by such plan and the results of a public hearing and public comments on such plan, and

(B) that establishes milestones for achievement of the requirements of this subsection.

SEC. 228. PUBLIC TRANSPORTATION PROGRAMS AND ACTIVITIES IN EXISTING FACILITIES AND ONE CAR PER TRAIN RULE.

(a) PUBLIC TRANSPORTATION PROGRAMS AND ACTIVITIES IN EXISTING FACILITIES

(1) IN GENERAL.—With respect to existing facilities used in the provision of designated public transportation services, it shall be considered discriminating, for purpose of Section 202 of this Act and Section 504 of the Rehabilitation Act of 1973 (29 U.S.C. 794), for a public entity to fail to operate a designated

public transportation program or activity conducted in such facilities that, when viewed in the entirety, the program or activity is readily accessible to and usable by individuals with disabilities.

(2) EXCEPTION.—Paragraph (1) shall not require a public entity to make structural changes to existing facilities in order to make such facilities accessible to individuals who use wheelchairs, unless and to the extent required by Section 227(a) (relating to alterations) or section 227(b) (relating to key stations).

(3) UTILIZATION.—Paragraph (1) shall not require a public entity to which paragraph (2) applies, to provide to individuals who use wheelchairs services made available to the general public at such facilities when such individuals could not utilize or benefit from such services provided at such facilities.

(b) ONE CAR PER TRAIN RULE.—

(1) GENERAL RULE.—Subject to paragraph (2), with respect to 2 or more vehicles operated as a train by a light or rapid rail system, for purposes of Section 202 of this Act and Section 504 of the Rehabilitation Act of 1973 (29 U.S.C. 794), it shall be considered discrimination for a public entity to fail to have at least 1 vehicle per train that is accessible to individuals with disabilities, including individuals who use wheelchairs, as soon as practicable but in no event later than the last day of the 5-year period beginning on the effective date of this section.

(2) HISTORIC TRAINS.—In order to comply with paragraph (1) with respect to the remanufacture of a vehicle of historic character which is to be used on a segment of a light or rapid rail system which is included on the National Register of Historic Places, if making such vehicle readily accessible to and usable by individuals with disabilities would significantly alter the historic character of such vehicle, the public entity which operates such system only have to make (or to purchase or lease a remanufactured vehicle with) those modifications which are necessary to meet the requirements of Section 222(c)(l) and which do not significantly alter the historic character of such vehicle.

SEC. 229. REGULATIONS.

(a) IN GENERAL.—Not later than 1 year after the date of enactment of this Act, the Secretary of Transportation shall issue regulations, in an accessible format, necessary for carrying out this part (other than section 223).

(b) STANDARDS—The regulations issued under this section and Section 223 shall include standards applicable to facilities and vehicles covered by this subtitle. The standards shall be consistent with the minimum guidelines and requirements issued by the Architectural and Transportation Barriers Compliance Board in accordance with section 504 of this Act.

SEC. 230. INTERIM ACCESSIBILITY REQUIREMENTS.

If final regulations have not been issued pursuant to Section 229, for new construction or alterations for which a valid and appropriate State or local building permit is obtained prior to the issuance of final regulations under such section, and for which the construction or alteration authorized by such permit begins within one year of the receipt of such permit and is completed under the terms of such permit, compliance with the Uniform Federal Accessibility Standards in effect at the time the building permit is issued shall suffice to satisfy the requirement that facilities be readily accessible to and usable by persons with disabilities as required under sections 226 and 227, except that, if such final regulations have not been issued one year after the Architectural and Transportation Barriers Compliance Board has issued the supplemental minimum guidelines required under section 504(a) of this Act, compliance with such supplemental minimum guidelines shall be necessary to satisfy the requirement that facilities be readily accessible to and usable by persons with disabilities prior to issuance of the final regulations.

SEC. 231. EFFECTIVE DATE.

(a) GENERAL RULE—Except as provided in subsection (b), this part shall become effective 18 months after the date of enactment of this Act.

(b) EXCEPTION.—Sections 222, 223 (other than subsection (a)), 224, 225, 227(b),228(b), and 229 shall become effective on the date of enactment of this Act.

PART II—PUBLIC TRANSPORTATION BY INTERCITY AND COMMUTER RAIL

SEC. 241. DEFINITIONS.

As used in this part:

(1) COMMUTER AUTHORITY.—The term "commuter authority" has the meaning given such term in section 103(8) of the Rail Passenger Service Act (45 U.S.C. 502(8)).

(2) COMMUTER RAIL TRANSPORTATION.—The term "commuter rail transportation" has the meaning given the term "commuter service" in section 103(9) of the Rail Passenger Service Act (45 U.S.C. 502(09)).

(3) INTERCITY RAIL TRANSPORTATION.—The term "intercity rail transportation" means transportation provided by the National Railroad Passenger Corporation.

(4) RAIL PASSENGER CAR.—The term "rail passenger car" means, with respect to intercity rail transportation, single-level and bi-level coach cars, single-level and bi-level dining cars, single-level and bi-level sleeping cars, sin-

gle-level and bi-level lounge cars, and food service cars.

(5) RESPONSIBLE PERSON.—The term responsible person means—

(A) in the case of a station more than 50 percent of which is owned by a public entity, such public entity;

(B) in the case of a station more than 50 percent of which is owned by a private party, the persons providing intercity or commuter rail transportation to such station, as allocated on an equitable basis by regulation by the Secretary of Transportation; and

(C) in a case where no party owns more than 50 percent of a station, the persons providing intercity or commuter rail transportation to such station and the owners of the station, other than private party owners, as allocated on an equitable basis by regulation by the Secretary of Transportation.

(6) STATION.—The term "station" means the portion of a property located appurtenant to a right-of-way on which intercity or commuter rail transportation is operated, where such portion is used by the general public and is related to the provision of such transportation, including passenger platforms, designated waiting areas, ticketing areas, restrooms, and, where a public entity providing rail transportation owns the property, concession areas, to the extent that such public entity exercises control over the selection, design, construction, or alteration of the property, but such term does not include flag stops.

SEC. 242. INTERCITY AND COMMUTER RAIL, ACTIONS CONSIDERED DISCRIMINATORY.

(a) INTERCITY RAIL TRANSPORTATION.—

(1) ONE CAR PER TRAIN RULE.—It shall be considered discrimination for purposes of section 202 of this Act and section 504 of the Rehabilitation Act of 1973 (29 U.S.C. 794) for a person who provides intercity rail transportation to fail to have at least one passenger car per train that is readily accessible to and usable by individuals with disabilities, including individuals who use wheelchairs, in accordance with regulations issued under section 244, as soon as practicable, but in no event later than 5 years after the date of enactment of this Act.

(2) NEW INTERCITY CARS.—

(A) GENERAL RULE.—Except as otherwise provided in this subsection with respect to individuals who use wheelchairs, it shall be considered discrimination for purposes of section 202 of this Act and section 504 of the Rehabilitation Act of 1973 (29 U.S.C. 794) for a person to purchase or lease any new rail passenger cars for use in intercity rail transportation, and for which a solicitation is made later than 30 days after the effective date of this section, unless all such rail cars are readily accessible to and usable by individuals with disabilities, including individuals who use wheel chairs, as prescribed by the Secretary of Transportation in regulations issued under section 244.

(B) SPECIAL RULE FOR SINGLE-LEVEL PASSENGER COACHES FOR INDIVIDUALS WHO USE WHEELCHAIRS.—Single-level passenger coaches shall be required to—

(i) be able to be entered by an individual who uses a wheelchair;

(ii) have space to park and secure a wheelchair;

(iii) have a seat to which a passenger in a wheelchair can transfer, and a space to fold and store such passenger's wheelchair; and

(iv) have a rest room usable by an individual who uses a wheelchair, only to the extent provided in paragraph (3).

(C) SPECIAL RULE FOR SINGLE-LEVEL DINING CARS FOR INDIVIDUALS WHO USE WHEELCHAIRS.—Single-level dining cars shall not be required to—

(i) be able to be entered from the station platform by an individual who uses a wheelchair; or

(ii) have a rest room usable by an individual who uses a wheelchair if no rest room is provided in such car for any passenger.

(D) SPECIAL RULE FOR BI-LEVEL DINING CARS FOR INDIVIDUALS WHO USE WHEELCHAIRS—Bi-level dining cars shall not be required to—

(i) be able to be entered by an individual who uses a wheelchair;

(ii) have space to park and secure a wheelchair;

(iii) have a seat to which a passenger in a wheelchair can transfer, or a space to fold and store such passenger's wheelchair; or

(iv) have a rest room usable by an individual who uses a wheelchair.

(3) ACCESSIBILITY OF SINGLE-LEVEL COACHES.—

(A) GENERAL RULE.—It shall be considered discrimination for purposes of section 202 of this Act and section 504 of the Rehabilitation Act of 1973 (29 U.S.C. 794) for a person who provides intercity rail transportation to fail to have on each train which includes one or more single-level rail passenger coaches—

(i) a number of spaces—

(I) to park and secure wheelchairs (to accommodate individuals who wish to remain in their wheelchairs) equal to not less than one-half of the number of single-level rail passenger coaches in such train; and

(II) to fold and store wheelchairs (to accommodate individuals who wish to transfer to coach seats) equal to not less than one-half of the number of single-level rail passenger coaches in such train, as soon as practicable, but in no event later than 5 years after the date of enactment of this Act; and

(ii) a number of spaces—

(I) to park and secure wheelchairs (to accommodate individuals who wish to remain in their wheelchairs) equal to not less than the total number of single-level rail passenger coaches in such train; and (II) to fold and store wheelchairs (to accommodate individuals who wish to transfer to coach seats) equal to not less than the total number of single-level rail passenger coaches in such train, as soon as practicable, but in no event later than 10 years after the date of enactment of this Act.

(B) LOCATION.—Spaces required by subparagraph (A) shall be located in single-level rail passenger coaches or food service cars.

(C) LIMITATION.—Of the number of spaces required on a train by subparagraph (A), not more than two spaces to park and secure wheelchairs nor more than two spaces to fold and store wheelchairs shall be located in any one coach or food service car.

(D) OTHER ACCESSIBILITY FEATURES. - Single-level rail passenger coaches and food service cars on which the spaces required by subparagraph (A) are located shall have a restroom usable by an individual who uses a wheelchair and shall be able to be entered from the station platform by an individual who uses a wheelchair.

(4) FOOD SERVICE—

(A) SINGLE-LEVEL DINING CARS.—On any train in which a single-level dining car is used to provide food service—

(i) if such single-level dining car was purchased after the date of enactment of this Act, table service in such car shall be provided to a passenger who uses a wheelchair if—

(I) the car adjacent to the end of the dining car through which a wheelchair may enter is itself accessible to a wheelchair;

(II) such passenger can exit to the platform from the car such passenger occupies, move down the platform, and enter the adjacent accessible car described in subclause (I) without the necessity of the train being moved within the station; and

(III) space to park and secure a wheelchair is available in the dining car at the time such passenger wishes to eat (if such passenger wishes to remain in a wheelchair), or space to store and fold a wheelchair is available in the dining car at the time such passenger wishes to eat (if such passenger wishes to transfer to a dining car seat); and

(ii) appropriate auxiliary aids and services, including a hard surface on which to eat, shall be provided to ensure that other equivalent food service is available to individuals with disabilities, including individuals who use wheelchairs, and to passengers traveling with such individuals.

Unless not practicable, a person providing intercity rail transportation shall place an accessible car adjacent to the end of a dining car described in clause (i) through which an individual who uses a wheelchair may enter.

B) BI-LEVEL DINING CARS.—On any train in which a bi-level dining car is used to provide food service—

(i) if such train includes a bi-level lounge car purchased after the date of enactment of this Act, table service in such lounge car shall be provided to individuals who use wheelchairs and to other passengers; and

(ii) appropriate auxiliary aids and services, including a hard surface on which to eat, shall be provided to ensure that other equivalent food service is available to individuals with disabilities, including individuals who use wheelchairs, and to passengers traveling with such individuals.

(b) COMMUTER RAIL TRANSPORTATION.—

(1) ONE CAR PER TRAIN RULE.—It shall be considered discrimination for purposes of section 202 of this Act and section 504 of the Rehabilitation Act of 1973 (29 U.S.C. 794) for a person who provides commuter rail transportation to fail to have at least one passenger car per train that is readily accessible to and usable by individuals with disabilities, including individuals who use wheelchairs, in accordance with regulations issued under section 244, as soon as practicable, but in no event later than 5 years after the date of enactment of this Act.

(2) NEW COMMUTER RAIL CARS.—

(A) GENERAL RULE.—It shall be considered discrimination for purposes of section 202 of this Act and section 504 of the Rehabilitation Act of 1973 (29 U.S.C. 794) for a person to purchase or lease any new rail passenger cars for use in commuter rail transportation, and for which a solicitation is made later than 30 days after the effective date of this section, unless all such rail cars are readily accessible to and usable by individuals with disabilities, including individuals who use wheelchairs, as prescribed by the Secretary of Transportation in regulations issued under section 244.

(B) ACCESSIBILITY.—For purposes of section 202 of this Act and section 504 of the Rehabilitation Act of 1973 (29 U.S.C. 794), a requirement that a rail passenger car used in commuter rail transportation be accessible to or readily accessible to and usable by individuals with disabilities, including individuals who use wheelchairs, shall not be construed to require—

(i) a rest room usable by an individual who uses a wheelchair if no rest room is provided in such car for any passenger;

(ii) space to fold and store a wheelchair; or

(iii) a seat to which a passenger who uses a wheelchair can transfer.

(c) USED RAIL CARS.—It shall be considered discrimination for purposes of section 202 of this Act and section 504 of the Rehabilitation Act of 1973 (29 U.S.C. 794) for a person to purchase or lease a used rail passenger car for use in intercity or commuter rail transportation, unless such person makes demonstrated good faith efforts to purchase or lease a used rail car that is readily accessible to and usable by individuals with disabilities, including individuals who use wheelchairs, as prescribed by the Secretary of Transportation in regulations issued under section 244.

(d) REMANUFACTURED RAIL CARS.—

(1) REMANUFACTURING.—It shall be considered discrimination for purposes of section 202 of this Act and section 504 of the Rehabilitation Act of 1973 (29 U.S.C. 794) for a person to remanufacture a rail passenger car for use in intercity or commuter rail transportation so as to extend its usable life for 10 years or more, unless the rail car, to the maximum extent feasible, is made readily accessible to and usable by individuals with disabilities, including individuals who use wheelchairs, as prescribed by the Secretary of Transportation in regulations issued under section 244.

(2) PURCHASE OR LEASE—It shall be considered discrimination for purposes of section 202 of this Act and section 504 of the Rehabilitation Act of 1973 (29 U.S.C. 794) for a person to purchase or lease a remanufactured rail passenger car for use in intercity or commuter rail transportation unless such car was remanufactured in accordance with paragraph (1).

(e) STATIONS.—

(1) NEW STATIONS.—It shall be considered discrimination for purposes of section 202 of this Act and section 504 of the Rehabilitation Act of 1973 (29 U.S.C. 794) for a person to build a new station for use in intercity or commuter rail transportation that is not readily accessible to and usable by individuals with disabilities, including individuals who use wheelchairs, as prescribed by the Secretary of Transportation in regulations issued under section 244.

(2) EXISTING STATIONS

(A) FAILURE TO MAKE READILY ACCESSIBLE.—

(i) GENERAL RULE.—It shall be considered discrimination for purposes of section 202 of this Act and section 504 of the Rehabilitation Act of 1973 (29 U.S.C. 794) for a responsible person to fail to make existing stations in the intercity rail transportation system, and existing key stations in commuter rail transportation systems, readily accessible to and usable by individuals with disabilities, including individuals who use wheelchairs, as prescribed by the Secretary of Transportation in regulations issued under section 244.

(ii) PERIOD FOR COMPLIANCE.—

(I) INTERCITY RAIL.—All stations in the intercity rail transportation system shall be made readily accessible to and usable by individuals with disabilities, including individuals who use wheelchairs, as soon as practicable, but in no event later than 20 years after the date of enactment of this Act.

(II) COMMUTER RAIL.—Key stations in commuter rail transportation systems shall be made readily accessible to and usable by individuals with disabilities, including individuals who use wheelchairs, as soon as practicable but in no event later than 3 years after the date of enactment of this Act, except that the time limit may be extended by the Secretary of Transportation up to 20 years after the date of enactment of this Act in a case where the raising of the entire passenger platform is the only means available of attaining accessibility or where other extraordinarily expensive structural changes are necessary to attain accessibility.

(iii) DESIGNATION OF KEY STATIONS.—Each commuter authority shall designate the key stations in its commuter rail transportation system, in consultation with individuals with disabilities and organizations representing such individuals, taking into consideration such factors as high ridership and whether such station serves as a transfer or feeder station. Before the final designation of key stations under this clause, a commuter authority shall hold a public hearing.

(iv) PLANS AND MILESTONES.—The Secretary of Transportation shall require the appropriate person to develop a plan for carrying out this subparagraph that reflects consultation with individuals with disabilities affected by such plan and that establishes milestones for achievement of the requirements of this subparagraph.

(B) REQUIREMENT WHEN MAKING ALTERATIONS.—

(i) GENERAL RULE.—It shall be considered discrimination, for purposes of section 202 of this Act and section 504 of the Rehabilitation Act of 1973 (29 U.S.C. 794). with respect to alterations of an existing station or part thereof in the intercity or commuter rail transportation systems that affect or could affect the usability of the station or part thereof, for the responsible person, owner, or person in control of the station to fail to make the alterations in such a manner that, to the maximum extent feasible, the altered portions of the station are readily accessible to and usable by individuals with disabilities, including individuals who use wheelchairs, upon completion of such alterations.

(ii) ALTERATIONS TO A PRIMARY FUNCTION AREA.—It shall be considered discrimination, for purposes of section 202 of this Act and section 504 of the Rehabilitation Act of 1973 (29 U.S.C. 794), with respect to alterations that affect or could affect the usability of or access to an area of the station containing a primary function, for the responsible person, owner, or person in control of the station to fail to make the alterations in such a manner that, to the maximum extent feasible, the path of travel to the altered area, and the bathrooms, telephones, and drinking fountains serving the altered area, are readily accessible to and usable by individuals with disabilities, including individuals who use wheelchairs, upon completion of such alterations, where such alterations to the path of travel or the bathrooms, telephones, and drinking fountains serving the altered area are not disproportionate to the overall alterations in terms of cost and scope (as determined under criteria established by the Attorney General).

(C) REQUIRED COOPERATION.—It shall be considered discrimination for purposes of section 202 of this Act and section 504 of the Rehabilitation Act of 1973 (29 U.S.C. 794) for an owner, or person in control, of a station governed by subparagraph (A) or (B) to fail to provide reasonable cooperation to a responsible person with respect to such station in that responsible person's efforts to comply with such subparagraph. An owner, or person in control, of a station shall be liable to a responsible person for any failure to provide reasonable cooperation as required by this subparagraph. Failure to receive reasonable cooperation required by this subparagraph shall not be a defense to a claim of discrimination under this Act.

SEC. 243. CONFORMANCE OF ACCESSIBILITY STANDARDS.

Accessibility standards included in regulations issued under this part shall be consistent with the minimum guidelines issued by the Architectural and Transportation Barriers Compliance Board under section 504(a) of this Act.

SEC. 244. REGULATIONS.

Not later than 1 year after the date of enactment of this Act, the Secretary of Transportation shall issue regulations, in an accessible format, necessary for carrying out this part.

SEC. 245. INTERIM ACCESSIBILITY REQUIREMENTS.

(a) STATIONS.—If final regulations have not been issued pursuant to section 241, for new construction or alterations for which a valid and appropriate State or local building permit is obtained prior to the issuance of final regulations under such section, and for which the construction or alteration authorized by such permit begins within one year of the receipt of such permit and is completed under the terms of such permit, compliance with the Uniform Federal Accessibility Standards in effect at the time the building permit is issued shall suffice to satisfy the requirement that stations be readily accessible to and usable by persons with disabilities as required under section 242(e), except that, if such final regulations have not been issued one year after the Architectural and Transportation Barriers Compliance Board has issued the supplemental minimum guidelines required under section 504(a) of this Act, compliance with such supplemental minimum guidelines shall be necessary to satisfy the requirement that stations be readily accessible to and usable by persons with disabilities prior to issuance of the final regulations.

(b) RAIL PASSENGER CARS.—If final regulations have not been issued pursuant to section 244, a person shall be considered to have complied with the requirements of section 242 (a) through (d) that a rail passenger car be readily accessible to and usable by individuals with disabilities, if the design for such car complies with the laws and regulations (including the Minimum Guidelines and Requirements for Accessible Design and such supplemental minimum guidelines as are issued under section 504(a) of this Act) governing accessibility of such cars, to the extent that such laws and regulations are not inconsistent with this part and are in effect at the time such design is substantially completed.

SEC. 246. EFFECTIVE DATE.

(a) GENERAL RULE.—Except as provided in subsection (b), this part shall become effective 18 months after the date of enactment of this Act.

(b) EXCEPTION.—Sections 242 and 244 shall become effective on the date of enactment of this Act.

TITLE III—PUBLIC ACCOMMODATIONS AND SERVICES OPERATED BY PRIVATE ENTITLES

SEC. 301. DEFINITIONS.

As used in this title:

(1) COMMERCE.—The term "commerce" means travel, trade, traffic, commerce, transportation, or communication—

(A) among the several States;

(B) between any foreign country or any territory or possession and any State; or

(C) between points in the same State but through another State or foreign country.

(2) COMMERCIAL FACILITIES—The term "commercial facilities" means facilities—

(A) that are intended for nonresidential use; and

(B) whose operations will affect commerce.

Such term shall not include railroad locomotives, railroad freight cars, railroad cabooses, railroad cars described in section 242 or covered under this title, railroad rights-of-way, or facilities that are covered or expressly exempted from coverage under the Fair Housing Act of 1968 (42 U.S.C. 3601 et seq.).

(3) DEMAND RESPONSIVE SYSTEM.—The term "demand responsive system" means any system of providing transportation of individuals by a vehicle, other than a system which is a fixed route system.

(4) FIXED ROUTE SYSTEM.—The term "fixed route system" means a system of providing transportation of individuals (other than by aircraft) on which a vehicle is operated along a prescribed route according to a fixed schedule.

(5) OVER-THE-ROAD BUS.—The term "over-the-road bus" means a bus characterized by an elevated passenger deck located over a baggage compartment.

(6) PRIVATE ENTITY.—The term "private entity" means any entity other than a public entity (as defined in section 201(1)).

(7) PUBLIC ACCOMMODATION.—The following private entities are considered public accommodations for purposes of this title, if the operations of such entities affect commerce—

(A) an inn, hotel, motel, or other place of lodging, except for an establishment located within a building that contains not more than five rooms for rent or hire and that is actually occupied by the proprietor of such establishment as the residence of such proprietor;

(B) a restaurant, bar, or other establishment serving food or drink;

(C) a motion picture house, theater, concert hall, stadium, or other place of exhibition or entertainment;

(D) an auditorium, convention center, lecture hall, or other place of public gathering;

(E) a bakery, grocery store, clothing store, hardware store, shopping center, or other sales or rental establishment;

(F) a laundromat, dry-cleaner, bank, barber shop, beauty shop, travel service, shoe repair service, funeral parlor, gas station, office of an accountant or lawyer, pharmacy, insurance office, professional office of a health care provider, hospital, or other service establishment;

(G) a terminal, depot, or other station used for specified public transportation;

(H) a museum, library, gallery, or other place of public display or collection;

(I) a park, zoo, amusement park, or other place of recreation;

(J) a nursery, elementary, secondary, undergraduate, or postgraduate private school, or other place of education;

(K) a day care center, senior citizen center, homeless shelter, food bank, adoption agency, or other social service center establishment; and

(L) a gymnasium, health spa, bowling alley, golf course, or other place of exercise or recreation.

(8) RAIL AND RAILROAD.—The terms rail and railroad have the meaning given the term "railroad" in section 202(e) of the Federal Railroad Safety Act of 1970 (45 U.S.C. 431(e)).

(9) READILY ACHIEVABLE.—The term "readily achievable" means easily accomplishable and able to be carried out without much difficulty or expense. In determining whether an action is readily achievable, factors to be considered include—

(A) the nature and cost of the action needed under this Act;

(B) the overall financial resources of the facility or facilities involved in the action; the number of persons employed at a such facility; the effect on expenses and and resources, or the impact otherwise of such action upon the operation of the facility;

(C) the overall financial resources of the covered entity; the overall size of the business of a covered entity with respect to the number of its employees; the number, type, and location of its facilities; and

(D) the type of operation or operations of the covered entity, including the composition, structure, and functions of the workforce of such entity; the geographic separateness, administrative or fiscal relationship of the facility or facilities in question to the covered entity.

(10) SPECIFIED PUBLIC TRANSPORTATION.—The term "specified public transportation" means transportation by bus, rail, or any other conveyance (other than by aircraft) that provides the general public with general or special service (including charter service) on a regular and continuing basis.

(11) VEHICLE.—The term "vehicle" does not include a rail passenger car, railroad locomotive, railroad freight car, railroad caboose, or a railroad car described in section 242 or covered under this title.

SEC. 302. PROHIBITION OF DISCRIMINATION BY PUBLIC ACCOMMODATIONS.

(a) GENERAL RULE.—NO individual shall be discriminated against on the basis of disability in the full and equal enjoyment of the goods, services, facilities, privileges, advantages, or accommodations of any place of public accommodation by any person who owns, leases (or leases to), or operates a place of public accommodation.

(b) CONSTRUCTION.—

(1) GENERAL PROHIBITION .—

(A) ACTIVITIES.—

(i) DENIAL OF PARTICIPATION.—It shall be discriminatory to subject an individual or class of individuals on the basis of a disability or disabilities of such individual or class, directly, or through contractual, licensing, or other arrangements, to a denial of the opportunity of the individual or class to participate in or benefit from the goods, services, facilities, privileges, advantages, or accommodations of an entity.

(ii) PARTICIPATION IN UNEQUAL BENEFIT.—It shall be discriminatory to afford an individual or class of individuals, on the basis of a disability or disabilities of such individual or class, directly, or through contractual, licensing, or other arrangements with the opportunity to participate in or benefit from a good, service, facility; privilege, advantage, or accommodation that is not equal to that afforded to other individuals.

(iii) SEPARATE BENEFIT.—It shall be discriminatory to provide an individual or class of individuals, on the basis of a disability or disabilities of such individual or class, directly, or through contractual, licensing, or other arrangements with a good, service, facility, privilege, advantage, or accommodation that is different or separate from that provided to other individuals, unless such action is necessary to provide the individual or class of individuals with a good, service, facility, privilege, advantage, or accommodation, or other opportunity that is as effective as that provided to others.

(iv) INDIVIDUAL OR CLASS OF INDIVIDUALS.—For purposes of clauses (i) through (iii) of this subparagraph, the term "individual or class of individuals" refers to the clients or customers of the covered public accommodation that enters into the contractual, licensing or other arrangement.

(B) INTEGRATED SETTINGS.—Goods, services, facilities, privileges, advantages, and accommodations shall be afforded to an individual with a disability in the most integrated setting appropriate to the needs of the individual.

(C) OPPORTUNITY TO PARTICIPATE.—Notwithstanding the existence of separate or different programs or activities provided in accordance with this section, an individual with a disability shall not be denied the opportunity to participate in such programs or activities that are not separate or different.

(D) ADMINISTRATIVE METHODS.—An individual or entity shall not, directly or through contractual or other arrangements, utilize standards or criteria or methods of administration—

(i) that have the effect of discriminating on the basis of disability; or

(ii) that perpetuate the discrimination of others who are subject to common administrative control.

(E) ASSOCIATION.—It shall be discriminatory to exclude or otherwise deny equal goods, services, facilities, privileges, advantages, accommodations, or other opportunities to an individual or entity because of the known disability of an individual with whom the individual or entity is known to have a relationship or association.

(2) SPECIFIC PROHIBITIONS.—

(A) DISCRIMINATION.—For purposes of subsection (a), discrimination includes—

(i) the imposition or application of eligibility criteria that screen out or tend to screen out an individual with a disability or any class of individuals with disabilities from fully and equally enjoying any goods, services, facilities, privileges, advantages, or accommodations, unless such criteria can be shown to be necessary for the provision of the goods, services, facilities, privileges, advantages, or accommodations being offered;

(ii) a failure to make reasonable modifications in policies, practices, or procedures, when such modifications are necessary to afford such goods, services, facilities, privileges, advantages, or accommodations to individuals with disabilities, unless the entity can demonstrate that making such modifications would fundamentally alter the nature of such goods, services, facilities, privileges, advantages, or accommodations;

(iii) a failure to take such steps as may be necessary to ensure that no individual with a disability is excluded, denied services, segregated or otherwise treated differently than other individuals because of the absence of auxiliary aids and services, unless the entity can demonstrate that taking such steps would fundamentally alter the nature of the good, service, facility, privilege, advantage, or accommodation being offered or would result in an undue burden;

(iv) a failure to remove architectural barriers, and communication barriers that are structural in nature, in existing facilities, and transportation barriers in existing vehicles and rail passenger cars used by an establishment for transporting individuals (not including barriers that can only be removed through the retrofitting of vehicles or rail passenger cars by the installation of a hydraulic or other lift), where such removal is readily achievable; and

(v) where an entity can demonstrate that the removal of a barrier under clause (iv) is not readily achievable, a failure to make such goods, services, facilities, privileges, advantages, or accommodations available through alternative methods if such methods are readily achievable.

(B) FIXED ROUTE SYSTEM.—

(i) ACCESSIBILITY.—It shall be considered discrimination for a private entity which operates a fixed route system and which is not subject to section 304 to purchase or lease a vehicle with a seating capacity in excess of 16 passengers (including the driver) for use on such system, for which a solicitation is made after the 30th day following the effective date of this subparagraph, that is not readily accessible to and usable by individuals with disabilities, including individuals who use wheelchairs.

(ii) EQUIVALENT SERVICE.—If a private entity which operates a fixed route system and which is not subject to section 304 purchases or leases a vehicle with a seating capacity of 16 passengers or less (including the driver) for use on such system after the effective date of this subparagraph that is not readily accessible to or usable by individuals with disabilities, it shall be considered discrimination for such entity to fail to operate such system so that, when viewed in its entirety, such system ensures a level of service to individuals with disabilities, including individuals who use wheelchairs, equivalent to the level of service provided to individuals without disabilities.

(C) DEMAND RESPONSIVE SYSTEM.—For purposes of subsection (a), discrimination includes—

(i) a failure of a private entity which operates a demand responsive system and which is not subject to section 304 to operate such system so that, when viewed in its entirety, such system ensures a level of service to individuals with disabilities, including individuals who use wheelchairs, equivalent to the level of service provided to individuals without disabilities; and

(ii) the purchase or lease by such entity for use on such system of a vehicle with a seating capacity in excess of 16 passengers (including the driver), for which solicitations are made after the 30th day following the effective date of this subparagraph, that is not readily accessible to and usable by individuals with disabilities (including individuals who use wheelchairs) unless such entity can demonstrate that such system, when viewed in its entirety, provides a level of service to individuals with disabilities equivalent to that provided to individuals without disabilities.

(D) OVER-THE-ROAD BUSES.—-

(i) LIMITATION ON APPLICABILITY.—Subparagraphs (B) and (C) do not apply to over-the-road buses.

(ii) ACCESSIBILITY REQUIREMENTS.—-For purposes of subsection (a), discrimination includes (I) the purchase or lease of an over-the-road bus which does not comply with the regulations issued under section 306(a)(2) by a private entity which provides transportation of individuals and which is not primarily engaged in the business of transporting people, and (II) any other failure of such entity to comply with such regulations.

(3) SPECIFIC CONSTRUCTION.—Nothing in this title shall require an entity to permit an individual to participate in or benefit from the goods, services, facilities, privileges, advantages and accommodations of such entity where such individual poses a direct threat to the health or safety of others. The term "direct threat" means a significant risk to the health or safety of others that cannot be eliminated by a modification of policies. practices, or procedures or by the provision of auxiliary aids or services.

SEC. 303. NEW CONSTRUCTION AND ALTERATIONS IN PUBLIC ACCOMMODATIONS AND COMMERCIAL FACILITIES.

(a) APPLICATION OF TERM.—Except as provided in subsection (b), as applied to public accommodations and commercial facilities, discrimination for purposes of section 302(a) includes—

(1) a failure to design and construct facilities for first occupancy later than 30 months after the date of enactment of this Act that are readily accessible to and

usable by individuals with disabilities, except where an entity can demonstrate that it is structurally impracticable to meet the requirements of such subsection in accordance with standards set forth or incorporated by reference in regulations issued under this title; and

(2) with respect to a facility or part thereof that is altered by, on behalf of, or for the use of an establishment in a manner that affects or could affect the usability of the facility or part thereof, a failure to make alterations in such a manner that, to the maximum extent feasible, the altered portions of the facility are readily accessible to and usable by individuals with disabilities, including individuals who use wheelchairs. Where the entity is undertaking an alteration that affects or could affect usability of or access to an area of the facility containing a primary function, the entity shall also make the alterations in such a manner that, to the maximum extent feasible, the path of travel to the altered area and the bathrooms. telephones, and drinking fountains serving the altered area, are not disproportionate to the overall alterations in the term of cost and scope (as 104 STAT. 359 determined under criteria established by the Attorney General).

(b) ELEVATOR.—Subsection (a) shall not be construed to require the installation of an elevator for facilities that are less than three stories or have less than 3,000 square feet per story unless the building is a shopping center, a shopping mall, or the professional office of a health care provider or unless the Attorney General determines that a particular category of such facilities requires the installation of elevators based on the usage of such facilities.

SEC. 304. PROHIBITION OF DISCRIMINATION IN SPECIFIED PUBLIC TRANSPORTATION SERVICES PROVIDED BY PRIVATE ENTITIES.

(a) GENERAL RULE.—No individual shall be discriminated against on the basis of disability in the full and equal enjoyment of specified public transportation services provided by a private entity that is primarily engaged in the business of transporting people and whose operations affect commerce.

(b) CONSTRUCTION.—For purposes of subsection (a), discrimination includes—

(1) the imposition or application by a entity described in subsection (a) of eligibility criteria that screen out or tend to screen out an individual with a disability or any class of individuals with disabilities from fully enjoying the specified public transportation services provided by the entity, unless such criteria can be shown to be necessary for the provision of the services being offered; (2) the failure of such entity to—

(A) make reasonable modifications consistent with those required under section 302(b)(2)(A)(ii);

(B) provide auxiliary aids and services consistent with the requirements of section 302(b)(2)(A)(iii); and

(C) remove barriers consistent with the requirements of section 302(b)(2)(A) and with the requirements of section 303(a)(2)

(3) the purchase or lease by such entity of a new vehicle (other than an automobile, a van with a seating capacity of less than 8 passengers, including the driver, or an over-the-road bus) which is to be used to provide specified public transportation and for which a solicitation is made after the 30th day following the effective date of this section, that is not readily accessible to and usable by individuals with disabilities, including individuals who use wheelchairs; except that the new vehicle need not be readily accessible to and usable by such individuals if the new vehicle is to be used solely in a demand responsive system and if the entity can demonstrate that such system, when viewed in its entirety, provides a level of service to such individuals equivalent to the level of service provided to the general public; (4)(A) the purchase or lease by such entity of an over-the-road bus which does not comply with the regulations issued under section 306(a)(2); and

(B) any other failure of such entity to comply with such regulations; and

(5) the purchase or lease by such entity of a new van with a seating capacity of less than 8 passengers, including the driver, which is to be used to provide specified public transportation and for which a solicitation is made after the 30th day following the effective date of this section that is not readily accessible to or usable by individuals with disabilities, including individuals who use wheelchairs; except that the new van need not be readily accessible to and usable by such individuals if the entity can demonstrate that the system for which the van is being purchased or leased, when viewed in its entirety, provides a level of service to such individuals equivalent to the level of service provided to the general public;

(6) the purchase or lease by such entity of a new rail passenger car that is to be used to provide specified public transportation, and for which a solicitation is made later than 30 days after the effective date of this paragraph, that is not readily accessible to and usable by individuals with disabilities, including individuals who use wheelchairs; and

(7) the remanufacture by such entity of a rail passenger car that is to be used to provide specified public transportation so as to extend its usable life for 10 years or more, or the purchase or lease by such entity of such a rail car, unless the rail car, to the maximum extent feasible, is made readily accessible to and usable by individuals with disabilities, including individuals who use wheelchairs.

(C) HISTORICAL OR ANTIQUATED CARS.—

(1) EXCEPTION.—To the extent that compliance with subsection (b)(2)(C) or (b)(7) would significantly alter the historic or antiquated character of a historical or antiquated rail passenger car, or a rail station served exclusively by

such cars, or would result in violation of any rule, regulation, standard, or order issued by the Secretary of Transportation under the Federal Railroad Safety Act of 1970, such compliance shall not be required.

(2) DEFINITION.—As used in this subsection, the term "historical or antiquated rail passenger car" means a rail passenger car—

(A) which is not less than 30 years old at the time of its use for transporting individuals;

(B) the manufacturer of which is no longer in the business of manufacturing rail passenger cars; and

(C) which—

(i) has a consequential association with events or persons significant to the past; or

(ii) embodies, or is being restored to embody, the distinctive characteristics of a type of rail passenger car used in the past, or to represent a time period which has passed.

SEC. 305. STUDY.

(a) PURPOSES.—The Office of Technology Assessment shall undertake a study to determine—

(1) the access needs of individuals with disabilities to over-the-road buses and over-the-road bus service; and

(2) the most cost-effective methods for providing access to over-the-road buses and over-the-road bus service to individuals with disabilities, particularly individuals who use wheelchairs, through all forms of boarding options.

(b) CONTENTS.—The study shall include, at a minimum, an analysis of the following: (1) The anticipated demand by individuals with disabilities for accessible over-the-road buses and over-the-road bus service. (2) The degree to which such buses and service, including any service required under sections 304(b)(4) and 306(a)(2), are readily accessible to and usable by individuals with disabilities.

(3) The effectiveness of various methods of providing accessibility to such buses and service to individuals with disabilities.

(4) The cost of providing accessible over-the-road buses and bus service to individuals with disabilities, including consideration of recent technological and cost saving developments in equipment and devices.

(5) Possible design changes in over-the-road buses that could enhance accessibility, including the installation of accessible restrooms which do not result in a reduction of seating capacity.

(6) The impact of accessibility requirements on the continuation of over-the-

road bus service, with particular consideration of the impact of such requirements on such service to rural communities.

(c) ADVISORY COMMITTEE.—In conducting the study required by subsection (a), the Office of Technology Assessment shall establish an advisory committee, which shall consist of—

(1) members selected from among private operators and manufacturers of over-the-road buses;

(2) members selected from among individuals with disabilities, particularly individuals who use wheelchairs, who are potential riders of such buses; and

(3) members selected for their technical expertise on issues included in the study, including manufacturers of boarding assistance equipment and devices. The number of members selected under each of paragraphs (1) and (2) shall be equal, and the total number of members selected under paragraphs (1) and (2) shall exceed the number of members selected under paragraph (3).

(d) DEADLINE.—The study required by subsection (a), along with recommendations by the Office of Technology Assessment, including any policy options for legislative action, shall be submitted to the President and Congress within 36 months after the date of the enactment of this Act. If the President determines that compliance with the regulations issued pursuant to section 306(a)(2)(B) on or before the applicable deadlines specified in section 306(a)(2)(B) will result in a significant reduction in intercity over-the-road bus service, the President shall extend each such deadline by 1 year.

(e) REVIEW.—In developing the study required by subsection (a), the Office of Technology Assessment shall provide a preliminary draft of such study to the Architectural and Transportation Barriers Compliance Board established under section 602 of the Rehabilitation Act of 1973 (29 U.S.C. 792). The Board shall have an opportunity to comment on such draft study, and any such comments by the Board made in writing within 120 days after the Board's receipt of the draft study shall be incorporated as part of the final study required to be submitted under subsection (d).

SEC. 306. REGULATIONS.

(a) TRANSPORTATION PROVISIONS.—

(1) GENERAL RULE.—Not later than 1 year after the date of the enactment of this Act, the Secretary of Transportation shall issue regulations in an accessible format to carry out sections 302(b)(2),(B) and (C) and to carry out section 304 (other than subsection (b)(4)).

(2) SPECIAL RULES FOR PROVIDING ACCESS TO OVER-THE-ROAD BUSES-

(A) INTERIM REQUIREMENTS.—

(i) ISSUANCE.—Not later than 1 year after the date of the enactment of this Act, the Secretary of Transportation shall issue regulations in an accessible format to carry out sections 304(b)(4) and 302(b)(2)(D)(ii) that require each private entity which uses an over-the-road bus to provide transportation of individuals to provide accessibility to such bus; except that such regulations shall not require any structural changes in over-the-road buses in order to provide access to individuals who use wheelchairs during the effective period of such regulations and shall not require the purchase of boarding assistance devices to provide access to such individuals.

(ii) EFFECTIVE PERIOD.—The regulations issued pursuant to this subparagraph shall be effective until the effective date of the regulations issued under subparagraph (B).

(B) FINAL REQUIREMENT.—

(i) REVIEW OF STUDY AND INTERIM REQUIREMENTS.—The Secretary shall review the study submitted under section 305 and the regulations issued pursuant to subparagraph (A).

(ii) ISSUANCE.—Not later than l year after the date of the submission of the study under section 305, the Secretary shall issue in an accessible format new regulations to carry out sections 304(b)(4) and 302(b)(2)(D)(ii) that require, taking into account the purposes of the study under section 305 and any recommendations resulting from such study, each private entity which uses an over-the-road bus to provide transportation to individuals to provide accessibility to such bus to individuals with disabilities, including individuals who use wheelchairs.

(iii) EFFECTIVE PERIOD.—Subject to section 305(d), the regulations issued pursuant to this subparagraph shall take effect—

(I) with respect to small providers of transportation (as defined by the Secretary), 7 years after the date of the enactment of this Act; and

(II) with respect to other providers of transportation, 6 years after such date of enactment.

(C) LIMITATION ON REQUIRING INSTALLATION OF ACCESSIBLE RESTROOMS.—The regulations issued pursuant to this paragraph shall not require the installation of accessible restrooms in over-the-road buses if such installation would result in a reduction of seating capacity.

(3) STANDARDS.—The regulations issued pursuant to this subsection shall include standards applicable to facilities and vehicles covered by sections 302(b)(2) and 304.

(b) OTHER PROVISIONS.—Not later than 1 year after the date of the enactment of this Act, the Attorney General shall issue regulations in an accessible format to carry out the provisions of this title not referred to in subsection (a) that include standards applicable to facilities and vehicles covered under section 302.

(c) CONSISTENCY WITH ATBCB GUIDELINES.—Standards included in regulations issued under subsections (a) and (b) shall be consistent with the minimum guidelines and requirements issued by the Architectural and Transportation Barriers Compliance Board in accordance with section 504 of this Act.

(d) INTERIM ACCESSIBILITY STANDARDS.—

(1) FACILITIES.—If final regulations have not been issued pursuant to this section, for new construction or alterations for which a valid and appropriate State or local building permit is obtained prior to the issuance of final regulations under this section, and for which the construction or alteration authorized by such permit begins within one year of the receipt of such permit and is completed under the terms of such permit, compliance with the Uniform Federal Accessibility Standards in effect at the time the building permit is issued shall suffice to satisfy the requirement that facilities be readily accessible to and usable by persons with disabilities as required under section 303, except that, if such final regulations have not been issued one year after the Architectural and Transportation Barriers Compliance Board has issued the supplemental minimum guidelines required under section 504(a) of this Act, compliance with such supplemental minimum guidelines shall be necessary to satisfy the requirement that facilities be readily accessible to and usable by persons with disabilities prior to issuance of the final regulations.

(2) VEHICLES AND RAIL PASSENGER CARS.—If final regulations have not been issued pursuant to this section, a private entity shall be considered to have complied with the requirements of this title, if any, that a vehicle or rail passenger car be readily accessible to and usable by individuals with disabilities, if the design for such vehicle or car complies with the laws and regulations (including the Minimum Guidelines and Requirements for Accessible Design and such supplemental minimum guidelines as are issued under section 504(a) of this Act) governing accessibility of such vehicles or cars, to the extent that such laws and regulations are not inconsistent with this title and are in effect at the time such design is substantially completed.

SEC. 307. EXEMPTIONS FOR PRIVATE CLUBS AND RELIGIOUS ORGANIZATIONS.

The provisions of this title shall not apply to private clubs or establishments exempted from coverage under Title II of the Civil Rights Act of 1964 (42 U.S.C. 2000-a(e)) or to religious organizations or entities controlled by religious organizations, including places of worship.

SEC. 308. ENFORCEMENT .

(a) IN GENERAL.—

(1) AVAILABILITY OF REMEDIES AND PROCEDURES.—The remedies

and procedures set forth in section 204(a) of the Civil Rights Act of 1964 (42 U.S.C. 2000a-3(a)) are the remedies and procedures this title provides to any person who is being subjected to discrimination on the basis of disability in violation of this title or who has reasonable grounds for believing that such person is about to be subjected to discrimination in violation of section 303. Nothing in this section shall require a person with a disability to engage in a futile gesture if such person has actual notice that a person or organization covered by this title does not intend to comply with its provisions.

(2) INJUNCTIVE RELIEF.—In the case of violations of sections 302(b)(2)(A)(IV) and section 303(a), injunctive relief shall include an order to alter facilities to make such facilities readily accessible to and usable by individuals with disabilities to the extent required by this title. Where appropriate, injunctive relief shall also include requiring the provision of an auxiliary aid or service, modification of a policy, or provision of alternative methods, to the extent required by this title.

(b) ENFORCEMENT BY THE ATTORNEY GENERAL

(1) DENIAL OF RIGHTS.—

(A) DUTY TO INVESTIGATE.—

(i) IN GENERAL.—The Attorney General shall investigate alleged violations of this title, and shall undertake periodic reviews of compliance of covered entities under this title.

(ii) ATTORNEY GENERAL CERTIFICATION.—On the application of a State or local government, the Attorney General may, in consultation with the Architectural and Transportation Barriers Compliance Board, and after prior notice and a public hearing at which persons, including individuals with disabilities, are provided an opportunity to testify against such certification, certify that a State law or local building code or similar ordinance that establishes accessibility requirements meets or exceeds the minimum requirements of this Act for the accessibility and usability of covered facilities under this title. At any enforcement proceeding under this section, such certification by the Attorney General shall be rebuttable evidence that such State law or local ordinance does meet or exceed the minimum requirements of this Act.

(B) POTENTIAL VIOLATION.—If the Attorney General has reasonable cause to believe that—

(i) any person or group of persons is engaged in a pattern or practice of discrimination under this title; or

(ii) any person or group of persons has been discriminated against under this title and such discrimination raises an issue of general public importance, the Attorney General may commence a civil action in any appropriate United States district court.

(2) AUTHORITY OF COURT.—In a civil action under paragraph (1)(B), the court—

(A) may grant any equitable relief that such court considers to be appropriate, including, to the extent required by this title—

(i) granting temporary, preliminary, or permanent relief;

(ii) providing an auxiliary aid or service, modification of policy, practice, or procedure, or alternative method; and

(iii) making facilities readily accessible to and usable by individuals with disabilities;

(B) may award such other relief as the court considers to be appropriate, including monetary damages to persons aggrieved when requested by the Attorney General; and

(C) may, to vindicate the public interest, assess a civil penalty against the entity in an amount—

(i) not exceeding $50,000 for a first violation; and

(ii) not exceeding $100,000 for any subsequent violation.

(3) SINGLE VIOLATION.—For purposes of paragraph (2)(C), in determining whether a first or subsequent violation has occurred, a determination in a single action, by judgment or settlement, that the covered entity has engaged in more than one discriminatory act shall be counted as a single violation.

(4) PUNITIVE DAMAGES.—For purposes of subsection (b)(2)(B), the term "monetary damages" and "such other relief" does not include punitive damages.

(5) JUDICIAL CONSIDERATION.—In a civil action under paragraph (1)(B), the court, when considering what amount of civil penalty, if any, is appropriate, shall give consideration to any good faith effort or attempt to comply with this Act by the entity. In evaluating good faith, the court shall consider, among other factors it deems relevant, whether the entity could have reasonably anticipated the need for an appropriate type of auxiliary aid needed to accommodate the unique needs of a particular individual with a disability.

SEC. 309. EXAMINATIONS AND COURSES.

Any person that offers examinations or courses related to applications, licensing, certification, or credentialing for secondary or post-secondary education, professional, or trade purposes shall offer such examinations or courses in a place and manner accessible to persons with disabilities or offer alternative accessible arrangements for such individuals.

SEC. 310. EFFECTIVE DATE.

(a) GENERAL RULE.—Except as provided in subsections (b) and (c), this title shall become effective 18 months after the date of the enactment of this Act.

(b) CIVIL ACTIONS.—Except for any civil action brought for a violation of section 303, no civil action shall be brought for any act or omission described in section 302 which occurs—

(1) during the first 6 months after the effective date, against businesses that employ 25 or fewer employees and have gross receipts of $1,000,000 or less; and

(2) during the first year after the effective date, against businesses that employ 10 or fewer employees and have gross receipts of $500,000 or less.

(c) EXCEPTION.—Sections 302(a) for purposes of section 302(b)(2)(B) and (C) only, 304(a) for purposes of section 304(b)(3) only, 304(b)(3), 305, and 306 shall take effect on the date of the enactment of this Act.

TITLE IV—TELECOMMUNICATIONS

SEC. 401. TELECOMMUNICATIONS RELAY SERVICES FOR HEARING-IMPAIRED AND SPEECH-IMPAIRED INDIVIDUALS.

(1)(a) TELECOMMUNICATIONS.—Title II of the Communications Act of 1934 (47 U.S.C. 201 et seq.) is amended by adding at the end thereof the following new section:

SEC. 225. TELECOMMUNICATIONS SERVICES FOR HEARING IMPAIRED AND SPEECH-IMPAIRED INDIVIDUALS.

(a) DEFINITIONS.—As used in this section—

(1) COMMON CARRIER OR CARRIER.—The term "common carrier" or "carrier" includes any common carrier engaged in interstate communication by wire or radio as defined in section 3(h) and any common carrier engaged in intrastate communication by wire or radio, notwithstanding sections 2(b) And 221(b).

(2) TDD.—The term "TDD" means a Telecommunications Device for the Deaf, which is a machine that employs graphic communication in the transmission of coded signals through a wire or radio communication system.

(3) TELECOMMUNICATIONS RELAY SERVICES.—The term "telecommunications relay services" means telephone transmission services that provide the ability for an individual who has a hearing impairment or speech impairment to engage in communication by wire or radio with a hearing individual in a manner that is functionally equivalent to the ability of an individual who does not have a hearing impairment or speech impairment to communicate using voice communication services by wire or radio. Such term includes services that enable two-way communication between an individual who uses a TDD or

other non-voice terminal device and an individual who does not use such a device.

(b) AVAILABILITY OF TELECOMMUNICATIONS RELAY SERVICES.—

(1) IN GENERAL.—In order to carry out the purposes established under section 1, to make available to all individuals in the United States a rapid, efficient nationwide communication service, and to increase the utility of the telephone system of the Nation, the Commission shall ensure that interstate and intrastate telecommunications relay services are available. to the extent possible and in the most efficient manner, to hearing-impaired and speech-impaired individuals in the United States.

(2) USE OF GENERAL AUTHORITY AND REMEDIES.—For the purposes of administering and enforcing the provisions of this section and the regulations prescribed thereunder, the Commission shall have the same authority, power, and functions with respect to common carriers engaged in intrastate communication as the Commission has in administering and enforcing the provisions of this title with respect to any common carrier engaged in interstate communication. Any violation of this section by any common carrier engaged in intrastate communication shall be subject to the same remedies, penalties, and procedures as are applicable to a violation of this Act by a common carrier engaged in interstate communication.

(c) PROVISION OF SERVICES.—Each common carrier providing telephone voice transmission services shall, not later than 3 years after the date of enactment of this section, provide in compliance with the regulations prescribed under this section, throughout the area in which it offers service, telecommunications relay services, individually, through designers, through a competitively selected vendor, or in concert with other carriers. A common carrier shall be considered to be in compliance with such regulations—

(1) with respect to intrastate telecommunications relay services in any State that does not have a certified program under subsection (f) and with respect to interstate telecommunications relay services, if such common carrier (or other entity through which the carrier is providing such relay services is in compliance with the Commission's regulations under subsection (d); or

(2) with respect to intrastate telecommunications relay services in any State that has a certified program under subsection (f) for such State, if such common carrier (or other entity through which the carrier is providing such relay services) is in compliance with the program certified under subsection (f) for such State.

(d) REGULATIONS.—

(1) IN GENERAL.—The Commission shall, not later than 1 year after the date of enactment of this section, prescribe regulations to implement this section, including regulations that—

(A) establish functional requirements, guidelines, and operations procedures for telecommunications relay services;

(B) establish minimum standards that shall be met in carrying out subsection (c);

(C) require that telecommunications relay services operate every day for 24 hours per day;

(D) require that users of telecommunications relay services pay rates no greater than the rates paid for functionally equivalent voice communication services with respect to such factors as the duration of the call, the time of day, and the distance from point of origination to point of termination;

(E) prohibit relay operators from failing to fulfill the obligations of common carriers by refusing calls or limiting the length of calls that use telecommunications relay services;

(F) prohibit relay operators from disclosing the content of any relayed conversation and from keeping records of the content of any such conversation beyond the duration of the call; and

(G) prohibit relay operators from intentionally altering a relayed conversation.

(2) TECHNOLOGY.—The Commission shall ensure that regulations prescribed to implement this section encourage, consistent with section 7(a) of this Act, the use of existing technology and do not discourage or impair the development of improved technology.

(3) JURISDICTIONAL SEPARATION OF COSTS.—

(A) IN GENERAL.—Consistent with the provisions of section 410 of this Act, the Commission shall prescribe regulations governing the jurisdictional separation of costs for the services provided pursuant to this section.

(B) RECOVERING COSTS.—Such regulations shall generally provide that costs caused by interstate telecommunications relay services shall be recovered from all subscribers for every interstate service and costs caused by intrastate telecommunications relay services shall be recovered from the intrastate jurisdiction. In a State that has a certified program under subsection (f), a State commission shall permit a common carrier to recover the costs incurred in providing intrastate telecommunications relay services by a method consistent with the requirements of this section.

(e) ENFORCEMENT.—

(1) IN GENERAL.—Subject to subsections (f) and (g), the Commission shall enforce this section.

(2) COMPLAINT.—The Commission shall resolve, by final order, a complaint alleging a violation of this section within 180 days after the date such complaint is filed.

(f) CERTIFICATION.—

(1) STATE DOCUMENTATION.—Any State desiring to establish a State program under this section shall submit documentation to the Commission that describes the program of such State for implementing intrastate telecommunications relay services and the procedures and remedies available for enforcing any requirements imposed by the State program.

(2) REQUIREMENTS FOR CERTIFICATION.—After review of such documentation, the Commission shall certify the State program if the Commission determines that—

(A) the program makes available to hearing-impaired and speech-impaired individuals, either directly, through designers, through a competitively selected vendor, or through regulation of intrastate common carriers, intrastate telecommunications relay services in such State in a manner that meets or exceeds the requirements of regulations prescribed by the Commission under subsection (d); and

(B) the program makes available adequate procedures and remedies for enforcing the requirements of the State program.

(3) METHOD OF FUNDING.—Except as provided in subsection (d), the Commission shall not refuse to certify a State program based solely on the method such State will implement for funding intrastate telecommunication relay services.

(4) SUSPENSION OR REVOCATION OF CERTIFICATION.—The Commission may suspend or revoke such certification if, after notice and opportunity for hearing, the Commission determines that such certification is no longer warranted. In a State whose program has been suspended or revoked, the Commission shall take such steps as may be necessary, consistent with this section, to ensure continuity of telecommunications relay services.

(g) COMPLAINT.—

(1) REFERRAL OF COMPLAINT.—If a complaint to the Commission alleges a violation of this section with respect to intrastate telecommunications relay services within a State and certification of the program of such State under subsection (f) is in effect, the Commission shall refer such complaint to such State.

(2) JURISDICTION OF COMMISSION.- After referring a complaint to a State under paragraph (1), the Commission shall exercise jurisdiction over such complaint only if-

(A) final action under such State program has not been taken on such State—

(i) within 180 days after the complaint is filed with such State; or

(ii) within a shorter period as prescribed by the regulations of such State; or

(B) the Commission determines that such State program is no longer qualified for certification under subsection (f).

(b) CONFORMING AMENDMENTS.—The Communications Act of 1934 (47 U.S.C. 151 et seq.) is amended—

(1) in section 2(b) (47 U.S.C. 152(b)), by striking "section 224" and inserting "sections 224 and 225"; and

(2) in section 221(b) (47 U.S.C. 221(b)), by striking "section 301" and inserting "sections 225 and 301".

SEC. 402. CLOSED-CAPTIONING OF PUBLIC SERVICE ANNOUNCEMENTS.

Section 711 of the Communications Act of 1934 is amended 47 USC 611. to read as follows:

SEC. 711. CLOSED-CAPTIONING OF PUBLIC SERVICE ANNOUNCEMENTS.

"Any television public service announcement that is produced or funded in whole or in part by any agency or instrumentality of Federal Government shall include closed captioning of the verbal content of such announcement. A television broadcast station licensee—

(1) shall not be required to supply closed captioning for any such announcement that fails to include it; and

(2) shall not be liable for broadcasting any such announcement without transmitting a closed caption unless the licensee intentionally fails to transmit the closed caption that was included with the announcement."

TITLE V—MISCELLANEOUS PROVISIONS

SEC. 501. CONSTRUCTION.

(a) IN GENERAL.—Except as otherwise provided in this Act, nothing in this Act shall be construed to apply a lesser standard than the standards applied under Title V of the Rehabilitation Act of 1973 (29 U.S.C. 790 et seq.) or the regulations issued by Federal agencies pursuant to such title.

(b) RELATIONSHIP TO OTHER LAWS.—Nothing in this Act shall be construed to invalidate or limit the remedies, rights, and procedures of any Federal Law or law of any State or political subdivision of any State or Jurisdiction that provides greater or equal protection for the rights of individuals with disabilities than are afforded by this Act. Nothing in this Act shall be construed to preclude the prohibition of, or the imposition of restrictions on, smoking in places of employment covered by title I, in transportation covered by Title II or III, or in places of public accommodation covered by Title III.

(c) INSURANCE.—Titles I through IV of this Act shall not be construed to prohibit or restrict—

(1) an insurer, hospital or medical service company, health maintenance organization, or any agent, or entity that administers benefit plans, or similar organizations from underwriting risks, classifying risks, or administering such risks that are based on or not inconsistent with State law; or

(2) a person or organization covered by this Act from establishing, sponsoring, observing or administering the terms of a bona fide benefit plan that are based on underwriting risks, classifying risks, or administering such risks that are based on or not inconsistent with State law; or

(3) a person or organization covered by this Act from establishing, sponsoring, observing or administering the terms of a bona fide benefit plan that is not subject to State laws that regulate insurance.

Paragraphs (1), (2), and (3) shall not be used as a subterfuge to evade the purposes of Title I and III.

(d) ACCOMMODATIONS AND SERVICES.—Nothing in this Act shall be construed to require an individual with a disability to accept an accommodation, aid, service, opportunity, or benefit which such individual chooses not to accept.

SEC. 502. STATE IMMUNITY.

A State shall not be immune under the eleventh amendment to the Constitution of the United States from an action in Federal or State court of competent jurisdiction for a violation of this Act. In any action against a State for a violation of the requirements of this Act, remedies (including remedies both at law and in equity) are available for such a violation to the same extent as such remedies are available for such a violation in an action against any public or private entity other than a State.

SEC. 503. PROHIBITION AGAINST RETALIATION AND COERCION.

(A) RETALIATION.—No person shall discriminate against any individual because such individual has opposed any act or practice made unlawful by this Act or because such individual made a charge, testified, assisted, or participated in any manner in an investigation, proceeding, or hearing under this Act.

(B) INTERFERENCE, COERCION, OR INTIMIDATION.—It shall be unlawful to coerce, intimidate, threaten, or interfere with any individual in the exercise or enjoyment of, or on account of his or her having exercised or enjoyed, or on account of his or her having aided or encouraged any other individual in the exercise or enjoyment of, any right granted or protected by this Act.

(C) REMEDIES AND PROCEDURES.—The remedies and procedures available under sections 107, 203, and 308 of this Act shall be available to aggrieved persons for violations of subsections (a) and (b), with respect to Title I, Title II and Title III, respectively.

SEC. 504. REGULATIONS BY THE ARCHITECTURAL AND TRANSPORTATION BARRIERS COMPLIANCE BOARD.

(a) ISSUANCE OF GUIDELINES.—Not later than 9 months after the date of enactment of this Act, the Architectural and Transportation Barriers Compliance Board shall issue minimum guidelines that shall supplement the existing Minimum Guidelines and Requirements for Accessible Design for purposes of Titles II and III of this Act.

(b) CONTENTS OF GUIDELINES.—The supplemental guidelines issued under subsection (a) shall establish additional requirements, consistent with this Act, to ensure that buildings, facilities. rail passenger cars, and vehicles are accessible, in terms of architecture and design, transportation, and communication, to individuals with disabilities.

(c) QUALIFIED HISTORIC PROPERTIES.—

(1) IN GENERAL.—The supplemental guidelines issued under subsection (a) shall include procedures and requirements for alterations that will threaten or destroy the historic significance of qualified historic buildup and facilities as defined in 4.1.7(1)(a) of the Uniform Federal Accessibility Standards.

(2) SITES ELIGIBLE FOR LISTING IN NATIONAL REGISTER.—With respect to alterations of buildings or facilities that are eligible for listing in the National Register of Historic Places under the National Historic Preservation Act (16 U.S.C. 470 et seq.), the guidelines described in paragraph (1) shall, at a minimum, maintain the procedures and requirements established in 4.1.7 (1) and (2) of the Uniform Federal Accessibility Standards.

(3) OTHER SITES.—With respect to alterations of buildings or facilities designated as historic under State or local law, the guidelines described in paragraph (1) shall establish procedures equivalent to those established by 4.1.7(1) (b) and (c) of the Uniform Federal Accessibility Standards, and shall require, at a minimum, compliance with the requirements established in 4.1.7(2) of such standards.

SEC. 505. ATTORNEY'S FEES.

In any action or administrative proceeding commenced pursuant to this Act, the court or agency, in its discretion, may allow the prevailing party, other than the United States, a reasonable attorney's fee. including litigation expenses, and costs, and the United States shall be liable for the foregoing the same as a private individual.

SEC. 506. TECHNICAL ASSISTANCE.

(a) PLAN FOR ASSISTANCE.—

(1) IN GENERAL.—Not later than 180 days after the date of enactment of this Act, the Attorney General, in consultation with the Chair of the Equal

Employment Opportunity Commission, the Secretary of Transportation, the Chair of the Architectural and Transportation Barriers Compliance Board, and the Chairman of the Federal Communications Commission, shall develop a plan to assist entities covered under this act, and other Federal agencies, in understanding the responsibility of such entities and agencies under this Act.

(2) PUBLICATION OF PLAN.—-The Attorney general shall publish the plan referred to in paragraph (1) for public comment in accordance with subchapter II of chapter 5 of title 5, United States Code (commonly known as the Administrative Procedure Act).

(b) AGENCY AND PUBLIC ASSISTANCE.—The Attorney General may obtain the assistance of other Federal agencies in carrying out subsection (a), including the National Council on Disability. the President's Committee on Employment of People with Disabilities, the Small Business Administration, and the Department of Commerce.

(c) IMPLEMENTATION.—

(1) RENDERING ASSISTANCE.—Each Federal agency that has responsibility under paragraph (2) for implementing this Act may render technical assistance to individuals and institutions that have rights or duties under the respective title or titles for which such agency has responsibility.

(2) IMPLEMENTATION OF TITLES.—

(A) TITLE I—The Equal Employment Opportunity Commission and the Attorney General shall implement the plan for assistance developed under subsection (a), for Title I.

(B) TITLE II.—

(i) SUBTITLE A.—The Attorney General shall implement such plan for assistance for subtitle A of Title II.

(ii) SUBTITLE B.—The Secretary of Transportation shall implement such plan for assistance for subtitle B of Title II.

(C) TITLE III.—The Attorney General, in coordination with the Secretary of Transportation and the Chair of the Architectural Transportation Barriers Compliance Board, shall implement such plan for assistance for Title III, except for section 304, the plan for assistance for which shall be implemented by the Secretary of Transportation.

(D) TITLE IV.—The Chairman of the Federal Communications Commission, in coordination with the Attorney General, shall implement such plan for assistance for Title IV.

(3) TECHNICAL ASSISTANCE MANUALS.—Each Federal agency that has responsibility under paragraph (2) for implementing this Act shall, as part of its implementation responsibilities, ensure the availability and provision of appropriate technical assistance manuals to individuals or entities with right or

duties under this Act no later than six months after applicable final regulations are published under Titles I, II, III, and IV.

(d) GRANTS AND CONTRACTS.—

(1) IN GENERAL.—Each Federal agency that has responsibility under subsection (c)(2) for implementing this Act may make grants or award contracts to effectuate the purposes of this section, subject to the availability of appropriations. Such grants and contracts may be awarded to individuals, institutions not organized for profit and no part of the net earnings of which inures to the benefit of any private shareholder or individual (including educational institutions), and association representing individuals who have rights or duties under this Act. Contracts may be awarded to entities organized for profit, but such entities may not be the recipients or grants described in this paragraph.

(2) DISSEMINATION OF INFORMATION.—Such grants and contracts, among other uses, may be designed to ensure wide dissemination of information about the rights and duties established by this Act and to provide information and technical assistance about techniques for effective compliance with this Act.

(e) FAILURE TO RECEIVE ASSISTANCE.—An employer, public accommodation, or other entity covered under this Act shall not be excused from compliance with the requirements of this Act because of any failure to receive technical assistance under this section, including any failure in the development or dissemination of any technical assistance manual authorized by this section.

SEC. 507. FEDERAL WILDERNESS AREAS.

(a) STUDY.—The National Council on Disability shall conduct a study and report on the effect that wilderness designations and wilderness land management practices have on the ability of individuals with disabilities to use and enjoy the National Wilderness Preservation System as established under the Wilderness Act (16 U.S.C. 1331 et seq.).

(b) SUBMISSION OF REPORT.—Not later than 1 year after the enactment of this Act, the National Council on Disability shall submit the report required under subsection (a) to Congress.

(c) SPECIFIC WILDERNESS ACCESS.—

(1) IN GENERAL.—Congress reaffirms that nothing in the Wilderness Act is to be construed as prohibiting the use of a wheelchair in a wilderness area by an individual whose disability requires use of a wheelchair, and consistent with the Wilderness Act no agency is required to provide any form of special treatment or accommodation, or to construct any facilities or modify any conditions of lands within a wilderness area in order to facilitate such use.

(2) DEFINITION.—For purposes of paragraph (1), the term "wheelchair"

means a device designed solely for use by a mobility-impaired person for locomotion, that is suitable for use in an indoor pedestrian area.

SEC. 508. TRANSVESTITES.

For the purposes of this Act, the term "disabled" or "disability" shall not apply to an individual solely because that individual is a transvestite.

SEC. 509. COVERAGE OF CONGRESS AND THE AGENCIES OF THE LEGISLATIVE BRANCH.

(a) COVERAGE OF THE SENATE.—

(1) COMMITMENT TO RULE XLII.—The Senate reaffirms its commitment to Rule XLII of the Standing Rules of the Senate which provides as follows:

"No member, officer, or employee of the Senate shall, with respect to employment by the Senate or any office thereof—

(a) fail or refuse to hire an individual;

(b) discharge an individual; or

(c) otherwise discriminate against an individual with respect to promotion, compensation, or terms, conditions, or privileges of employment on the basis of such individual's race, color, religion, sex, national origin, age, or state of physical handicap.".

(2) APPLICATION TO SENATE EMPLOYMENT.—The rights and protections provided pursuant to this Act, the Civil Rights Act of 1990 (S. 2104, 101st Congress), the Civil Rights Act of 1964, the Age Discrimination in Employment Act of 1967, and the Rehabilitation Act of 1973 shall apply with respect to employment by the United States Senate.

(3) INVESTIGATION AND ADJUDICATION OF CLAIMS.—All claims raised by any individual with respect to Senate employment, pursuant to the Act referred to in paragraph (2), shall be investigated and adjudicated by the Select Committee on Ethics, pursuant to S. Res. 338, 88th Congress, as amended, or such other entity as the Senate may designate.

(4) RIGHTS OF EMPLOYEES.—The Committee on Rules and Administration shall ensure that Senate employees are informed of their rights under the Acts referred to in paragraph (2).

(5) APPLICABLE REMEDIES.—When assigning remedies to individuals found to have a valid claim under the Acts referred to in paragraph (2), the Select Committee on Ethics, or such other entity as the Senate may designate, should to the extent practicable apply the same remedies applicable to all other employees covered by the Acts referred to in paragraph (2). Such remedies shall apply exclusively.

(6) MATTERS OTHER THAN EMPLOYMENT.—

(A) IN GENERAL.—The rights and protections under this Act shall, subject to subparagraph (B), apply with respect to the conduct of the House of Representatives regarding matters other than employment.

(B) REMEDIES.—The Architect of the Capitol shall establish remedies and procedures to be utilized with respect to the rights and protections provided pursuant to subparagraph (A). Such remedies and procedures shall apply exclusively, after approval in accordance with subparagraph (C).

(C) APPROVAL .—For purposes of subparagraph (B), the Architect of the Capitol shall submit proposed remedies and procedures to the Speaker of the House of Representatives. The remedies and procedures shall be effective upon the approval of the Speaker, after consultation with the House Office Building Commission.

(7) EXERCISE OF RULEMAKING POWER.—Notwithstanding any of the provision of law, enforcement and adjudication of the rights and protections referred to in paragraph (2) and (6)(A) shall be within the exclusive jurisdiction of the United States Senate. The provisions of paragraph (1), (3), (4), (5), (6)(B), and (6)(C) are enacted by the Senate as an exercise of the rule-making power of the Senate, with full recognition of the right of the Senate to change its rules, in any manner, and to the same extent, as in the case of any rule of the Senate.

(b) COVERAGE OF THE HOUSE OF REPRESENTATIVES.

(1) IN GENERAL—Notwithstanding any other provision of this Act shall, subject to paragraphs (2) and (3), apply in their entirety to the House of Representatives.

(2) EMPLOYMENT IN THE HOUSE.—

(A) APPLICATION.—The rights and protections under this Act shall, subject to subparagraph (B), apply with respect to any employee in an employment position in the House of Representatives and any employing authority of the House of Representatives.

(B) ADMINISTRATION.—

(i) IN GENERAL.—In the administration of this paragraph, the remedies and procedures made applicable pursuant to the resolution described in clause (ii) shall apply exclusively.

(ii) RESOLUTION.—The resolution referred to in clause (i) is House Resolution 15 of the One Hundred First Congress, as agreed to January 3, 1989, or any other provisions of, or is a successor to, the Fair Employment Practices Resolution (House Resolution 558 of the One Hundredth Congress, as agreed to October 4, 1988).

(C) EXERCISE OF RULEMAKING POWER.—The provisions of subparagraph (B) are enacted by the House of Representatives as an exercise of the rulemaking power of the House of Representatives, with full recognition of the right of the House to change its rules, in the same manner, and to the same extent as in the case of any other rule of the House.

(3) MATTERS OTHER THAN EMPLOYMENT.—

(A) IN GENERAL.—The rights and protections under this Act shall, subject to subparagraph (B), apply with respect to the conduct of the House of Representatives regarding matters other than employment.

(B) REMEDIES.—The Architect of the Capitol shall establish remedies and procedures to be utilized with respect to the rights and protections provided pursuant to subparagraph (A). Such remedies and procedures shall apply exclusively, after approval in accordance with paragraph (C).

(C) APPROVAL.—For purposes of subparagraph (B), the Architect of the Capitol shall submit proposed remedies and procedures to the Speaker of the House of Representatives. The remedies and procedures shall be effective upon the approval of the Speaker, after consultation with the House Office Building Commission.

(c) INSTRUMENTALITIES OF CONGRESS.—

(1) IN GENERAL.—The rights and protections under this Act shall subject to paragraph (2), apply with respect to the conduct of each instrumentality of the Congress.

(2) ESTABLISHMENT OF REMEDIES AND PROCEDURES BY INSTRUMENTALITIES.—The chief official of each instrumentality of the Congress shall establish remedies and procedures to be utilized with respect to the rights and protections provided pursuant to paragraph (1). Such remedies and procedures shall apply exclusively.

(3) REPORT TO CONGRESS.—The chief official of each instrumentality of the Congress shall, after establishing remedies and procedures for purposes of paragraph (2), submit to the Congress a report describing the remedies and procedures.

(4) DEFINITION OF INSTRUMENTALITIES.—For purposes of this section, instrumentalities of the Congress include the following: the Architect of the Capitol, the Congressional Budget Office, the General Accounting Office, the Government Printing Office, the Library of Congress, the Office of Technology Assessment, and the United States Botanic Garden.

(5) CONSTRUCTION.—Nothing in this section shall alter the enforcement procedures for individuals with disabilities provided in the General Accounting Office Personnel Act of 1980 and regulations promulgated pursuant to that Act.

SEC. 510. ILLEGAL USE OF DRUGS.

(a) IN GENERAL.—For purposes of this Act, the term "individual with a disability" does not include an individual who is currently engaging in the illegal use of drugs, when the covered entity acts on the basis of such use.

(b) RULES OF CONSTRUCTION.—Nothing in subsection (a) shall be construed to exclude as an individual with a disability an individual who—

(1) has successfully completed a supervised drug rehabilitation program and is no longer engaging in the illegal use of drugs, or has otherwise been rehabilitated successfully and is no longer engaging in such use;

(2) is participating in a supervised rehabilitation program and is no longer engaging in such use; or

(3) is erroneously regarded as engaging in such use, but is not engaging in such use; except that it shall not be a violation of this Act for a covered entity to adopt or administer reasonable policies or procedures, including but not limited to drug testing, designed to ensure that an individual described in paragraph (1) or (2) is no longer engaging in the illegal use of drugs; however, nothing in this section shall be construed to encourage, prohibit, restrict, or authorize the conducting of testing for the illegal use of drugs.

(c) HEALTH AND OTHER SERVICES.—Notwithstanding subsection (a) and section 511(b)(3), an individual shall not be denied health services, or services provided in connection with drug rehabilitation, on the basis of the current illegal use of drugs if the individual is otherwise entitled to such services.

(d) DEFINITION OF ILLEGAL USE OF DRUGS.—

(1) IN GENERAL.—The term "illegal use of drugs" means the use of drugs, the possession or distribution of which is unlawful under the Controlled Substances Act (21 U.S.C. 812). Such term does not include the use of a drug taken under supervision by a licensed health care professional, or other uses authorized by he Controlled Substances Act or other provisions of Federal law.

(2) DRUGS.—The term "drug" means a controlled substance, as defined in schedules I through V of section 202 of the Controlled Substance Act.

SEC. 511. DEFINITIONS.

(a) HOMOSEXUALITY AND BISEXUALITY.—For purposes of the definition of "disability" in section 3(2), homosexuality and bisexuality are not impairments and as such are not disabilities under this Act.

(b) CERTAIN CONDITIONS.—Under this Act, the term "disability" shall not include—

(1) transvestism. transsexualism, pedophilia, exhibitionism, voyeurism, gender identity disorders not resulting from physical impairments, or other sexual behavior disorders;

(2) compulsive gambling, kleptomania, or pyromania; or

(3) psychoactive substance use disorders resulting from current illegal use of drugs.

SEC. 512. AMENDMENTS TO THE REHABILITATION ACT.

(a) DEFINITION OF HANDICAPPED INDIVIDUAL.—Section 7(8) of the Rehabilitation Act of 1973 (29 U.S.C. 706(8)) is amended by redesignating subparagraph (C) as subparagraph (D), and by insert ing after subparagraph (B) the following subparagraph:

(C)(i) For purposes of Title V, the term "individual with handicaps" does not include an individual who is currently engaging in the illegal use of drugs, when a covered entity acts on the basis of such use.

(ii) Nothing in clause (i) shall be construed to the handicaps an individual who—

(I) has successfully completed a supervised drug rehabilitation program and is no longer engaging in the illegal use of drugs, or has otherwise been rehabilitated successfully and is no longer engaging in such use;

(II) is participating in a supervised rehabilitation program and is no longer engaging in such use;

(III) is erroneously regarded as engaging in such use, but is not engaging in such use; except that it shall not be a violation of this Act for a covered entity to adopt or administer reasonable policies or procedures, including but not limited to drug testing, designed to ensure that an individual described in subclause (I) or (II) is no longer engaging in the illegal use of drugs.

(iii) Notwithstanding clause (i), for purposes of programs and activities providing health services and services provided under Titles I, II and III, an individual shall not be excluded from the benefits of such programs or activities on the basis of his or her current illegal use of drugs if he or she is otherwise entitled to such services.

(iv) For purposes of prograMs and activities providing educational services, local educational agencies may take disciplinary action pertaining to the use or possession of illegal drugs or alcohol against any handicapped student who currently is engaging in the illegal use of drugs or in the use of alcohol to the same extent that such disciplinary action is taken against nonhandicapped students. Furthermore, the due process procedures at 34 CFR 104.36 shall not apply to such disciplinary actions.

(v) For purposes of sections 503 and 504 as such sections relate to employment, the term "individual with handicaps" does not include any individual who is an alcoholic whose current use of alcohol prevents such individual from performing the duties of the job in question or whose employment, by reason of such current alcohol abuse, would constitute a direct threat to property or the safety of others.

(b) DEFINITION OF ILLEGAL DRUGS—

Section 7 of the Rehabilitation Act of 1973 (29 U.S.C. 706) is amended by adding at the end the following new paragraph:

(A) The term "drug" means a controlled substance, as defined in schedules I through V of section 202 of the Controlled Substances Act (21 U.S.C. 812).

(B) The term "illegal use of drugs" means the use of drugs, the possession or distribution of which is unlawful under the Controlled Substances Act. Such term does not include the use of a drug taken under supervision by a licensed health care professional, or other uses authorized by the Controlled Substances Act or other provisions of Federal law.".

(C) CONFORMING AMENDMENTS—

Section 7(8)(B) of the Rehabilitation Act of 1973 (29 U.S.C. 706(8)(B)) is amended—

(1) in the first sentence, by striking "Subject to the second sentence of this subparagraph," and inserting "Subject to subparagraphs (C) and (D),"; and

(2) by striking the second sentence.

SEC. 513. ALTERNATIVE MEANS OF DISPUTE RESOLUTION.

Where appropriate and to the extent authorized by law, the use of alternative means of dispute resolution, including settlement negotiations, conciliation, facilitation. mediation, fact-finding. mini-trials and arbitration, is encouraged to resolve disputes arising under this Act.

SEC. 514. SEVERABILITY.

Should any provision in this Act be found to be unconstitutional by a court of law, such provision shall be severed from the remainder of the Act, and such action shall not affect the enforceability of the remaining provisions of the Act, Approved July 26, 1990.

Appendix B

Technical Assistance Manual for the Americans with Disabilities Act

TABLE OF OF CONTENTS

MANUAL

INTRODUCTION

The Equal Employment Opportunity Commission (EEOC) is issuing this Technical Assistance Manual as part of an active technical assistance program to help employers, other covered entities, and persons with disabilities learn about their obligations and rights under the employment provisions of the Americans with Disabilities Act (Title I of the ADA). ADA requirements for nondiscrimination in employment become effective for employers with 25 or more employees and other covered entities on July 26, 1992, and for employers with 15 to 24 employees on July 26, 1994.

The Manual provides guidance on the practical application of legal requirements established in the statute and EEOC regulations. It also provides a directory of resources to aid in compliance. The Manual is designed to be updated periodically with supplements as the Commission develops further policy guidance and identifies additional resources.

Part One of the Manual explains key legal requirements in practical terms, including:

- who is protected by, and who must comply with, the ADA;
- what the law permits and prohibits with respect to establishing qualification standards, assessing the qualifications and capabilities of people with disabilities to perform specific jobs, and requiring medical examinations and other inquiries;
- the nature of the obligation to make a reasonable accommodation;
- how the law's nondiscrimination requirements apply to aspects of the employment process such as promotion, transfer, termination, compensation, leave, fringe benefits and contractual arrangements;
- how ADA provisions regarding drug and alcohol use affect other legal obligations and employer policies concerning drugs and alcohol; and
- how ADA requirements affect workers' compensation policies and practices.

The manual explains many employment provisions through the use of examples. These examples are used only to illustrate the particular point or principle to which they relate in the text and should not be taken out of context as statements of EEOC policy that would apply in different circumstances.

Part Two of the Manual is a Resource Directory listing public and private agencies and organizations that provide information, expertise, and technical assistance on many aspects of employing people with disabilities, including reasonable accommodation.

EEOC has published informational booklets on the ADA for employers and for people with disabilities, and will provide other written and audiovisual educational materials; it will provide ADA training for people with disabilities, for employers and other covered entities, and will participate in meetings and training programs of various organizations. EEOC also has established a free "800" number "Helpline" to respond to individual requests for information and assistance.

The Commission's technical assistance program will be separate and distinct from its enforcement responsibilities. Employers who seek information or assistance from EEOC will not be subject to any enforcement action because of such inquiries. The Commission believes that the majority of employers wish to comply voluntarily with the ADA, and will do so if guidance and technical assistance are provided.

To obtain additional single copies of this Manual or other ADA informational materials, call EEOC at 1-800-669-EEOC (voice) or 1-800-800-3302 (TDD) or write to EEOC Office of Communications and Legislative Affairs, 1801 L Street, N.W., Washington, D.C. 20507. Copies of these materials also are available in braille, large print, audio tape, and electronic file on computer disk. To obtain copies in an accessible format, call the EEOC Office of Equal Employment Opportunity at (202) 663-4395 or (202) 663-4398 (voice); (202) 663-4399 (TDD) or write this office at the address above.

HOW TO USE THIS MANUAL

The information in this Manual is presented in an order designed to explain the ADA's basic employment nondiscrimination requirements. The first three chapters provide an overview of Title I legal requirements and discuss in detail the basic requirement not to discriminate against a "qualified individual with a disability," including the requirement for reasonable accommodation. The following chapters apply these legal requirements to specific employment practices and activities. Readers familiar with Title I legal requirements may wish to go directly to chapters that address specific practices. However, in many cases, these chapters refer back to the earlier sections to fully explain the requirements that apply.

The following summary of Manual chapters may be helpful in locating specific types of information.

Chapter I. Provides a summary of Title I legal requirements with cross-references to the chapters where these requirements are discussed.

Chapter II. Looks at the definitions of "an individual with a disability" and a "qualified individual with a disability," drawing upon guidance set out in EEOC's Title I regulation and interpretive appendix. These definitions are important, because an individual is only protected by the ADA if s/he meets both definitions. In addition, the second definition incorporates the ADA's basic employment nondiscrimination requirement, by defining a "qualified" individual as a person who can "perform the essential functions of a job . . . with or without reasonable accommodation.'' Chapter II also provides practical guidance on identifying "essential" job functions.

Chapter III. Provides guidance on the obligation to make a "reasonable accommodation," including why reasonable accommodation is necessary for nondiscrimination and what is required. This chapter also provides many examples of reasonable accommodations for people with different types of disabilities in different jobs. The following chapters provide further guidance on making reasonable accommodations in the employment practices described in those chapters.

Chapter IV. Explains how to establish qualification standards and selection criteria that do not discriminate under the ADA including standards necessary to assure health and safety in the workplace.

Chapter V. Provides guidance on nondiscrimination in recruitment and selection, including important requirements regarding Preemployment inquiries—Among other issues, this chapter discusses nondiscrimination in advertising. recruiting application forms, and the overall application process. including interviews and testing.

Chapter VI. Discusses ADA requirements applicable to medical examinations and medical inquiries, including the different requirements that apply before making a job offer, after making a conditional job offer, and after an individual is employed.

Chapter VII. Discusses and illustrates the obligation to apply ADA nondiscrimination requirements to all other employment. practices and activities, and to all terms, conditions, and benefits of employment. In particular, the chapter looks at the application of ADA requirements to promotion and advancement opportunities, training, evaluation, and employee benefits such as insurance. The chapter also discusses the ADA's prohibition of discrimination on the basis of a "relationship or association with a person with disability."

Chapter VII. Discusses ADA requirements related to employment policies regarding drug and alcohol abuse.

Chapter IX. Provides further guidance on ADA requirements as they relate to workers' compensation practices.

Chapter X. Describes the enforcement provisions of the ADA and how they will be applied by EEOC.

TITLE I: AN OVERVIEW OF LEGAL REQUIREMENTS

This chapter of the manual provides a brief overview of the basic requirements of Title I of the ADA. Following chapters look at these and other requirements in more detail and illustrate how they apply to specific employment practices.

Who Must Comply with Title I of the ADA?

Private employers, state and local governments, employment agencies, labor unions, and joint labor-management committees must comply with Title I of the ADA. The ADA calls these "covered entities." For simplicity, this manual generally refers to all covered entities as "employers," except where there is a specific reason to emphasize the responsibilities of a particular type of entity.

An employer cannot discriminate against qualified applicants and employees on the basis of disability. The ADA's requirements ultimately will apply to employers with 15 or more employees. To give smaller employers more time to prepare for compliance, coverage is phased in two steps as follows:

NUMBER OF EMPLOYEES	COVERAGE BEGINS
25 or more	July 26, 1992
15 or more	July 26, 1994

Covered employers are those who have 25 or more employees (1992) or 15 or more employees (1994), including part-time employees, working for them for 20 or more calendar weeks in the current or preceding calendar year. The ADA's definition of "employee" includes U.S. citizens who work for American companies, their subsidiaries, or firms controlled by Americans outside the USA. However, the Act provides an exemption from coverage for any action in compliance with the ADA which would violate the law of the foreign country in which a workplace is located.

(Note that state and local governments, regardless of size, are covered by employment nondiscrimination requirements under Title II of the ADA as of January 26, 1992. See *Coordination of Overlapping Federal Requirements* below.)

The definition of "employer" includes persons who are "agents" of the employer, such as managers, supervisors, foremen, or others who act for the employer, such as agencies used to conduct background checks on candidates. Therefore, the employer is responsible for actions of such persons that may violate the law. These coverage requirements are similar to those of Title VII of the Civil Rights Act of 1964.

Special Situations

Religious organizations are covered by the ADA, but they may give employment preference to people of their own religion or religious organization.

> *For example:* A church organization could require that its employees be members of its religion. However, it could not discriminate in employment on the basis of disability against members of its religion.

The *legislative branch* of the U.S. Government is covered by the ADA, but is governed by different enforcement procedures established by the Congress for its employees.

Certain individuals appointed by elected officials of state and local governments also are covered by the special enforcement procedures established for Congressional employees.

Who Is Exempt?

Executive agencies of the U.S. Government are exempt from the ADA, but these agencies are covered by similar nondiscrimination requirements and additional affirmative employment requirements under Section 501 of the Rehabilitation Act of 1973. Also exempted from the ADA (as they are from Title VII of the Civil Rights Act) are corporations fully owned by the U.S. Government, Indian tribes, and bona fide private membership clubs that are not labor organizations and that are exempt from taxation under the Internal Revenue Code.

Who Is Protected by Title I?

The ADA prohibits employment discrimination against "*qualified individuals with disabilities.*" A qualified individual with a disability is:

> an individual with a disability who meets the skill, experience, education, and other job-related requirements of a position held or desired, and who, with or without reasonable accommodation, can perform the essential function of a job.

To understand who is and who is not protected by the ADA, it is first necessary to understand the Act's definition of an "individual with a disability" and then determine if the individual meets the Act's definition of a "qualified individual with a disability."

The ADA definition of individual with a disability is very specific. A person with a "disability" is an individual who:

- has a physical or mental impairment that substantially limit one or more of his/her major life activities;
- has a record of such an impairment; or
- is regarded as having such an impairment.

(See Chapter II.)

Individuals Specifically not Protected by the ADA

The ADA specifically states that certain individuals are not protected by its provisions:

Persons who currently use drugs illegally

Individuals who currently use drugs illegally are not individuals with disabilities protected under the Act when an employer takes action because of their continued use of drugs. This includes people who use prescription drugs illegally as well as those who use illegal drugs.

However, people who have been rehabilitated and do not currently use drugs illegally, or who are in the process of completing a rehabilitation program may be protected by the ADA. (See Chapter VIII.)

Other Specific Exclusions

The Act states that homosexuality and bisexuality are not impairments and therefore are not disabilities under the ADA. In addition, the Act specifically excludes a number of behavior disorders from the definition of "individual with a disability." (See Chapter II.)

Employment Practices Regulated by Title I of the ADA

Employers cannot discriminate against people with disabilities in regard to any employment practices or terms, conditions, and privileges of employment. This prohibition covers all aspects of the employment process, including:

- application
- testing
- hiring
- assignments
- evaluation
- disciplinary actions
- training
- promotion
- medical examinations
- layoff/recall
- termination
- compensation
- leave
- benefits

Actions which Constitute Discrimination

The ADA specifies types of actions that may constitute discrimination. These actions are discussed more fully in the following chapters, as indicated:

1) Limiting, segregating, or classifying a job applicant or employee in a way that adversely affects employment opportunities for the applicant or employee because of his or her disability. (See Chapter VII.)

2) Participating in a contractual or other arrangement or relationship that subjects an employer's qualified applicant or employee with a disability to discrimination. (See Chapter VII.)

3) Denying employment opportunities to a qualified individual because s/he has a relationship or association with a person with a disability. (See Chapter VII.)

4) Refusing to make reasonable accommodation to the known physical or mental limitations of a qualified applicant or employee with a disability unless the accommodation would pose an undue hardship on the business. (See Chapters III. and VII.)

5) Using qualification standards, employment tests, or other selection criteria that screen out or tend to screen out an individual with a disability unless they are job-related and necessary for the business. (See Chapter IV.)

6) Failing to use employment tests in the most effective manner to measure actual abilities. Tests must accurately reflect the skills, aptitude, or other factors being measured, and not the impaired sensory, manual, or speaking skills of an employee or applicant with a disability (unless those are the skills the test is designed to measure). (See Chapter V.)

7) Denying an employment opportunity to a qualified individual because s/he has a relationship or association with an individual with a disability. (See Chapter VII.)

8) Discriminating against an individual because s/he has opposed an employment practice of the employer or filed a complaint, testified, assisted, or participated in an investigation, proceeding, or hearing to enforce provisions of the Act. (See Chapter X.)

Reasonable Accommodation and the Undue Hardship Limitation

Reasonable Accommodation

Reasonable accommodation is a critical component of the ADA's assurance of nondiscrimination. Reasonable accommodation is any change in the work environment or in the way things are usually done that results in equal employment opportunity for an individual with a disability.

An employer must make a reasonable accommodation to the known physical or mental limitations of a qualified applicant or employee with a disability unless it can show that the accommodation would cause an undue hardship on the operation of its business.

Some examples of reasonable accommodation include:

- making existing facilities used by employees readily accessible to, and usable by, an individual with a disability;
- job restructuring;
- modifying work schedules;
- reassignment to a vacant position;
- acquiring or modifying equipment or devices;
- adjusting or modifying examinations, training materials, or policies;
- providing qualified reader or interpreters.

An employer is not required to lower quality or quantity standards to make an accommodation. Nor is an employer obligated to provide personal use items, such as glasses or hearing aids, as accommodations.

Undue Hardship

An employer is not required to provide an accommodation if it will impose an undue hardship on the operation of its business. Undue hardship is defined by the ADA as an action that is:

> "excessively costly, extensive, substantial, or disruptive, or that would fundamentally alter the nature or operation of the business."

In determining undue hardship, factors to be considered include the nature and cost of the accommodation in relation to the size, the financial resources, the nature and structure of the employer's operation, as well as the impact of the accommodation on the specific facility providing the accommodation. (See Chapter III.)

Health or Safety Defense

An employer may require that an individual not pose a "direct threat" to the health or safety of himself/herself or others. A health or safety risk can only be considered if it is "a significant risk of substantial harm." Employers cannot deny an employment opportunity merely because of a slightly increased risk. An assessment of "direct threat" must be strictly based on valid medical analyses and/or other objective evidence, and not on speculation. Like any qualification standard, this requirement must apply to all applicants and employees, not just to people with disabilities.

If an individual appears to pose a direct threat because of a disability, the employer must first try to eliminate or reduce the risk to an acceptable level with reasonable accommodation. If an effective accommodation cannot be found, the employer may refuse to hire an applicant or discharge an employee who poses a direct threat. (See Chapter IV.)

Pre-employment Inquiries and Medical Examination

An employer may not ask a job applicant about the existence, nature, or severity of a disability. **Applicants** may be asked about their ability to perform specific job functions. An employer may not make medical inquiries or conduct a medical examination until after a job offer has been made. A job offer may be conditioned on the results of a medical examination or inquiry, but only if this is required for all entering employees in similar jobs. Medical examinations of employees must be job-related and consistent with the employer's business needs. (See Chapters V. and VI.)

Drug and Alcohol Use

It is not a violation of the ADA for employers to use drug tests to find out if applicants or employees are currently illegally using drugs. Tests for illegal use of drugs are not subject to the ADA's restrictions on medical examinations. Employers may hold illegal users of drugs and alcoholics to the same performance and conduct standards as other employees. (See Chapter VIII.)

Enforcement and Remedies

The U.S. Equal Employment Opportunity Commission (EEOC) has responsibility for enforcing compliance with Title I of the ADA. An individual with a disability who believes that s/he has been discriminated against in employment can file a charge with EEOC. The procedures for processing charges of discrimination under the ADA are the same as those under Title VII of the Civil Rights Act of 1964. (See Chapter X.)

Remedies that may be required of an employer who is found to have discriminated against an applicant or employee with a disability include compensatory and punitive damages, back pay, front pay, restored benefits, attorney's fees, reasonable accommodation, reinstatement, and job offers. (See Chapter X.)

Posting Notices

An employer must post notices concerning the provisions of the ADA. The notices must be accessible, as needed, to persons with visual or other reading disabilities. A new equal employment opportunity (EEO) poster, containing ADA provisions and other federal employment nondiscrimination provisions may be obtained by writing EEOC at 1801 L Street N.W., Washington, D.C., 20507, or calling 1-800-669-EEOC or 1-800-800-3302 (TDD).

Coordination of Overlapping Federal Requirements

Employers covered by Title I of the ADA also may be covered by other federal requirements that prohibit discrimination on the basis of disability. The ADA directs the agencies with enforcement authority for these legal requirements to coordinate their activities to prevent duplication and avoid conflicting standards. Overlapping requirements exist for both public and private employers.

Title II of the ADA, enforced by the U.S. Department of Justice, prohibits discrimination in all **state and local government programs and activities** including employment, after January 26, 1992.

The Department of Justice regulations implementing Title II provide that EEOC's Title I regulations will constitute the employment nondiscrimination requirements for those state and local governments covered by Title I governments with 25 or more employees after July 26, 1992; governments with 15 or more employees after July 26, 1994). If a government is not covered by Title I, or until it is covered, the Title II employment nondiscrimination requirements will be those in the Department of Justice coordination regulations applicable to federally assisted programs under Section 504 of the Rehabilitation Act of 1973, which prohibits discrimination on the basis of disability by recipients of federal financial assistance.

Section 504 employment requirements in most respects are the same as those of Title I, because the ADA was based on the Section 504 regulatory requirements. (Note that governments receiving federal financial assistance, as well as federally funded private entities, will continue to be covered by Section 504.)

In addition, some **private employers** are covered by Section 503 of the Rehabilitation Act. Section 503 requires nondiscrimination and affirmative action by federal contractors and subcontractors to employ and advance individuals with disabilities, and is enforced by the Office of Federal Contract Compliance Programs (OFCCP) in the U.S. Department of Labor.

The EEOC, the Department of Labor, the Department of Justice and the other agencies that enforce Section 504 (i.e., Federal agencies with programs of financial assistance) will coordinate their enforcement efforts under the ADA and the Rehabilitation Act, to assure consistent standards and to eliminate unnecessary duplication. (See Chapter X.)

II. WHO IS PROTECTED BY THE ADA? INDIVIDUAL WITH A DISABILITY QUALIFIED INDIVIDUAL WITH A DISABILITY

2.1 Introduction

The ADA protects qualified individuals with disabilities from employment discrimination. Under other laws that prohibit employment discrimination, it usually is a simple matter to know whether an individual is covered because of his or her race, color, sex, national origin or age. But to know whether a person is covered by the employment provisions of the ADA can be more complicated. It is first necessary to understand the Act's very specific definitions of **"disability"** and **"qualified individual with a disability."** Like other determinations under the ADA, deciding who is a "qualified" individual is a case-by-case process, depending on the circumstances of the particular employment situation.

2.2 Individual with a Disability

The ADA has a three-part definition of "disability." This definition, based on the definition under the Rehabilitation Act, reflects the specific types of discrimination experienced by people with disabilities. Accordingly, it is not the same as the definition of disability in other laws, such as state workers' compensation laws or other federal or state laws that provide benefits for people with disabilities and disabled veterans.

Under the ADA, an *individual with a disability* is a person who has:

- a physical or mental **impairment** that **substantially limits** one or more **major life activities;**
- a **record** of such an impairment; or
- is **regarded** as having such an impairment.

2.1(a) An Impairment that Substantially Limits Major Life Activities

The first part of this definition has three major subparts that further define who is and who is not protected by the ADA.

(i) A Physical or Mental Impairment

A *physical impairment* is defined by the ADA as:

> "any physiological disorder, or condition, cosmetic disfigurement, or anatomical loss affecting one or more of the following body systems: neurological, musculoskeletal, special sense organs, respiratory (including speech organs), cardiovascular, reproductive, digestive, genito-urinary, hemic and lymphatic, skin, and endocrine."

A *mental impairment* is defined by the ADA as:

> "[a]ny mental or psychological disorder, such as mental retardation, organic brain syndrome, emotional or mental illness, and specific learning disabilities. "

Neither the statute nor EEOC regulations list all diseases or conditions that make up "physical or mental impairments," because it would be impossible to provide a comprehensive list, given the variety of possible impairments.

A person's impairment is determined without regard to any medication or assistive device that s/he may use.

> *For example:* A person who has epilepsy and uses medication to control seizures, or a person who walks with an artificial leg would be considered to have an impairment, even if the medicine or prosthesis reduces the impact of that impairment.

An impairment under the ADA is a *physiological* or *mental disorder;* simple physical characteristics, therefore, such as eye or hair color, left-handedness, or height or weight within a normal range, are not impairments. A physical condition that is not the result of a physiological disorder, such as pregnancy, or a predisposition to a certain disease would not be an impairment. Similarly, personality traits such as poor judgment, quick temper or irresponsible behavior, are not themselves impairments. Environmental, cultural, or economic disadvantages, such as lack of education or a prison record also are not impairments.

For example: A person who cannot read due to dyslexia is an individual with a disability because dyslexia, which is a learning disability, is an impairment. But a person who cannot read because she dropped out of school is not an individual with a disability, because lack of education is not an impairment.

"Stress" and "depression" are conditions that may or may not be considered impairments, depending on whether these conditions result from a documented physiological or mental disorder.

For example: A person suffering from general "stress" because of job or personal life pressures would not be considered to have an impairment. However, if this person is diagnosed by a psychiatrist as having an identifiable stress disorder, s/he would have an impairment that may be a disability.

A person who has a contagious disease has an impairment. For example, infection with the Human Immunodeficiency Virus (HIV) is an impairment. The Supreme Court has ruled that an individual with tuberculosis which affected her respiratory system had an impairment under Section 04 of the Rehabilitation Act.* However, although a person who has a contagious disease may be covered by the ADA, an employer would not have to hire or retain a person whose contagious disease posed a direct threat to health or safety, if no reasonable accommodation could reduce or eliminate this threat. (See *Health and Safety Standards,* Chapter IV.)

(ii) Major Life Activities.

To be a disability covered by the ADA, an impairment must substantially limit one or more **major life activities.** These are activities that an average person can perform with little or no difficulty. Examples are:

- walking
- peaking
- breathing
- performing manual tasks
- working
- seeing
- hearing
- learning
- caring for oneself

**School Board of Nassau County v. Arline*, 480 U.S. 273 (1987).

These are examples only. Other activities such as sitting, standing, lifting, or reading are also major life activities.

(iii) Substantially Limits

An impairment is only a "disability" under the ADA if it *substantially limits* one or more major life activities. An individual must be unable to perform, or be significantly limited in the ability to perform, an activity compared to an average person in the general population.

The regulations provide three factors to consider in determining whether a person's impairment substantially limits a major life activity.

- its nature and severity;
- how long it will last or is expected to last;
- it permanent or long term impact, or expected impact.

These factors must be considered because, generally, it is not the name of an impairment or a condition that determines whether a person is protected by the ADA, but rather the effect of an impairment or condition on the life of a particular person. Some impairments, such as blindness, deafness, HIV infection or AIDS, are by their nature substantially limiting, but many other impairments may be disabling for some individuals but not for others, depending on the impact on their activities.

> *For example:* Although cerebral palsy frequently significantly restricts major life activities such as speaking, walking and performing manual tasks, an individual with very mild cerebral palsy that only slightly interferes with his ability to speak and has no significant impact on other major life activities is not an individual with a disability under this part of the definition.

The determination as to whether an individual is substantially limited must always be based on the effect of an impairment on *that* individual's life activities.

> *For example:* An individual who had been employed as a receptionist-clerk sustained a back injury that resulted in considerable pain. The pain permanently restricted her ability to walk, sit, stand, drive, care for her home, and engage in recreational activities. Another individual who had been employed as a general laborer had sustained a back injury, but was able to continue an active life, including recreational sports, and had obtained a new position as a security guard. The first individual was found by a court to be an individual with a disability; the second individual was found not significantly restricted in any major life activity, and therefore not an individual with a disability.

Sometimes, an individual may have two or more impairments, neither of which by itself substantially limits a major life activity, but that together have this effect. In such a situation, the individual has a disability.

For example: A person has a mild form of arthritis in her wrists and hands and a mild form of osteoporosis. Neither impairment by itself substantially limits a major life activity. Together, however, these impairments significantly restrict her ability to lift and perform manual tasks. She has a disability under the ADA.

Temporary Impairments

Employers frequently ask whether "temporary disabilities" are covered by the ADA. How long an impairment lasts is a factor to be considered, but does not by itself determine whether a person has a disability under the ADA. The basic question is whether an impairment "substantially limits" one or more major life activities. This question is answered by looking at the *extent, duration,* and *impact* of the impairment. Temporary, non-chronic impairments that do not last for a long time and that have little or no long term impact usually are not disabilities.

For example: Broken limbs, sprains, concussions, appendicitis, common colds, or influenza generally would not be disabilities. A broken leg that heals normally within a few months, for example, would not be a disability under the ADA. However, if a broken leg took significantly longer than the normal healing period to heal, and during this period the individual could not walk, s/he would be considered to have a disability. Or, if the leg did not heal properly, and resulted in a permanent impairment that significantly restricted walking or other major life activities, s/he would be considered to have a disability.

Substantially Limited in Working

It is not necessary to consider if a person is substantially limited in the major life activity of "working" if the person is substantially limited in any other major life activity.

For example: If a person is substantially limited in seeing, hearing, or walking, there is no need to consider whether the person is also substantially limited in working.

In general, a person will not be considered to be substantially limited in working if s/he is substantially limited in performing only a **particular** job for one employer, or unable to perform a very specialized job in a particular field.

For example: A person who cannot qualify as a commercial airline pilot because of a minor vision impairment, but who could qualify as a co-pilot or a pilot for a courier service, would not be considered substantially limited in working just because he could not perform a particular job. Similarly, a baseball pitcher who develops a bad elbow and can no longer pitch would not be substantially limited in working because he could no longer perform the specialized job of pitching in baseball.

But a person need not be totally unable to work in order to be considered substantially limited in working. The person must be significantly restricted in the ability to perform either a *class of jobs* or a *broad range of jobs in various classes.* compared to an average person with similar training, skills, and abilities.

The regulations provide factors to help determine whether a person is substantially limited in working. These include:

- the **type of job** from which the individual has been disqualified because of the impairment;
- the **geographical area** in which the person may reasonably expect to find a job;
- the **number and type of jobs using similar training, knowledge, skill, or abilities** from which the individual is disqualified within the geographical area, and/or
- the **number and types of other jobs in the area that do not involve similar training, knowledge, kill, or abilities** from which the individual also is disqualified because of the impairment.

For example: A person would be considered significantly restricted in a "class of jobs" if a back condition prevents him from working in any heavy labor job. A person would be considered significantly limited in the ability to perform "a broad range of jobs in various classes" if she has an allergy to a substance found in most high-rise office buildings in the geographic area in which she could reasonably seek work, and the allergy caused extreme difficulty in breathing. In this case, she would be substantially limited in the ability to perform the many different kinds of jobs that are performed in high-rise buildings. By contrast, a person who has a severe allergy to a substance in the particular office in which she works but who is able to work in many other offices that do not contain this substance, would not be significantly restricted in working.

For example: A computer programmer develops a vision impairment that does not substantially limit her ability to see, but because of poor contrast is unable to distinguish print on computer screens. Her impairment prevents her from working as a computer operator, programmer, instructor, or systems analyst. She is substantially limited in working, because her impairment prevents her from working in the class of jobs requiring use of a computer.

In assessing the "number" of jobs from which a person might be excluded by an impairment, the regulations make clear that it is only necessary to indicate an approximate number of jobs from which an individual would be excluded (such as "few," "many," "most"), compared to an average person with similar training, skills and abilities, to show that the individual would be significantly limited in working.

Specific Exclusion

A person **who currently illegally use drugs is not protected by the ADA,** as an "individual with a disability", when an employer acts on the basis of such use. However, former drug addicts who have been successfully rehabilitated may be protected by the Act. (See Chapter VIII). (See also discussion below of a person "regarded as" a drug addict.)

Homosexuality and **bisexuality** are not impairments and therefore are not disabilities covered by the ADA. The Act also states that the term "disability" does not include the following sexual and behavioral disorders:

- transvestitism, transsexualism, pedophilia, exhibitionism, voyeurism, gender identity disorders not resulting from physical impairments, or other sexual behavior disorders;
- compulsive gambling, kleptomania, or pyromania; or
- psychoactive substance use disorders resulting from current illegal use of drugs.

The discussion so far has focused on the first part of the definition of an "individual with a disability," which protects people who currently *have* an impairment that substantially limits a major life activity. The second and third parts of the definition protect people who may or may not actually have such an impairment, but who may be subject to discrimination because they *have a record of* or are *regarded as* having such an impairment.

2.2(b) Record of a Substantially Limiting Condition

This part of the definition protects people who have a history of a disability from discrimination, whether or not they currently are substantially limited in a major life activity.

> *For example:* It protects people with a history of cancer, heart disease, or other debilitating illness, whose illnesses are either cured, controlled or in remission. It also protects people with a history of mental illness.

This part of the definition also protects people who may have been *misclassified* or *misdiagnosed* as having a disability.

> *For example:* It protects a person who may at one time have been erroneously classified as having mental retardation or having a learning disability. These people have a record of disability. (If an employer relies on any

record [such as an educational, medical or employment record] containing such information to make an adverse employment decision about a person who currently is qualified to perform a job, the action is subject to challenge as a discriminatory practice.)

Other examples of individuals who have a record of disability, and of potential violations of the ADA if an employer relies on such a record to make an adverse employment decision:

- A job applicant formerly was a patient at a state institution. When very young she was misdiagnosed as being psychopathic and this misdiagnosis was never removed from her records. If this person is otherwise qualified for a job, and an employer does not hire her based on this record, the employer has violated the ADA.
- A person who has a learning disability applies for a job as secretary/receptionist. The employer reviews records from a previous employer indicating that he was labeled as mentally retarded." Even though the person's resume shows hat he meets all requirements for the job, the employer does not interview him because he doesn't want to hire a person who has mental retardation. This employer has violated the ADA.
- A job applicant was hospitalized for treatment for cocaine addiction several years ago. He has been successfully rehabilitated and has not engaged in the illegal use of drugs since receiving treatment. This applicant has a record of an impairment that substantially limited his major life activities. If he is qualified to perform a job, it would be discriminatory to reject him based on the record of his former addiction.

In the last example above, the individual was protected by the ADA because his drug **addiction** was an impairment that substantially limited his major life activities. However, if an individual had a record of casual drug use, s/he would not be protected by the ADA, because casual drug use, as opposed to addiction, does not substantially limit a major life activity.

To be protected by the ADA under this part of the definition, a person must have a record of a physical or mental impairment that *substantially limits one or more major life activities.* A person would not be protected, for example, merely because s/he has a record of being a "disabled veteran," or a record of "disability" under another Federal statute or program unless this person also met the ADA definition of an individual with a record of a disability.

2.2(c) Regarded as Substantially Limited

This part of the definition protects people who are not substantially limited in a major life activity from discriminatory actions taken because they are perceived to have such a limitation. Such protection is necessary, because, as the Supreme Court has stated and the Congress has reiterated, "society's myths and fears about disability and disease are as handicapping as are the physical limitations that flow from actual impairments."

The legislative history of the ADA indicates that Congress intended this part of the definition to protect people from a range of discriminatory actions based on "myths, fears and stereotypes" about disability, which occur even when a person does not have a substantially limiting impairment.

An individual may be protected under this part of the definition in three circumstances:

1. The individual may have an impairment which is not substantially limiting, but is *treated by* the employer *as having such an impairment.*

   For example: An employee has controlled high blood pressure which does not substantially limit his work activities. If an employer reassigns the individual to a less strenuous job because of unsubstantiated fear that the person would suffer a heart attack if he continues in the present job, the employer has "regarded" this person as disabled.

2. The individual has an impairment that is substantially limiting because of *attitudes* of others toward the condition.

   For example: An experienced assistant manager of a convenience store who had a prominent facial scar was passed over for promotion to store manager. The owner promoted a less experienced part-time clerk, because he believed that customers and vendors would not want to look at this person. The employer discriminated against her on the basis of disability, because he perceived and treated her as a person with a substantial limitation.

3. The individual may have *no* impairment at all, but is *regarded* by an employer as *having* a *substantially limiting impairment.*

   For example: An employer discharged an employee based on a rumor that the individual had HIV disease. This person did not have any impairment, but was treated as though she had a substantially limiting impairment.

This part of the definition protects people who are "perceived" as having disabilities from employment decisions based on stereotypes, fears, or misconceptions about disability. It applies to decisions based on unsubstantiated concerns about **productivity, safety, insurance, liability, attendance, cots of accommodation, accessibility, worker' compensation costs or acceptance by coworkers and customers.**

Accordingly, if an employer makes an adverse employment decision based on unsubstantiated beliefs or fears that a person's perceived disability will cause problems in areas such as those listed above, and cannot show a legitimate, nondiscriminatory reason for the action, that action would be discriminatory under this part of the definition.

2.3 Qualified Individual with a Disability

To be protected by the ADA, a person must not only be an individual with a disability, but must be *qualified.* An employer is not required to hire or retain an individual who is not qualified to perform a job. The regulations define a *qualified individual with a disability* as a person with a disability who:

> "satisfies the requisite skill, experience, education and other job-related requirements of the employment position such individual holds or desires, and who, with or without reasonable accommodation can perform the essential functions of such position."

There are two basic steps in determining whether an individual is "qualified" under the ADA:

(1) Determine if the individual meets necessary prerequisites for the job, such as:

- education;
- work experience;
- training;
- skills;
- licenses;
- certificates;
- other job-related requirements, such as good judgment or ability to work with other people.

For example: The first step in determining whether an accountant who has cerebral palsy is qualified for a certified public accountant job is to determine if the person is a licensed CPA. If not, s/he is not qualified. Or, if it is a company's policy that all its managers have at least three years' experience working with the company, an individual with a disability who has worked for two years for the company would not be qualified for a managerial position.

This first step is sometimes referred to as determining if an individual with a disability is **"otherwise qualified."** Note, however, that if an individual meets all job prerequisites except those that s/he cannot meet because of a disability, and alleges discrimination because s/he is "otherwise qualified" for a job, the employer would have to show that the requirement that screened out this person is "job related and consistent with business necessity." (See Chapter IV)

If the individual with a disability meets the necessary job prerequisites:

(2) Determine if the individual can perform the *essential functions* of the job, *with or without reasonable accommodation.* This second step, a key aspect of nondiscrimination under the ADA, has two parts:

- Identifying *"essential functions of the job"*; and
- Considering whether the person with a disability can perform these functions, unaided or with a *"reasonable accommodation."*

The ADA requires an employer to focus on the essential functions of a job to determine whether a person with a disability is qualified. This is an important nondiscrimination requirement. Many people with disabilities who can perform essential job functions are denied employment because they cannot do things that are only marginal to the job.

> *For example:* A file clerk position description may state that the person holding the job answers the telephone, but if in fact the basic functions of the job are to file and retrieve written materials, and telephones actually or usually are handled by other employees, a person whose hearing impairment prevents use of a telephone and who is qualified to do the basic file clerk functions should not be considered unqualified for this position.

2.3(a) Identifying the Essential Functions of a Job

Sometimes it is necessary to identify the essential functions of a job in order to know whether an individual with a disability is "qualified" to do the job. The regulations provide guideposts on identifying the essential functions of the job. The first consideration is **whether employees in the position actually are required to perform the function.**

> *For example:* A job announcement or job description for a secretary or receptionist may state that typing is a function of the job. If, in fact, the employer has never or seldom required an employee in that position to type, this could not be considered an essential function.

If a person holding a job does perform a function, the next consideration is whether removing that function would fundamentally change the job.

The regulations list several reasons why a function could be considered essential:

1. **The position exists to perform the function.**

   For example:

- A person is hired to proofread documents. The ability to proofread accurately is an essential function, because this is the reason that this position exists.
- A company advertises a position for a "floating" supervisor to substitute when regular supervisors on the day, night, and graveyard shifts are absent. The only reason this position exists is to have someone who can work on any of the three shifts in place of an absent superior. Therefore, the ability to work at any time of day is an essential function of the job.

2. **The are a limited number of other employees available to perform the function, or among whom the function can be distributed.**

   This may be a factor because there are only a few other employees, or because of fluctuating demands of a business operation.

For example: It may be an essential function for a file clerk to answer the telephone if there are only three employees in a very busy office and each employee has to perform many different tasks. Or, a company with a large workforce may have periods of very heavy labor-intensive activity alternating with less active periods. The heavy work flow during peak periods may make performance of each function essential, and limit an employer's flexibility to reassign a particular function.

3. A function is highly specialized, and the person in the position is hired for special expertise or ability to perform it.

   For example: A company wishes to expand its business with Japan. For a new sales position, in addition to sales experience, it requires a person who can communicate fluently in the Japanese language. Fluent communication in the Japanese language is an essential function of the job.

The regulation also lists several types of evidence to be considered in determining whether a function is essential. This list is not all-inclusive, and factors not on the list may be equally important as evidence. Evidence to be considered includes:

a. The employer's judgment

An employer's judgment as to which functions are essential is important evidence. However, the legislative history of the ADA indicates that Congress did not intend that this should be the only evidence, or that it should be the prevailing evidence. Rather, the employer's judgment is a factor to be considered along with other relevant evidence.

However, the consideration of various kinds of evidence to determine which functions are essential does not mean that an employer will be second-guessed on production standards, setting the quality or quantity of work that must be performed by a person holding a job, or be required to set lower standards for the job.

For example: If an employer requires its typists to be able to accurately type 75 words per minute, the employer is not required to show that such speed and accuracy are "essential" to a job or that less accuracy or speed would not be adequate. Similarly, if a hotel requires its housekeepers to thoroughly clean 16 room per day, it does not have to justify this standard as "essential." However, in each case, if a person with a disability is disqualified by such a standard, the employer should be prepared to show that it does in fact require employees to perform at this level, that these are not merely paper requirements and that the standard was not established for a discriminatory reason.

b. A written job description prepared before advertising or interviewing applicants for a job

The ADA does not require an employer to develop or maintain job descriptions. A written job description that is prepared before advertising or interviewing applicants for a job will be considered as evidence along with other relevant factors. However, the job description will not be given greater weight than other relevant evidence.

A written job description may state that an employee performs a certain essential function. The job description will be evidence that the function is essential, but if individuals currently performing the job do not in fact perform this function, or perform it very infrequently, a review of the actual work performed will be more relevant evidence than the job description.

If an employer uses written job descriptions, the ADA does not require that they be limited to a description of essential functions or that "essential functions" be identified. However, if an employer wishes to use a job description as evidence of essential functions, it should in some way identify those functions that the employer believes to be important in accomplishing the purpose of the job.

If an employer uses written job descriptions, they should be reviewed to be sure that they accurately reflect the actual functions of the current job. Job descriptions written years ago frequently are inaccurate.

For example: A written job description may state that an employee reads temperature and pressure gauges and adjusts machine controls to reflect these readings. The job description will be evidence that these functions are essential. However, if this job description is not up-to-date, and in fact temperature and pressure are now determined automatically, the machine is controlled by a computer and the current employee does not perform the stated functions or does so very infrequently, a review of actual work performed will be more relevant evidence of what the job requires.

In identifying an essential function to determine if an individual with a disability is qualified, the employer should focus on the *purpose* of the function and the *result* to be accomplished, rather than the manner in which the function presently is performed. An individual with a disability may be qualified to perform the function if an accommodation would enable this person to perform the job in a different way, and the accommodation does not impose an undue hardship. Although it may be essential that a function be performed, frequently it is not essential that it be performed in a particular way.

For example: In a job requiring use of a computer, the essential function is the ability o access, input, and retrieve information from the computer. It is not "essential" that a person in this job enter information manually, or visually read the information on the computer screen. Adaptive devices or computer software can enable a person without arms or a person with impaired vision to perform the essential functions of the job.

Similarly, an essential function of a job on a loading dock may be to move heavy packages from the dock to a storage room, rather than to lift and carry packages from the dock to the storage room. (See also discussion of *Job*

Analysis and Essential Functions of a Job, below).

If the employer intends to use a job description as evidence of essential functions, the job description must be prepared *before* advertising or interviewing for a job; a job description prepared after an alleged discriminatory action will not be considered as evidence.

c. The amount of time spent performing the function

For example: If an employee spends most of the time or a majority of the time operating one machine, this would be evidence that operating this machine was an essential function.

d. The consequences of not requiring a person in the job to perform a function

Sometimes a function that is performed infrequently may be essential because there will be serious consequences if it is not performed.

For example:

- An airline pilot spends only a few minutes of a flight landing a plane, but landing the plane is an essential function because of the very serious consequences if the pilot could not perform this function.
- A firefighter may only occasionally have to carry a heavy person from a burning building, but being able to perform this function would be essential to the firefighter's job.
- A clerical worker may spend only a few minutes a day answering the telephones, but this could be an essential function if no one else is available to answer the phones at that time, and business calls would go unanswered.

e. The terms of a collective bargaining agreement

Where a collective bargaining agreement lists duties to be performed in particular jobs, the terms of the agreement may provide evidence of essential functions. However, like a position description, the agreement would be considered along with other evidence, such as the actual duties performed by people in these jobs.

f. Work experience of people who have performed a job in the past and work experience of people who currently perform similar job

The work experience of previous employees in a job and the experience of current employees in similar jobs provide pragmatic evidence of actual duties performed. The employer should consult such employees and observe their work operations to identify essential job functions, since the tasks actually performed provide significant evidence of these functions.

g. Other relevant factors

The *nature of the work operation* and the employer' *organizational structure* may be factors in determining whether a function is essential.

For example:

- A particular manufacturing facility receives large orders for its product intermittently. These orders must be filled under very tight deadlines. To meet these deadlines, it is necessary that each production worker be able to perform a variety of different tasks with different requirements. All of these tasks are essential functions for a production worker at that facility. However, another facility that receives orders on a continuous basis finds it most efficient to organize an assembly line process, in which each production worker repeatedly performs one major task. At this facility, this single task may be the only essential function of the production worker's job.
- An employer may structure production operations to be carried out by a "team" of workers. Each worker performs a different function, but every worker is required, on a rotating basis, to perform each different function. In this situation, all the functions may be considered to be essential for the job, rather than the function that any one worker performs at a particular time.

Changing Essential Job Functions

The ADA does not limit an employers ability to establish or change the content, nature, or functions of a job. It is the employer's province to establish what a job is and what functions are required to perform it. The ADA simply requires that an individual with a disability's qualifications for a job are evaluated in relation to its essential functions.

> *For example:* A grocery store may have two different jobs at the checkout stand, one titled, "checkout clerk" and the other "bagger." The essential functions of the checkout clerk are entering the price for each item into a cash register, receiving money, making change, and passing items to the bagger. The essential functions of the bagging job are putting items into bags, giving the bags to the customer directly or placing them in grocery carts.

For legitimate business reasons, the tore management decides to combine the two jobs in a new job called "checker-bagger." In the new job, each employee will have to perform the essential functions of both former jobs. Each employee now must enter prices in a new, faster computer-scanner, put the items in bags, give the bags to the customer or place them in carts. The employee holding this job would have to perform all of these functions. There may be some aspects of each function, however, that are not "essential" to the job, or some possible modification in the way these functions are performed, that would enable a person employed as a "checker" whose disability prevented performance of all the bagging operations to do the new job.

> *For example:* If the checker's disability made it impossible to lift any item over one pound, s/he might not be qualified to perform the essential bagging functions of the new job. But if the disability only precluded lifting

items of more than 20 pounds, it might be possible for this person to perform the bagging functions, except for the relatively few instances when items or loaded bags weigh more than 20 pounds. If other employees are available who could help this individual with the few heavy items, perhaps in exchange for some incidental functions that they perform, or if this employee could keep filled bags loads under 20 pounds, then bagging loads over 20 pounds would not be an essential function of the new job.

2.3(b) Job Analysis and the "Essential Functions" of a Job

The ADA does not require that an employer conduct a job analysis or any particular form of job analysis to identify the essential functions of a job. The information provided by a job analysis may or may not be helpful in properly identifying essential job functions, depending on how it is conducted.

The term "job analysis" generally is used to describe a formal process in which information about a specific job or occupation is collected and analyzed. Formal job analysis may be conducted by a number of different methods. These methods obtain different kinds of information that is used for different purposes. Some of these methods will not provide information sufficient to determine if an individual with a disability is qualified to perform "essential" job functions.

For example: One kind of formal job analysis looks at specific job tasks and classifies jobs according to how these tasks deal with data, people, and objects. This type of job analysis is used to set wage rates for various jobs; however, it may not be adequate to identify the essential functions of a *particular* job, as required by the ADA. Another kind of job analysis looks at the kinds of knowledge, skills, and abilities that are necessary to perform a job. This type of job analysis is used to develop selection criteria for various jobs. The information from this type of analysis sometimes helps to measure the importance of certain skills, knowledge and abilities, but it does not take into account the fact that people with disabilities often can perform essential functions using other skills and abilities.

Some job analysis methods ask current employees and their supervisors to rate the importance of general characteristics necessary to perform a job, such as "strength," "endurance" or "intelligence," without linking these characteristics to *specific* job functions or specific tasks that are part of a function. Such general information may not identify, for example, whether upper body or lower body "strength" is required, or whether muscular endurance or cardiovascular "endurance" is needed to perform a particular job function. Such information, by itself, would not be sufficient to determine whether an individual who has particular limitations can perform an essential function with or without an accommodation.

As already stated, the ADA does not require a formal job analysis or any particular method of analysis to identify the essential functions of a job. A small employer may wish to conduct an informal analysis by observing and consulting with people who perform the job or have previously performed it and their supervisors. If possible, it is advisable to observe and consult with several workers under a range of conditions, to get a better idea of all job functions and the different ways they may be performed. Production records and workloads also may be relevant factors to consider.

To identify essential job functions under the ADA, a job analysis should focus on the purpose of the job and the importance of actual job functions in achieving this purpose. Evaluating "importance" may include consideration of the frequency with which a function is performed, the amount of time spent on the function, and the consequences if the function is not performed. The analysis may include information on the work environment (such as unusual heat cold, humidity, dust, toxic substances or stress factors). The job analysis may contain information on the manner in which a job currently is performed, but should not conclude that ability to perform the job **in that manner** is an essential function, unless there is no other way to perform the function without causing undue hardship. A job analysis will be most helpful for purposes of the ADA if it focuses on the **results** or **outcome** of a function, not solely on the way it customarily is performed.

For example:

- An essential function of a computer programmer job might be described as "ability to develop programs that accomplish necessary objectives," rather than "ability to manually write programs." Although a person currently performing the job may write these programs by hand, that is not the essential function, because programs can be developed directly on the computer.
- If a job requires mastery of information contained in technical manuals, this essential function would be "ability to learn technical material," rather than "ability to read technical manuals." People with visual and other reading impairments could perform this function using other means, such as audio tapes.
- A job that requires objects to be moved from one place to another should state this essential function. The analysis may note that the person in the job "lifts 50 pound cartons to a height of 3 or 4 feet and loads them into truck-trailers 5 hours daily," but should not identify the "ability to *manually* lift and load 50 pound cartons" as an essential function unless this is the only method by which-the function can be performed without causing an undue hardship.

A job analysis that is focused on outcomes or results also will be helpful in establishing appropriate qualification standards, developing job descriptions, conducting interviews, and selecting people in accordance with ADA requirements. It will be particularly useful in helping to identify accommodations that will enable an individual with specific functional abilities and limitations to perform the job. (See Chapter III.)

2.8(c) Perform Essential Function "With or Without Reasonable Accommodation"

Many individuals with disabilities are qualified to perform the essential functions of jobs without need of any accommodation. However, if an individual with a disability who is otherwise qualified cannot perform one or more essential job functions because of his or her disability, the employer, in assessing whether the person is qualified to do the job, must consider whether there are modifications or adjustments that would enable the person to perform these functions. Such modifications or adjustments are called **"reasonable accommodations."**

Reasonable accommodation is a key nondiscrimination requirement under the ADA. An employer must first consider reasonable accommodation in determining whether an individual with a disability is qualified; reasonable accommodation also must be considered when making many other employment decisions regarding people with disabilities. The following chapter discusses the employer's obligation to provide reasonable accommodation and the limits to that obligation. The chapter also provides examples of reasonable accommodations.

III. THE REASONABLE ACCOMMODATION OBLIGATION

3.1 Overview of Legal Obligation

- An employer must provide a reasonable accommodation to the known physical or mental limitations of a qualified applicant or employee with a disability unless it can show that the accommodation would impose an undue hardship on the business.
- Reasonable accommodation is any modification or adjustment to a job, an employment practice, or the work environment that makes it possible for an individual with a disability to enjoy an equal employment opportunity.
- The obligation to provide a reasonable accommodation applies to all aspects of employment. This duty is ongoing and may arise any time that a person's disability or job changes.
- An employer cannot deny an employment opportunity to a qualified applicant or employee because of the need to provide reasonable accommodation, unless it would cause an undue hardship.
- An employer does not have to make an accommodation for an individual who is not otherwise qualified for a position.
- Generally, it is the obligation of an individual with a disability to request a reasonable accommodation.
- A qualified individual with a disability has the right to refuse an accommodation. However, if the individual cannot perform the essential functions of

the job without the accommodation, s/he may not be qualified for the job.

- If the cost of an accommodation would impose an undue hardship on the employer, the individual with a disability should be given the option of providing the accommodation or paying that portion of the cost which would constitute an undue hardship.

3.2 Why Is a Reasonable Accommodation Necessary?

Reasonable accommodation is a key nondiscrimination requirement of the ADA because of the special nature of discrimination faced by people with disabilities. Many people with disabilities can perform jobs without any need for accommodations. But many others are excluded from jobs that they are qualified to perform because of unnecessary barriers in the workplace and the work environment. The ADA recognizes that such barriers may discriminate against qualified people with disabilities just as much as overt exclusionary practices. For this reason, the ADA requires **reasonable accommodation** as a means of overcoming unnecessary barriers that prevent or restrict employment opportunities for otherwise qualified individuals with disabilities.

People with disabilities are restricted in employment opportunities by many different kinds of barriers. Some face physical barriers that make it difficult to get into and around a work site or to use necessary work equipment. Some are excluded or limited by the way people communicate with each other. Others are excluded because of rigid work schedules that allow no flexibility for people with special needs caused by disability. Many are excluded only by barriers in other people's minds; these include unfounded fears, stereotypes, presumptions, and misconceptions about job performance, safety, absenteeism, costs, or acceptance by co-workers and customers.

Under the ADA, when an individual with a disability is qualified to perform the essential functions of a job except for functions that cannot be performed because of related limitations and existing job barriers, an employer must try to find a reasonable accommodation that would enable this person to perform these functions. The reasonable accommodation should reduce or eliminate unnecessary barriers between the individual's abilities and the requirements for performing the essential job functions.

3.3 What Is a Reasonable Accommodation?

Reasonable accommodation is a modification or adjustment to a job, the work environment, or the way things usually are done that enables a qualified individual with a disability to enjoy an equal employment opportunity. An equal employment opportunity means an opportunity to attain the same level of performance or to enjoy equal benefits and privileges of employment as are available to a similarly-situated employee without a disability. The ADA requires reasonable accommodation in three aspects of employment:

- **to ensure equal opportunity in the application process;**
- **to enable a qualified individual with a disability to perform the essential function of a job; and**
- **to enable an employee with a disability to enjoy equal benefits and privileges of employment.**

Reasonable Accommodation in the Application Process
Reasonable accommodation must be provided in the job application process to enable a qualified applicant to have an equal opportunity to be considered for a job.

For example: A person who uses a wheelchair may need an accommodation if an employment office or interview site is not accessible. A person with a visual disability or a person who lacks manual dexterity may need assistance in filling out an application form. Without such accommodations, these individuals may have no opportunity to be considered for a job.

(See Chapter V. for further discussion of accommodations in the application process).

Accommodations to Perform the Essential Functions of a Job
Reasonable accommodation must be provided to enable a qualified applicant to perform the essential functions of the job s/he is seeking, and to enable a qualified employee with a disability to perform the essential functions of a job currently held. Modifications or adjustments may be required in the work environment, in the manner or circumstances in which the job customarily is performed, or in employment policies. Many accommodations of this nature are discussed later in this chapter.

Accommodations to Ensure Equal Benefits of Employment
Reasonable accommodations must be provided to enable an employee with a disability to enjoy benefits and privileges of employment equal to those enjoyed by similarly situated non disabled employees.

For example: Employees with disabilities must have equal access to lunchrooms, employee lounges, rest rooms, meeting rooms, and other employer-provided or sponsored services such as health programs, transportation, and social events. (See Chapter VII for further discussion of this requirement).

3.4 Some Basic Principle of Reasonable Accommodation

A reasonable accommodation must be an effective accommodation. It must provide an opportunity for a person with a disability to achieve the same level of performance or to enjoy benefits or privileges equal to those of a similarly-situated non disabled person. However, the accommodation does not have to ensure equal results or provide exactly the same benefits or privileges.

For example: An employer provides an employee lunchroom with food and beverages on the second floor of a building that has no elevator. If it would be an undue hardship to install an elevator for an employee who uses a wheelchair, the employer must provide a comparable facility on the first floor. The facility does not have to be exactly the same as that on the second floor, but must provide food, beverages and space for the disabled employee to eat with co-workers. It would not be a reasonable accommodation merely to provide a place for this employee to eat by himself. Nor would it be a reasonable accommodation to provide a separate facility for the employee if access to the common facility could be provided without undue hardship. For example, if the lunchroom was only several steps up, a portable ramp could provide access.

The reasonable accommodation obligation applies only to accommodations that reduce barriers to employment related to a person's disability; it does not apply to accommodations that a disabled person may request for some other reason.

For example: Reassignment is one type of accommodation that may be required under the ADA. If an employee whose job requires driving loses her sight, reassignment to a vacant position that does not require driving would be a reasonable accommodation, if the employee is qualified for that position with or without an accommodation. However, if a blind computer operator working at an employer's Michigan facility requested reassignment to a facility in Florida because he prefers to work in a warmer climate, this would not be a reasonable accommodation required by the ADA. In the second case, the accommodation is not needed because of the employee's disability.

A reasonable accommodation need not be the best accommodation available. as long as it is effective for the purpose; that is, it gives the person with a disability an equal opportunity to be considered for a job, to perform the essential functions of the job, or to enjoy equal benefits and privileges of the job.

For example: An employer would not have to hire a full-time reader for a blind employee if a co-worker is available as a part-time reader when needed, and this will enable the blind employee to perform his job duties effectively.

An employer is not required to provide an accommodation that is primarily for personal use. Reasonable accommodation applies to modifications that specifically assist an individual in performing the duties of a particular job. Equipment or devices that assist a person in daily activities on and off the job are considered personal items that an employer is not required to provide. However, in some cases, equipment that otherwise would be considered "personal" may be required as an accommodation if it is specifically designed or required to meet job-related rather than personal needs.

For example: An employer generally would not be required to provide personal items such as eyeglasses, a wheelchair, or an artificial limb. However, the employer might be required to provide a person who has a visual impairment with glasses that are specifically needed to use a computer monitor. Or, if deep pile carpeting in a work area makes it impossible for an individual to use a manual wheelchair, the employer may need to replace the carpet, place a usable surface over the carpet in areas used by the employee, or provide a motorized wheelchair.

The ADA's requirements for certain types of adjustments and modifications to meet the reasonable accommodation obligation do not Prevent an employer from Providing accommodations beyond those required by the ADA.

For example: "Supported employment" programs may provide free job coaches and other assistance to enable certain individuals with severe disabilities to learn and/or to progress in jobs. These programs typically require a range of modifications and adjustments to customary employment practices. Some of these modifications may also be required by the ADA as reasonable accommodations. However, supported employment programs may require modifications beyond those required under the ADA, such as restructuring of essential job functions. Many employers have found that supported employment programs are an excellent source of reliable productive new employees. Participation in these programs advances the underlying goal of the ADA—to increase employment opportunities for people with disabilities. Making modifications for supported employment beyond those required by the ADA in no way violates the ADA.

Some Examples of Reasonable Accommodation

The statute and EEOC's regulations provide examples of common types of reasonable accommodation that an employer may be required to provide, but many other accommodations may be appropriate for particular situations. Accommodations may include:

- making facilities readily accessible to and usable by an individual with a disability;
- restructuring a job by reallocating or redistributing marginal job functions;
- altering when or how an essential job function is performed;
- part-time or modified work schedules;
- obtaining or modifying equipment or devices;
- modifying examinations, training materials or policies;
- providing qualified readers and interpreters;
- reassignment to a vacant position;

- permitting use of accrued paid leave or unpaid leave for necessary treatment;
- providing reserved parking for a person with a mobility impairment;
- allowing an employee to provide equipment or devices that an employer is not required to provide.

These and other types of reasonable accommodation are discussed in the pages that follow. However, the examples in this Manual cannot cover the range of potential accommodations, because every reasonable accommodation must be determined on an individual basis. A reasonable accommodation always must take into consideration two unique factors:

- the specific abilities and functional limitation of a particular applicant or employee with a disability; and
- the specific functional requirements of a particular job.

In considering an accommodation, the focus should be on the abilities and limitations of the **individual,** not on the name of 8 disability or a particular physical or mental condition. This is necessary because people who have any particular disability may have very different abilities and limitations. Conversely, people with different kinds of disabilities may have similar functional limitations.

> *For example:* If it is an essential function of a job to press a foot pedal a certain number of times a minute and an individual with a disability applying for the job has some limitation that makes this difficult or impossible, the accommodation process should focus on ways that *this person* might be able to do the job function, not on the nature of her disability or on how persons with this kind of disability generally might be able to perform the Job.

3.6 Who Is Entitled to a Reasonable Accommodation?

As detailed in Chapter II, an individual is entitled to a reasonable accommodation if s/he:

> meets the ADA definition of "a qualified individual with a disability" (meets all prerequisites for performing the essential functions of a job [being considered for a job or enjoying equal benefits and privileges of a job] except any that cannot be met because of a disability).

If there is a reasonable accommodation that will enable this person to perform the essential functions of a job (be considered, or receive equal benefits, etc.), the employer is obligated to provide it, unless it would impose an undue hardship on the operation of the business.

When Is an Employer Obligated to Make a Reasonable Accommodation?

An employer is obligated to make an accommodation only to the *known* limitations of an otherwise qualified individual with a disability. In general, it is the responsibility of the applicant or employee with a disability to inform the employer that an accommodation is needed to participate in the application process, to perform essential job functions or to receive equal benefits and privileges of employment. An employer is not required to provide an accommodation if unaware of the need.

However, the employer is responsible for **notifying** job applicants and employees of its obligation to provide accommodations for otherwise qualified individuals with disabilities.

The ADA requires an employer to **post notices** containing the provisions of the ADA, including the reasonable accommodation obligation, in conspicuous places on its premises. Such notices should be posted in employment offices and other places where applicants and employees can readily see them. EEOC provides posters for this purpose. (See Chapter I for additional information on the required notice.)

Information about the reasonable accommodation obligation also can be included in job application forms, job vacancy notices, and in personnel manuals, and may be communicated orally.

An applicant or employee does not have to specifically request a "reasonable accommodation," but must only let the employer know that some adjustment or change is needed to do a job because of the limitations caused by a disability.

If a job applicant or employee has a "hidden" disability—one that is not obvious—it is up to that individual to make the need for an accommodation known. If an applicant has a known disability, such as a visible disability, that appears to limit, interfere with, or prevent the individual from performing job-related functions, the employer may ask the applicant to describe or demonstrate how s/he would perform the function with or without a reasonable accommodation. Chapter V provides guidance on how to make such an inquiry without violating the ADA prohibition against pre-employment inquiries in the application and interview process.

If an employee with a known disability is not performing well or is having difficulty in performing a job, the employer should assess whether this is due to a disability. The employer may inquire at any time whether the employee needs an accommodation.

Documentation of Need for Accommodation

If an applicant or employee requests an accommodation and the need for the accommodation is not obvious, or if the employer does not believe that the accommodation is needed, the employer may request documentation of the individual's functional limitations to support the request.

For example: An employer may ask for written documentation from a doctor, psychologist, rehabilitation counselor, occupational or physical therapist, independent living specialist, or other professional with knowledge of the person's functional limitations. Such documentation might indicate, for example, that this person cannot lift more than 15 pounds without assistance.

3.7 How Does an Employer Determine What Is a Reasonable Accommodation?

When a qualified individual with a disability requests an accommodation, the employer must make a reasonable effort to provide an accommodation that is *effective for the individual* (gives the individual an equally effectiveopportunity to apply for a job, perform essential job functions, or enjoy equal benefits and privileges).

In many cases an appropriate accommodation will be obvious and can be made without difficulty and at little or no cost. Frequently, the individual with a disability can suggest a simple change or adjustment, based on his or her life or work experience.

An employer should always consult the person with the disability as the first step in considering an accommodation. Often this person can suggest much simpler and less costly accommodations than the employer might have believed necessary.

> *For example:* A small employer believed it necessary to install a special lower drinking fountain for an employee using a wheelchair, but the employee indicated that he could use the existing fountain if paper cups were provided in a holder next to the fountain.

However, in some cases, the appropriate accommodation may not be so easy to identify. The individual requesting the accommodation may not know enough about the equipment being used or the exact nature of the worksite to suggest an accommodation, or the employer may not know enough about the individual's functional limitations in relation to specific job tasks.

In such cases, the employer and the individual with a disability should work together to identify the appropriate accommodation. EEOC regulations require, when necessary, an informal, interactive process to find an effective accommodation. The process is described below in relation to an accommodation that will enable an individual with a disability to perform the essential functions of a job. However, the same approach can be used to identify accommodations for job applicants and accommodations to provide equal benefits and privileges of employment.

3.8 A Process for Identifying a Reasonable Accommodation

1. **Look at the particular job involved. Determine its purpose and its essential functions.**

Chapter II recommended that the essential functions of the job be identified before advertising or interviewing for a job. However, it is useful to reexamine the specific job at this point to determine or confirm its essential functions and requirements.

2. **Consult with the individual with a disability to find out his or her specific physical or mental abilities and limitations** as they relate to the essential job functions. Identify the barriers to job performance and assess how these barriers could be overcome with an accommodation.

3. **In consultation with the individual, identify potential accommodations and assess how effective** each would be in enabling the individual to perform essential job functions. If this consultation does not identify an appropriate accommodation, technical assistance is available from a number of sources, many without cost. There are also financial resources to help with accommodation costs. (See *Financial and Technical Assistance for Accommodations*. 4.1 below).

4. If there are several effective accommodations that would provide an equal employment opportunity, consider **the preference of the individual** with a disability and **select the accommodation** that **best serves the needs of the individual and the employer.**

If more than one accommodation would be effective for the individual with a disability, or if the individual would prefer to provide his or her own accommodation, the individual's preference should be given first consideration. However, the employer is free to choose among effective accommodations, and may choose one that is less expensive or easier to provide.

The fact that an individual is willing to provide his or her own accommodation does not relieve the employer of the duty to provide this or another reasonable accommodation should this individual for any reason be unable or unwilling to continue to provide the accommodation.

Examples of the Reasonable Accommodation Process

- A "sack-handler" position requires that the employee in this job pick up 50 pound sacks from a loading dock and carry them to the storage room. An employee who is disabled by a back impairment requests an accommodation. The employer analyzes the job and finds that its real purpose and essential function is to *move* the sacks from the loading dock to the store room. The person in the job does not necessarily have to lift and carry the sacks. The employer consults with the employee to determine his exact physical abilities and limitations. With medical documentation, it is determined that this person can lift 50 pound sacks to waist level, but cannot carry them to the storage room. A number of potential accommodations are identified: use of a dolly, a hand-truck or a cart. The employee prefers the dolly. After considering the relative cost, efficiency, and availability of the alternative accommodations, and after considering the preference of the employee, the employer provides the dolly as an accommodation. In this case, the employer found the dolly to be the most cost-effective accommodation, as well as the one preferred by the employee. If the employer had found a hand-truck to be as efficient, it could have provided the hand-truck as a reasonable accommodation.

A company has an opening for a warehouse foreman. Among other functions, the job requires checking stock for inventory, completing bills of lading and other reports, and using numbers. To perform these functions, the foreman must have good math skills. An individual with diabetes who has good experience performing similar warehouse supervisory functions applies for the job. Part of the application process is a computerized test for math skills, but the job itself does not require use of a computer. The applicant tells the employer that although he has no problem reading print, his disability causes some visual impairment which makes it difficult to read a computer screen. He says he can take the test if it is printed out by the computer. However, this accommodation won't work, because the computer test is interactive, and the questions change based on the applicant's replies to each previous question. Instead, the employer offers a reader as an accommodation; this provides an effective equivalent method to test the applicant's math skills.

An individual with a disability is not required to accept an accommodation if the individual has not requested an accommodation and does not believe that one is needed. However, if the individual refuses an accommodation necessary to perform essential job functions, and as a result cannot perform those functions, the individual may not be considered qualified.

For example: An individual with a visual impairment that restricts her field of vision but who is able to read would not be required to accept a reader as an accommodation. However, if this person could not read accurately unaided, and reading is an essential function of the job, she would not be qualified for the job if she refused an accommodation that would enable her to read accurately.

3.9 The Undue Hardship Limitation

An employer is not required to make a reasonable accommodation if it would impose an *undue hardship* on the operation of the business. However, if a particular accommodation would impose an undue hardship, the employer must consider whether there are alternative accommodations that would not impose such hardship.

An undue hardship is an action that requires **"significant difficulty or expense"** in relation to the size of the employer, the resources available, and the nature of the operation.

Accordingly, whether a particular accommodation will impose an undue hardship must always be determined on a **case-by-case** basis. An accommodation that poses an undue hardship for one employer at a particular time may not pose an undue hardship for another employer, or even for the same employer at another time. In general, a larger employer would be expected to make accommodations requiring greater effort or expense than would be required of a smaller employer. The concept of undue hardship includes any action that is:

- **unduly costly;**
- **extensive;**
- **substantial;**
- **disruptive; or**
- **that would fundamentally alter the nature or operation of the business.**

The statute and regulations provide **factors to be considered** in determining whether an accommodation would impose an undue hardship on a particular business:

1. **The nature and net cost of the accommodation needed.** The cost of an accommodation that is considered in determining undue hardship will be the actual cost to the employer. Specific Federal tax credits and tax deductions are available to employers for making accommodations required by the ADA, and there are also sources of funding to help pay for some accommodations. If an employer can receive tax credits or tax deductions or partial funding for an accommodation, only the *net* cost to the employer will be considered in a determination of undue hardship. (See *Financial and Technical Assistance for Accommodations,* 4.1 below);

2. **The financial resources of the facility making the accommodation, the number of employees at this facility, and the effect on expenses and resource of the facility.**

If an employer has only one facility, the cost and impact of the accommodation will be considered in relation to the effect on expenses and resources of that facility. However, if the facility is part of a larger entity that is covered by the ADA, factors 3. and 4. below also will be considered in determinations of undue hardship.

3. **The overall financial resources, size, number of employees, and type and location of facilities of the entity covered by the ADA** (if the facility involved in the accommodation is part of a larger entity).

4. **The type of operation of the covered entity, including the structure and function of the workforce, the geographic separateness, and the administrative or fiscal relationship of the facility involved in making the accommodation to the larger entity.**

Factor 4. may include consideration of special types of employment operations, on a case-by-case basis, where providing a particular accommodation might be an undue hardship.

For example: It might "fundamentally alter" the nature of a temporary construction site or be unduly costly to make it physically accessible to an employee using a wheelchair, if the terrain and structures are constantly changing as construction progresses.

Factor 4. will be considered, along with factors 2. and 3., where a covered entity operates more than one facility, in order to assess the financial resources actually available to the facility making the accommodation, in light of the interrelationship between the facility and the covered entity. In some cases, consideration of the resources of the larger covered entity may not be justified, because the particular facility making the accommodation may not have access to those resources.

For example: A local, independently owned fast food franchise of a national company that receives no funding from that company may assert that it would be an undue hardship to provide an interpreter to enable a deaf applicant for store manager to participate in weekly staff meetings, because its own resources are inadequate and it has no access to resources of the national company. If the financial relationship between the national company and the local company is limited to payment of an annual franchise fee, only the resources of the local franchise would be considered in determining whether this accommodation would be an undue hardship. However, if the facility was part of a national company with financial and administrative control over all of its facilities, the resources of the company as a whole would be considered in making this determination.

5. The impact of the accommodation on the operation of the facility that is making the accommodation.

This may include the impact on the ability of other employees to perform their duties and the impact on the facility's ability to conduct business.

An employer may be able to show that providing a particular accommodation would be unduly disruptive to its other employees or to its ability to conduct business.

For example: If an employee with a disability requested that the thermostat in the workplace be raised to a certain level to accommodate her disability, and this level would make it uncomfortably hot for other employees or customers, the employer would not have to provide this accommodation. However, if there was an alternative accommodation that would not be an undue hardship, such as providing a space heater or placing the employee in a room with a separate thermostat, the employer would have to provide that accommodation.

For example: A person with a visual impairment who requires bright light to see well applies for a waitress position at an expensive nightclub. The club maintains dim lighting to create an intimate setting, and lowers its lights further during the floor show. If the job applicant requested bright lighting as an accommodation so that she could see to take orders, the employer could assert that this would be an undue hardship, because it would seriously affect the nature of it operation.

In determining whether an accommodation would cause an undue hardship, an employer may consider the impact of an accommodation on the ability of other employees to do their jobs. However, an employer may not claim undue hardship solely because providing an accommodation has a negative impact on the **morale** of other employees. Nor can an employer claim undue hardship because of "disruption" due to employees' fears about, or prejudices toward, a person's disability.

For example: If restructuring a job to accommodate an individual with a disability creates a heavier workload for other employees, this may constitute an undue hardship. But if other employees complain because an individual with a disability is allowed to take additional unpaid leave-or to have a special flexible work schedule as a reasonable accommodation, such complaints or other negative reactions would not constitute an undue hardship.

For example: If an employee objects to working with an individual who has a disability because the employee feels uncomfortable or dislikes being near this person, this would not constitute an undue hardship. In this case, the problem is caused by the employee's fear or prejudice toward the individual's disability, not by an accommodation.

Problems of employee morale and employee negative attitudes should be addressed by the employer through appropriate consultations with supervisors and, where relevant, with union representatives. Employers also may wish to provide supervisors, managers and employees with "awareness" training, to help overcome fears and misconceptions about disabilities, and to inform them of the employer's obligations under the ADA.

Other Cost Issues

An employer may not claim undue hardship simply because the cost of an accommodation is high in relation to an employee's wage or salary. When enacting the ADA "factors" for determining undue hardship, Congress rejected a proposed amendment that would have established an undue hardship if an accommodation exceeded 10% of an individual's salary. This approach was rejected because it would unjustifiably harm lower-paid workers who need accommodations. Instead, Congress dearly established that the focus for determining undue hardship should be the resources available to the employer.

If an employer finds that the cost of an accommodation would impose an undue hardship and no funding is available from another source, an applicant or employee with a disability should be offered the option of paying for the portion of the cost that constitutes an undue hardship, or of providing the accommodation.

For example: If the cost of an assistive device is $2000, and an employer believes that it can demonstrate that spending more than $1500 would be an undue hardship, the individual with a disability should be offered the option of paying the additional $500. Or, if it would be an undue hardship for an employer to purchase brailling equipment for a blind applicant, the applicant should be offered the option of providing his own equipment (if there is no other effective accommodation that would not impose an undue hardship).

The terms of a collective bargaining agreement may be relevant in determining whether an accommodation would impose an undue hardship.

For example: A worker who has a deteriorated disc condition and cannot perform the heavy labor functions of a machinist job, requests reassignment to a vacant clerk's job as a reasonable accommodation. If the collective bargaining agreement has specific seniority lists and requirements governing each craft, it might be an undue hardship to reassign this person if others had seniority for the clerk's job.

However, since both the employer and the union are covered by the ADA's requirements, including the duty to provide a reasonable accommodation, the employer should consult with the union and try to work out an acceptable accommodation.

To avoid continuing conflicts between a collective bargaining agreement and the duty to provide reasonable accommodation, employers may find it helpful to seek a provision in agreements negotiated after the effective date of the ADA permitting the employer to take all actions necessary to comply with this law. (See Chapter VII.)

3.10 Examples of Reasonable Accommodations

1. Making Facilities Accessible and Usable

The ADA establishes different requirements for accessibility under different sections of the Act. A **private employer's** obligation to make its facilities accessible to its job applicants and employees under Title I of the ADA differs from the obligation of a place of **public accommodation** to provide access in existing facilities to its customers and clients, and from the obligations of public accommodations and **commercial facilities** to provide accessibility in renovated or newly constructed buildings under Title III of the Act. The obligation of a **state and local government** to provide access for applicants and employees under Title I also differs from its obligation to provide accessibility under Title II of the ADA.

The employer's obligation under Title I is to provide access for an *individual* applicant to participate in the job application process, and for an *individual* employee with a disability to perform the essential functions of his/her job, including access to a building, to the work site, to needed equipment, and to all facilities used by employees. The employer must provide such access unless it would cause an undue hardship.

Under Title I, an employer is not required to make its existing facilities accessible until a particular applicant or employee with a particular disability needs an accommodation, and then the modifications should meet that individual's work needs. The employer does not have to make changes to provide access in places or facilities that will not be used by that individual for employment related activities or benefits.

In contrast, Title III of the ADA requires that places of public accommodation (such as banks, retail stores, theaters, hotels and restaurants) make their goods and services accessible generally, to all people with disabilities. Under Title III, existing buildings and facilities of a public accommodation must be made accessible by removing architectural barriers or communications barriers that are structural in nature, if this is "readily achievable." If this is not "readily achievable," services must be provided to people with disabilities in some alternative manner if this is "readily achievable."

The obligation for state and local governments to provide "program accessibility" in existing facilities under Title II also differs from their obligation to provide access as employers under Title I. Title II requires that these governments operate each service, program or activity in existing facilities so that, when viewed in its entirety, it is readily accessible to and usable by persons with disabilities, unless this would cause a "fundamental alteration" in the nature of the program or service, or would result in "undue financial and administrative burdens."

In addition, private employers that occupy commercial facilities or operate places of public accommodation and state and local governments must conform to more extensive accessibility requirements under Title III and Title II when making alterations to existing facilities or undertaking new construction. (See *Requirements for Renovation and New Construction* below.)

The accessibility requirements under Title II and III are established in Department of Justice regulations. Employers may contact the Justice Department's **Office on the American with Disabilities Act** for information on these requirements and for copies of the regulations with applicable accessibility guidelines.

When making changes to meet an individual's needs under Title I, an employer will find it helpful to consult the applicable Department of Justice accessibility guidelines as a starting point. It is advisable to make changes that conform to these guidelines, if they meet the individual's needs and do not impose an undue hardship, since such changes will be useful in the future for accommodating others. However, even if a modification meets the standards required under Title II or III, further adaptations may be needed to meet the needs of a *particular* individual.

For example: A restroom may be modified to meet standard accessibility requirements (including wider door and stalls, and grab bars in specified locations) but it may be necessary to install a lower grab bar for a very short person in a wheelchair so that this person can transfer from the chair to the toilet.

Although the requirement for accessibility in employment is triggered by the needs of a particular individual, employers should consider initiating changes that will provide general accessibility, particularly for job applicants, since it is likely that people with disabilities will apply for jobs in the future.

For example: Employment offices and interview facilities should be accessible to people using wheelchairs and others with mobility impairments. Plans also should be in place for making job information accessible and for communicating with people who have visual or hearing impairments. (See Chapter V. for additional guidance on accommodation in the application process.)

Accessibility to Perform the Essential Functions of the Job

The obligation to provide accessibility for a qualified individual with a disability includes accessibility of the job site itself and all work-related facilities.

Examples of accommodations that may be needed to make facilities accessible and usable include:

- installing a ramp at the entrance to a building;
- removing raised thresholds;
- reserving parking spaces close to the work site that are wide enough to allow people using wheelchairs to get in and out of vehicles;
- making restrooms accessible, including toilet stalls, sinks, soap, and towels; rearranging office furniture and equipment;
- making a drinking fountain accessible (for example, by installing a paper cup dispenser);
- making accessible, and providing an accessible "path of travel" to, equipment and facilities used by an employee, such as copying machines, meeting and training rooms, lunchrooms and lounges;
- removing obstacles that might be potential hazards in the path of people without vision;
- adding flashing lights when alarm bells are normally used, to alert an employee with a hearing impairment to emergencies.

Requirements for Renovation or New Construction

While an employer's requirements for accessibility under Title I relate to accommodation of an individual, as described above employers will have more extensive accessibility requirements under Title II or III of the ADA if they make renovations to their facilities or undertake new construction.

Title III of the ADA requires that any alterations to, or new construction of **"commercial facilities,"** as well as places of **public accommodation,** made after January 26, 1992, must conform to the "ADA Accessibility Guidelines" (incorporated in Department of Justice Title III regulations). "Commercial facilities" are defined as any nonresidential facility whose operations affect commerce, including office buildings, factories and warehouses; therefore, the facilities of most employers will be subject to this requirement. An alteration is any change that affects the "usability" of a facility; it does not include normal maintenance, such as painting, roofing or changes to mechanical or electrical systems, unless the changes affect the "usability" of the facility.

For example: If, during remodeling or renovation, a doorway is relocated, the new doorway must be wide enough to meet the requirements of the ADA Accessibility Guidelines.

Under Title III, all newly constructed public accommodations and commercial facilities for which the last building permit is certified after January 26, 1992, and which are occupied after January 26, 1993, must be accessible in accordance with the standards of the ADA Accessibility Guidelines. However, Title III does not require elevators in facilities under 3 stories or with less than 3000 square feet per floor, unless the building is a shopping center, mall, professional office of a health provider, or public transportation station.

Under Title II, any alterations to, or new construction of, State or local government facilities made after January 26, 1992, must conform either with the ADA Accessibility Guidelines (however, the exception regarding elevators does not apply to State or local governments) or with the Uniform Federal Accessibility Standards. Facilities under design on January 26, 1992 must comply with this requirement if bids were invited after that date.

Providing accessibility in remodeled and new buildings usually can be accomplished at minimal additional cost. Over time, fully accessible new and remodeled buildings will reduce the need for many types of individualized reasonable accommodations. Employers planning alterations to their facilities or new construction should contact the **Office on the Americans with Disabilities Act** in the **U.S. Department of Justice** for information on accessibility requirements, including the *ADA Accessibility Guidelines* and the *Uniform Federal Accessibility Guidelines*. Employers may get specific technical information and guidance on accessibility by calling, toll-free, the Architectural and Transportation Barriers Compliance Board, at 1-800-USA-ABLE.

2. Job Restructuring

Job restructuring or job modification is a form of reasonable accommodation which enables many qualified individuals with disabilities to perform jobs effectively. Job restructuring as a reasonable accommodation may involve reallocating or redistributing the marginal functions of a job. However, an employer is not required to reallocate essential functions of a job as a reasonable accommodation. Essential functions, by definition, are those that a qualified individual must perform, with or without an accommodation.

> *For example:* Inspection of identification cards is generally an essential function of the job of a security job. If a person with a visual impairment could not verify the identification of an individual using the photo and other information on the card, the employer would not be required to transfer this function to another employee.

Job restructuring frequently is accomplished by exchanging marginal functions of a job that cannot be performed by a person with a disability for marginal job functions performed by one or more other employees.

> *For example:* An employer may have two jobs, each containing essential functions and a number of marginal functions. The employer may hire an individual with a disability who can perform the essential functions of one job and some, but not all, of the marginal functions of both jobs. As an accommodation, the employer may redistribute the marginal functions so that all of the functions that can be performed by the person with a disability are in this person's job and the remaining marginal functions are transferred to the other job.

Although an employer is not required to reallocate essential job functions, it may be a reasonable accommodation to modify the essential functions of a job by changing **when** or **how** they are done.

For example:

- An essential function that is usually performed in the early morning might be rescheduled to be performed later in the day, if an individual has a disability that makes it impossible to perform this function in the morning, and this would not cause an undue hardship.
- A person who has a disability that makes it difficult to write might be allowed to computerize records that have been maintained manually.
- A person with mental retardation who can perform job tasks but has difficulty remembering the order in which to do the tasks might be provided with a list to check off each task; the checklist could be reviewed by a supervisor at the end of the day.

Technical assistance in restructuring or modifying jobs for individuals with specific limitations can be obtained from state vocational rehabilitation agencies and other organizations with expertise in job analysis and job restructuring for people with various disabilities.

3. Modified Work Schedules

An employer should consider modification of a regular work schedule as a reasonable accommodation unless this would cause an undue hardship. Modified work schedules may include flexibility in work hours or the work week, or part-time work, where this will not be an undue hardship.

Many people with disabilities are fully qualified to perform jobs with the accommodation of a modified work schedule. Some people are unable to work a standard 9-5 work day, or a standard Monday to Friday work week; others need some adjustment to regular schedules.

Some examples of modified work schedules as a reasonable accommodation:

An accountant with a mental disability required two hours off, twice weekly, for sessions with a psychiatrist. He was permitted to take longer lunch breaks and to make up the time by working later on those days.

A machinist has diabetes and must follow a strict schedule to keep blood sugar levels stable. She must eat on a regular schedule and take insulin at set times each day. This means that she cannot work the normal shift rotations for machinists. As an accommodation, she is assigned to one shift on a permanent basis.

An employee who needs kidney dialysis treatment is unable to work on two days because his treatment is only available during work hours on weekdays. Depending on the nature of his work and the nature of the employer's operation, it may be possible, without causing an undue hardship, for him to work Saturday and Sunday in place of the two weekdays, to perform work assignments at home on the weekend, or to work three days a week as part-time employee.

People whose disabilities may need modified work schedules include those who require special medical treatment for their disability (such as cancer patients, people who have AIDS, or people with mental illness); people who need rest periods (including some people who have multiple sclerosis, cancer, diabetes, respiratory conditions, or mental illness); people whose disabilities (such as diabetes) are affected by eating or sleeping schedules; and people with mobility and other impairments who find it difficult to use public transportation during peak hours, or who must depend upon special para-transit schedules.

4. Flexible Leave Policies

Flexible leave policies should be considered as a reasonable accommodation when people with disabilities require time off from work because of their disability. An employer is not required to provide additional paid leave as an accommodation, but should consider allowing use of accrued leave, advanced leave, or leave without pay, where this will not cause an undue hardship.

People with disabilities may require special leave for a number of reasons related to their disability, such as:

- medical treatment related to the disability;
- repair of a prosthesis or equipment;
- temporary adverse conditions in the work environment (for example, an air-conditioning breakdown causing temperature above 85 degrees could seriously harm the condition of a person with multiple sclerosis);
- training in the use of an assistive device or a dog guide. (However, if an assistive device is used at work and provided as a reasonable accommodation, and if other employees receive training during work hours, the disabled employee should receive training on this device during work hours, without need to take leave.)

5. Reassignment to a Vacant Position

In general, the accommodation of reassignment should be considered only when an accommodation is not possible in an employee's present job, or when an accommodation in the employee's present job would cause an undue hardship. Reassignment also may be a reasonable accommodation if both that this is more appropriate than employer and employee agree accommodation in the present job.

Consideration of reassignment is only required for **employees.** An employer is not required to consider a different position for a job applicant if s/he is not able to perform the essential functions of the position s/he is applying for, with or without reasonable accommodation.

Reassignment may be an appropriate accommodation when an employee becomes disabled, when a disability becomes more severe, or when changes or technological developments in equipment affect the job performance of an employee with a disability. If there is no accommodation that will enable the person to perform the present job, or if it would be an undue hardship for the employer to provide such accommodation, reassignment should be considered.

Reassignment may not be used to limit, segregate, or otherwise discriminate against an employee with a disability. An employer may not reassign people with disabilities only to certain undesirable positions, or only to certain offices or facilities.

Reassignment should be made to a position equivalent to the one presently held in terms of pay and other job status, if the individual is qualified for the position and if such a position is vacant or will be vacant within a reasonable amount of time. A "reasonable amount of time" should be determined on a case-by-case basis, considering relevant factors such as the types of jobs for which the employee with a disability would be qualified; the frequency with which such jobs become available; the employer's general policies regarding reassignments of employees; and any specific policies regarding sick or injured employees.

For example: If there is no vacant position available at the time that an individual with a disability requires a reassignment, but the employer knows that an equivalent position for which this person is qualified will become vacant within one or two weeks, the employer should reassign the individual to the position when it becomes available.

An employer may reassign an individual to a lower graded position if there are no accommodations that would enable the employee to remain in the current position and there are no positions vacant or soon to be vacant for which the employee is qualified (with or without an accommodation). In such a situation, the employer does not have to maintain the individual's salary at the level of the higher graded position, unless it does so for other employees who are reassigned to lower graded positions.

An employer is not required to create a new job or to bump another employee from a job in order to provide reassignment as a reasonable accommodation. Nor is an employer required to promote an individual with a disability to make such an accommodation.

6. Acquisition or Modification of Equipment and Devices

Purchase of equipment or modifications to existing equipment may be effective accommodations for people with many types of disabilities.

There are many devices that make it possible for people to overcome existing barriers to performing functions of a job. These devices range from very simple solutions, such as an elastic band that can enable a person with cerebral palsy to hold a pencil and write, to "high-tech" electronic equipment that can be operated with eye or head movements by people who cannot use their hands.

There are also many ways to modify standard equipment 80 as to enable people with different functional limitations to perform jobs effectively and safely.

Many of these assistive devices and modifications are inexpensive. Frequently, applicants and employees with disabilities can suggest effective low cost device or equipment. They have had a great deal of experience in accommodating their disabilities, and many are informed about new and available equipment. Where the job requires special adaptations of equipment, the employer and the applicant or employee should use the process described earlier (see 3.8) to identify the exact functional abilities and limitations of the individual in relation to functional job needs, and to determine what type of assistance may be needed.

There are many sources of technical assistance to help identify and locate devices and equipment for specific job applications. An employer may be able to get information needed simply by telephoning the *Job Accommodation Network,* a free consulting service on accommodations, or other sources listed under "Accommodations" in the *Resource Directory*. Employers who need further assistance may use resources such as vocational rehabilitation specialists, occupational therapists and Independent Living Centers who will come on site to conduct a job analysis and recommend appropriate equipment or job modifications.

As indicated above (see 3.4), an employer is only obligated to provide equipment that is needed to perform a job; there is no obligation to provide equipment that the individual uses regularly in daily life, such as glasses, a hearing aid or a wheelchair. However, as previously stated, the employer may be obligated to provide items of this nature if special adaptations are required to perform a job.

For example: It may be a reasonable accommodation to provide an employee with a motorized wheelchair if her job requires movement between buildings that are widely separated, and her disability prevents her operation of a wheelchair manually for that distance, or if heavy, deep-pile carpeting prevents operation of a manual wheelchair.

In some cases, it may be a reasonable accommodation to allow an applicant or employee to provide and use equipment that an employer would not be obligated to provide.

For example: It would be a reasonable accommodation to allow an individual with a visual disability to provide his own guide dog.

Some examples of equipment and devices that may be reasonable accommodations:

- TDDs (Telecommunication Devices for the Deaf make it possible for people with hearing and/or speech impairments to communicate over the telephone;
- telephone amplifiers are useful for people with hearing impairments;
- special software for standard computers and other equipment can enlarge print or convert print documents to spoken words for people with vision and/or reading disabilities;
- tactile markings on equipment in brailled or raised print are helpful to people with visual impairments;
- telephone headsets and adaptive light switches can be used by people with cerebral palsy or other manual disabilities;
- talking calculators can be used by people with visual or reading disabilities;
- speaker phones may be effective for people who are amputees or have other mobility impairments.

Some examples of effective low cost assistive devices as reported by the Job Accommodation Network and other sources:

- A timer with an indicator light allowed a medical technician who was deaf to perform laboratory tests. Cost $27.00;
- A clerk with limited use of her hands was provided a "lazy Susan" file holder

that enabled her to reach all materials needed for her job. Cost $85.00;

- A groundskeeper who had limited use of one arm was provided a detachable extension arm for a rake. This enabled him to grasp the handle on the extension with the impaired hand and control the rake with the functional arm. Cost $20.00;
- A desk layout was changed from the right to left side to enable a data entry operator who is visually impaired to perform her job. Cost $0;
- A telephone amplifier designed to work with a hearing aid allowed a plant worker to retain his job and avoid transfer to a lower paid job. Cost $24.00;
- A blind receptionist was provided a light probe which allowed her to determine which lines on the switchboard were ringing, on hold, or in use. (A light-probe gives an audible signal when held over an illuminated source.) Cost $50.00 to $100.00;
- A person who had use of only one hand, working in a food service position could perform all tasks except opening cans. She was provided with a one-handed can opener. Cost $35.00;
- Purchase of a light weight mop and a smaller broom enabled an employee with Downs syndrome and congenital heart problems to do his job with minimal strain. Cost under $40;
- A truck driver had carpal tunnel syndrome which limited his wrist movement and caused extreme discomfort in cold weather. A special wrist splint used with a glove designed for skin divers made it possible for him to drive even in extreme weather conditions. Cost $55.00;
- A phone headset allowed an insurance salesman with cerebral palsy to write while talking to clients. Rental cost $6.00 per month;
- A simple cardboard form, called a jig, made it possible for a person with mental retardation to properly fold jeans as a stock clerk in a retail store. Cost $0.

Many recent technological innovations make it possible for people with severe disabilities to be very productive employees. Although some of this equipment is expensive, Federal tax credits, tax deductions, and other sources of financing are available to help pay for higher cost equipment.

> *For example:* A company hired a person who was legally blind as a computer operator. The State Commission for the Blind paid half of the cost of a braille terminal. Since all programmers were provided with computers, the cost of the accommodation to this employer was only one-half of the difference in cost between the braille terminal and a regular computer. A smaller company also would be eligible for a tax credit for such cost. (See *Tax Credit for Small Business,* **4.1a** below)

7. Adjusting and Modifying Examinations, Training Materials, and Policies

An employer may be required to modify. adjust, or make other reasonable accommodations in a way that tests and training are administered in order to provide equal employment opportunities for qualified individuals with disabilities. Revisions to other employment policies and practices also may be reasonable accommodations.

a. Tests and Examinations

Accommodations may be needed to assure that tests or examinations measure the actual **ability** of an individual to perform job functions, rather than reflecting limitations caused by the disability. The ADA requires that tests be given to people who have sensory, speaking, or manual impairment in a format that does not require the use of the impaired skill, unless that is the job-related skill the test is designed to measure.

For example: An applicant who has dyslexia, which causes difficulty in reading, should be given an oral rather than a written test, unless reading is an essential function of the job. Or, an individual with visual disability or a learning disability might be allowed more time to take a test, unless the test is designed to measure speed required on a job.

The employer is only required to provide a reasonable accommodation for a test if the individual with a disability requests such an accommodation. But the employer has an obligation to inform job applicants in advance that a test will be given, so that an individual who needs an accommodation can make such a request. (See Chapter V. for further guidance on accommodations in testing.)

b. Training

Reasonable accommodation should be provided, when needed, to give employees with disabilities equal opportunity for training to perform their jobs effectively and to progress in employment. Needed accommodations may include:

- providing accessible training sites;
- providing training materials in alternate formats to accommodate a disability.

  For example: An individual with a visual disability may need training materials on tape, in large print, or on a computer diskette. A person with mental retardation may need materials in simplified language or may need help in understanding test instructions;

- modifying the manner in which training is provided.

  For example: It may be a reasonable accommodation to allow more time for training or to provide extra assistance to people with learning disabilities or people with mental impairments.

  Additional guidance on accommodations in training is provided in Chapter VII.

c. Other Policies

Adjustments to various existing policies may be necessary to provide reasonable accommodation. As discussed above (see **3.10.3** and **3.10.4**), modifications to existing leave policies and regular work hours may be required as accommodations. Or, for example, a company may need to modify a policy prohibiting animals in the work place, so that a visually impaired person can use a guide dog. Policies on providing information to employees may need adjustment to assure that all information is available in accessible formats for employees with disabilities. Policies on emergency evacuations should be adjusted to provide effective accommodations for people with different disabilities. (See Chapter VI).

8. Providing Qualified Readers

It may be a reasonable accommodation to provide a reader for a qualified individual with a disability, if this would not impose an undue hardship.

> *For example:* A court has held under the Rehabilitation Act that it was not an undue hardship for a large state agency to provide full-time readers for three blind employees, in view of its very substantial budget. However, it may be an undue hardship for a smaller agency or business to provide such an accommodation.

In some job situations a reader may be the most effective and efficient accommodation, but in other situations alternative accommodations may enable an individual with a visual disability to perform job tasks just as effectively.

When an applicant or employee has a visual disability, the employer and the individual should use the "process" outlined in **3.8** above to identify specific limitations of the individual in relation to specific needs of the job and to assess possible accommodations.

> *For example:* People with visual impairments perform many jobs that do not require reading. Where reading is an essential job function, depending on the nature of a visual impairment and the nature of job tasks, print magnification equipment or a talking computer may be more effective for the individual and less costly for an employer than providing another employee as a reader. Where an individual has to read lengthy documents, a reader who transcribes documents onto tapes may be a more effective accommodation.

Providing a reader does not mean that it is necessary to hire a first time employee for this service. Few jobs require an individual to spend all day reading. A reader may be a part time employee or full-time employee who performs other duties. However, the person who reads to a visually impaired employee must read well enough to enable the individual to perform his or her job effectively. It would not be a reasonable accommodation to provide a reader whose poor skills hinder the job performance of the individual with a disability.

9. Providing Qualified interpreters

Providing an interpreter on an "as-needed" basis may be a reasonable accommodation for a person who is deaf in some employment situations, if this does not impose an undue hardship.

If an individual with a disability is otherwise qualified to perform essential job functions, the employers basic obligation is to provide an accommodation that will enable this person to perform the job effectively. A person who is deaf or hearing-impaired should be able to communicate effectively with others as required by the duties of the job. Identifying the needs of the individual in relation to specific job tasks will determine whether or when an interpreter may be needed. The resources available to the employer would be considered in determining whether it would be an undue hardship to provide such an accommodation.

For example: It may be necessary to obtain a qualified interpreter for a job interview, because for many jobs the applicant and interviewer must communicate fully and effectively to evaluate whether the applicant is qualified to do the job. Once hired, however, if the individual is doing clerical work, research, computer applications, or other job tasks that do not require much verbal communication an interpreter may only be needed occasionally. Interpretation may be necessary for training situations, staff meetings or an employee party, so that this person can fully participate in these functions. Communication on the job may be handled through different means, depending on the situation, such as written notes, "signing" by other employees who have received basic sign language training, or by typing on a computer or typewriter.

People with hearing impairments have different communication needs and use different modes of communication. Some use signing in American Sign Language, but others use sign language that has different manual codes. Some people rely on an oral interpreter who silently mouths words spoken by others to make them easier to lip read. Many hearing-impaired people use their voices to communicate, and some combine talking and signing. The individual should be consulted to determine the most effective means of communication.

Communication between a person who is deaf and others through a supervisor and/or co-worker with basic sign language training may be sufficient in many job situations. However, where extensive discussions or complex subject matter is involved, a trained interpreter may be needed to provide effective communication. Experienced interpreters usually have received special training and may be certified by a professional interpreting organization or state or local Commission serving people who are deaf.

10. Other Accommodations

There are many other accommodations that may be effective for people with different disabilities in different jobs. The examples of accommodations in EEOC regulations and the examples in this Manual are not the only types of accommodations that may be required. Some other accommodations that may be appropriate include:

- making transportation provided by the employer accessible;
- providing a personal assistant for certain job-related functions, such as a page turner for a person who has no hands, or a travel attendant to act as a sighted guide to assist a blind employee on occasional business trips.
- use of a job coach for people with mental retardation and other disabilities who benefit from individualized on-the-job training and services provided at no cost by vocational rehabilitation agencies in "supported employment" programs.

3.11 Financial and Technical Assistance for Accommodations

a. Financial Assistance

There are several sources of financial assistance to help employers make accommodations and comply with ADA requirements.

1. Tax Credits for Small Business (Section 44 of the Internal Revenue Code)
In 1990, Congress established a special tax credit to help smaller employers make accommodations required by the ADA. An eligible small business may take a tax credit of up to $5000 per year for accommodations made to comply with the ADA. The credit is available for one-half the cost of "eligible access expenditures" that are more than $250 but less than $10,250.

> *For example:* If an accommodation cost $10,250, an employer could get a tax credit of $5000 ($10,250 minus $250, divided by 2). If the accommodation cost $7000, a tax credit of $3375 would be available.

An *eligible small business* is one with gross receipts of $1 million or less for the taxable year, or 30 or fewer full time employees.

"Eligible access expenditures" for which the tax credit may be taken include the types of accommodations required under Title I of the ADA as well as accessibility requirements for commercial facilities and places of public accommodation under Title III. "Eligible access expenditures" include:

- removal of architectural, communication, physical, or transportation barriers to make the business accessible to, or usable by, people with disabilities.
- providing qualified interpreters or other methods to make communication accessible to people with hearing disabilities;
- providing qualified readers, taped texts, or other methods to make information accessible to people with visual disabilities; and/or
- acquiring or modifying equipment or devices for people with disabilities.

To be eligible for the tax credit, changes made to remove barriers or to provide services, materials or equipment must meet technical standards of the ADA Accessibility Guidelines, where applicable

2. Tax Deduction for Architectural and Transportation Barrier Removal (Section 190 of the Internal Revenue Code)
Any business may take a full tax deduction, up to $15,000 per year, for expenses of removing specified architectural or transportation barriers. Expenses covered include costs of removing barriers created by steps, narrow doors, inaccessible parking spaces, toilet facilities, and transportation vehicles. **Both** the tax credit and the tax deduction are available to eligible small businesses.

For example: If a small business makes a qualified expenditure of $24,000, it may take the $5000 tax *credit* for the initial $10,250 and, if the remaining $13,750 qualifies under Section i90, may *deduct* that amount from its taxable income. However, a business may not receive a double benefit for the same expense: for example, it may not take both the tax credit and the tax deduction for $10,000 spent to renovate bathrooms.

Information on the Section 44 tax credit and the Section 190 tax deduction can be obtained from a local IRS office, or by contacting the Office of Chief Counsel, Internal Revenue Service.

3. Targeted Jobs Tax Credit
Tax credits also are available under the Targeted Jobs Tax Credit Program (TJTCP) for employers who hire individuals with disabilities referred by state or local vocational rehabilitation agencies, State Commissions on the Blind and the U.S. Department of Veterans Affairs and certified by a State Employment Service. This program promotes hiring of several "disadvantaged" groups, including people with disabilities.

Under the TJTCP, a tax credit may be taken for 40% of the first $6000 of an employee's first-year salary. This program must be re authorized each year by Congress, and currently has been extended through June 30, 1992. Information about this program can be obtained from the State Employment Services or from State Governor's Committees on the Employment of People with Disabilities.

4. Other Funding Sources
State or local vocational rehabilitation agencies and State Commissions for the Blind can provide financial assistance for equipment and accommodations for their clients. The U.S. Department of Veterans Affairs also provides financial assistance to disabled veterans for equipment needed to help perform jobs. Some organizations that serve people with particular types of disabilities also provide financial assistance for needed accommodations. Other types of assistance may be available in the community. For example, some Independent Living Centers provide transportation service to the workplace for people with disabilities.

b. Technical Assistance

There are many sources of technical assistance to help employers make effective accommodations for people with different disabilities in various job situations. Many of these resources are available without cost. Major resources for information, assistance, and referral to local specialized resources are 10 new *ADA Regional Business and Disability Technical Assistance Centers* that have been funded by Congress specifically to help implement the ADA. These Centers have been established to provide information, training and technical assistance to employers and all other entities covered by the ADA and to people with disabilities. The Centers also can refer employers to local technical assistance sources. Other resources include:

- State and local vocational rehabilitation agencies
- **Independent Living Centers** in some 400 communities around the country provide technical assistance to employers and people with disabilities on accessibility and other accommodations and make referrals to specialized sources of assistance.
- **The Job Accommodation Network** (JAN) a free national consultant service, available through a toll-free number, helps employers make individualized accommodations.
- **ABLEDATA,** a computerized database of disability-related products and services, conducts customized information searches on worksite modifications, assistive devices and other accommodations.
- **The President's Committee on Employment of People with Disabilities** provides technical information, including publications with practical guidance on job analysis and accommodations.
- **Governors' Committees on Employment of People with Disabilities** in each State, allied with the President's Committee, are local resources of information and technical assistance.

IV. ESTABLISHING NONDISCRIMINATORY QUALIFICATION STANDARDS AND SELECTION CRITERIA

4.1 Introduction

The ADA does not prohibit an employer from establishing job-related qualification standards, including education, skills, work experience, and physical and mental standards necessary for job performance, health and safety.

The Act does not interfere with an employer's authority to establish appropriate job qualifications to hire people who can perform jobs effectively and safely, and to hire the best qualified person for a job. ADA requirements are designed to assure that people with disabilities are not excluded from jobs that they can perform.

ADA requirements apply to all selection standards and procedures, including. but not limited to:

- education and work experience requirements;
- physical and mental requirements;
- safety requirements; paper and pencil tests;
- physical or psychological tests;
- interview questions; and rating systems;

4.2 Overview of Legal Obligations

- Qualification standards or selection criteria that screen out or tend to screen out an individual with a disability on the basis of disability must be **job-related and consistent with business necessity.**
- Even if a standard is job-related and consistent with business necessity, if it screens out an individual with a disability on the basis of disability, the employer **must consider** if the individual could meet the standard with a **reasonable accommodation.**
- An employer is not required to lower existing production standards applicable to the quality or quantity of work for a given job in considering qualifications of an individual with a disability, if these standards are uniformly applied to all applicants and employees in that job.
- If an individual with a disability cannot perform a marginal function of a job because of a disability, an employer may base a hiring decision only on the individual's ability to perform the *essential* functions of the job, with or without a reasonable accommodation.

4.3 What Is Meant by "Job-Related" and "Consistent with Business Necessity"

1. Job-Related

If a qualification standard, test or other selection criterion operates to screen out an individual with a disability, or a class of such individuals on the basis of disability, it must be a legitimate measure or qualification for the *specific* job it is being used for. It is not enough that it measures qualifications for a general class of Jobs.

For example: A qualification standard for a secretarial job of "ability to take shorthand dictation" is not job-related if the person in the particular secretarial job actually transcribes taped dictation.

The ADA does not require that a qualification standard or selection criterion apply only to the "essential functions" of a job. A "job related" standard or selection criterion may evaluate or measure all functions of a job and employers may continue to select and hire people who can perform all of these functions. It is only when an individual's disability prevents or impedes performance of marginal job functions that the ADA requires the employer to evaluate this individual's qualifications solely on his/her ability to perform the essential functions of the job, with or without an accommodation.

For example: An employer has a job opening for an administrative assistant. The essential functions of the job are administrative and organizational. Some occasional typing has been part of the job, but other clerical staff are available who can perform this marginal job function. There are two job applicants. One has a disability that makes typing very difficult, the other has no disability and can type. The employer may not refuse to hire the first applicant because of her inability to type, but must base a job decision on the relative ability of each applicant to perform the essential administrative and organizational job functions, with or without accommodation. The employer may not screen out the applicant with a disability because of the need to make an accommodation to perform the essential job functions. However, if the first applicant could not type for a reason not related to her disability (for example, if she had never learned to type) the employer would be free to select the applicant who could best perform all of the job functions.

2. Business Necessity

"Business necessity" will be interpreted under the ADA as it has been interpreted by the courts under Section 504 of the Rehabilitation Act.

Under the ADA, as under the Rehabilitation Act:

> If a test or other selection criterion excludes an individual with a disability *because of* the disability and does not relate to the *essential functions of a job,* it is not consistent with business necessity.

This standard is similar to the legal standard under Title VII of the Civil Rights Act which provides that a selection procedure which screens out a disproportionate number of persons of a particular race, sex or national origin "class" must be justified as a "business necessity." However, under the ADA the standard may be applied to an *individual* who is screened out by a selection procedure because of disability, as well as to a class of persons. It is not necessary to make statistical comparisons between a group of people with disabilities and people who are not disabled to show that a person with a disability is screened out by a selection standard.

Disabilities vary so much that it is difficult, if not impossible, to make general determinations about the effect of various standards, criteria and procedures on "people with disabilities." Often, there may be little or no statistical data to measure the impact of a procedure on any "class" of people with a particular disability compared to people without disabilities. As with other determinations under the ADA, the exclusionary effect of a selection procedure usually must be looked at in relation to a particular individual who has particular limitations caused by a disability.

Because of these differences, the federal *Uniform Guidelines on Employee*

Selection Procedures that apply to selection procedures on the basis of race, sex, and national origin under Title VII of the Civil Rights Act and other Federal authorities *do not apply* under the ADA to selection procedures affecting people with disabilities.

A standard may be job-related but not justified by business necessity, because it does not concern an essential function of a job.

For example: An employer may ask candidates for a clerical job if they have a driver's license, because it would be desirable to have a person in the job who could occasionally run errands or take packages to the post office in an emergency. This requirement is "job-related," but it relates to an **incidental,** not an **essential,** job function. If it disqualifies a person who could not obtain a driver's license because of a disability, it would not be justified as a "business necessity" for purposes of the ADA.

Further, the ADA requires that even if a qualification standard or selection criterion is job-related and consistent with business necessity, it may not be used to exclude an individual with a disability if this individual could satisfy the legitimate standard or selection criterion with a reasonable accommodation.

For example: It may be job-related and necessary for a business to require that a secretary produce letters and other documents on a word processor. But it would be discriminatory to reject a person whose disability prevented manual keyboard operation, but who could meet the qualification standard using a computer assistive device, if providing this device would not impose an undue hardship.

4.4 Establishing Job-Related Qualification Standards

The ADA does not restrict an employer's authority to establish needed job qualifications, including requirements related to:

- education;
- skills;
- work experience;
- licenses or certification;
- physical and mental abilities;
- health and safety; or
- other job-related requirements, such as judgment, ability to work under pressure or interpersonal skills.

Physical and Mental Qualification Standards

An employer may establish physical or mental qualifications that are necessary to perform specific jobs (for example, jobs in the transportation and construction industries; police and fire fighter jobs; security guard jobs) or to protect health and safety.

However, as with other job qualification standards, if a physical or mental qualification standard screens out an individual with a disability or a class of individuals with disabilities, the employer must be prepared to show that the standard is:

- **job-related and**
- **consistent with business necessity.**

Even if a physical or mental qualification standard is job-related and necessary for a business, if it is applied to exclude an otherwise qualified individual with a disability, the employer must consider whether there is a reasonable accommodation that would enable *this person* to meet the standard. The employer does not have to consider much accommodations in establishing a standard, but only when an otherwise qualified person with a disability requests an accommodation.

For example: An employer has a forklift operator job. The essential function of the job is mechanical operation of the forklift machinery. The job has a physical requirement of ability to lift a 70 pound weight, because the operator must be able to remove and replace the 70 pound battery which powers the forklift. This standard is job-related. However, it would be a reasonable accommodation to eliminate this standard for an otherwise qualified forklift operator who could not lift a 70 pound weight because of a disability, if other operators or employees are available to help this person remove and replace the battery.

Evaluating Physical and Mental Qualification Standards Under the ADA
Employers generally have two kinds of physical or mental standards:

1. Standards that may exclude an entire class of individuals with disabilities.

   For example: No person who has epilepsy, diabetes, or a heart or back condition is eligible for a job.

2. Standards that measure a physical or mental ability needed to perform a job.

   For example: The person in the job must be able to lift x pounds for x hours daily, or run x miles in x minutes.

Standards That Exclude an Entire Class of Individuals with Disabilities
"Blanket" exclusions of this kind usually have been established because employers believed them to be necessary for health or safety reasons. Such standards also may be used to screen out people who an employer fears, or assumes, may cause higher medical insurance or workers' compensation costs, or may have a higher rate of absenteeism.

Employers who have such standards should review them carefully. In most cases, they will not meet ADA requirements.

The ADA recognizes legitimate employer concerns and the requirements of other laws for health and safety in the workplace. An employer is not required to hire or retain an individual who would pose a "direct threat" to health or safety (see below). But the ADA requires an *objective assessment of a particular individual's current ability* to perform a job safely and effectively. Generalized "blanket" exclusions of an entire group of people with a certain disability prevent such an individual consideration. Such class-wide exclusions that do not reflect up-to-date medical knowledge and technology, or that are based on fears about future medical or workers' compensation costs, are unlikely to survive a legal challenge under the ADA. (However, the ADA recognizes employers' obligations to comply with Federal laws that mandate such exclusions in certain occupations. [See *Health and Safety Requirements of Other Federal or State Laws* below.])

The ADA requires that:

- any determination of a direct threat to health or safety must be based on an *individualized* assessment of objective and specific evidence about a particular *individual's* present ability to perform essential job functions, not on general assumptions or speculations about a disability. (See *Standards Necessary for Health and Safety: A "Direct Threat"* below).

For example: An employer who excludes all persons who have epilepsy from jobs that require use of dangerous machinery will be required to look at the life experience and work history of an *individual* who has epilepsy. The individual evaluation should take into account the type of job, the degree of seizure control, the type(s) of seizures (if any), whether the person has an "aura" (warning of seizure), the person's reliability in taking prescribed anticonvulsant medication, and any side effects of such medication. Individuals who have no seizures because they regularly take prescribed medication, or who have sufficient advance warning of a seizure so that they can stop hazardous activity, would not pose a "direct threat" to safety.

Standards that Measure Needed Physical or Mental Ability to Perform a Job

Specific physical or mental abilities may be needed to perform certain types of jobs.

For example: Candidates for jobs such as airline pilots, policemen and firefighters may be required to meet certain physical and psychological qualifications.

In establishing physical or mental standards for such jobs, an employer does not have to show that these standards are "job related," justified by "business necessity" or that they relate only to "essential" functions of the job. However, if such a standard screens out an otherwise qualified individual with a disability, the employer must be prepared to show that the standard, as applied, is job-related and consistent with business necessity under the ADA. And, even if this can be shown, the employer must consider whether this individual could meet the standard with a **reasonable accommodation.**

For example: A police department that requires all its officers to be able to make forcible arrests and to perform all job functions in the department might be able to justify stringent physical requirements for all officers, if in fact they are all required to be available for any duty in an emergency.

However, if a position in a mailroom required as a qualification standard that the person in the job be able to reach high enough to place and retrieve packages from foot high shelves, an employer would have to consider whether there was an accommodation that would enable a person with a disability that prevented reaching that high to perform these essential functions. Possible accommodations might include lowering the shelf-height, providing a step stool or other assistive device.

Physical Agility Tests

An employer may give a physical agility test to determine physical qualifications necessary for certain jobs prior to making a job offer if it is simply an agility test and not a medical examination. Such a test would not be subject to the prohibition against pre-employment medical examinations if given to all similarly situated applicants or employees, regardless of disability. However, if an agility test screens out or tends to screen out an individual with a disability or a class of such individuals because of disability, the employer must be prepared to show that the test is job-related and consistent with business necessity and that the test or the job cannot be performed with a reasonable accommodation.

It is important to understand the distinction between physical agility tests and prohibited pre-employment medical inquiries and examinations. One difference is that agility tests do not involve medical examinations or diagnoses by a physician, while medical examinations may involve a doctor.

For example: At the pre-offer stage, a police department may conduct an agility test to measure a candidate's ability to walk, run, jump, or lift in relation to specific job duties, but it cannot require the applicant to have a medical screening before taking the agility test. Nor can it administer a medical examination before making a conditional job offer to this person.

Some employers currently may require a medical screening before administering a physical agility test to assure that the test will not harm the applicant. There are two ways that an employer can handle this problem under the ADA:

- the employer can request the applicant's physician to respond to a very restricted inquiry which describes the specific agility test and asks: "Can this person safely perform this test?"

- the employer may administer the physical agility test after making a conditional job offer, and in this way may obtain any necessary medical information, as permitted under the ADA. (See Chapter VI.) The employer may find it more cost-efficient to administer such tests only to those candidates who have met other job qualifications.

4.5 Standards Necessary for Health and Safety: A "Direct Threat"

An employer may require as a qualification standard that an individual not pose a "direct threat" to the health or safety of the individual or others, if this standard is applied to all applicants for a particular job. However, an employer must meet very specific and stringent requirements under the ADA to establish that such a "direct threat" exists.

The employer must be prepared to show that there is:

- *significant* risk of substantial harm;
- the *specific* risk must be identified;
- it must be a *current* risk, not one that is speculative or remote;
- the assessment of risk must be based on objective medical or other factual evidence regarding a particular individual; and
- even if a genuine significant risk of substantial harm exists, the employer must consider whether the risk can be eliminated or reduced below the level of a "direct threat" by *reasonable accommodation.*

Looking at each of these requirements more closely:

1. Significant risk of substantial harm

An employer cannot deny an employment opportunity to an individual with a disability merely because of a slightly increased risk. The employer must be prepared to show that there is a **significant risk,** that is, **a high probability of substantial harm,** if the person were employed.

The assessment of risk *cannot be based on mere speculation* unrelated to the individual in question

For example: An employer cannot assume that a person with cerebral palsy who has restricted manual dexterity cannot work in a laboratory because s/he will pose a risk of breaking vessels with dangerous contents. The abilities or limitations of a particular individual with cerebral palsy must be evaluated.

2. The specific risk must be identified

If an individual has a disability, the employer must identify the aspect of the disability that would pose a direct threat, considering the following factors:

- the **duration** of the risk.

  For example: An elementary school teacher who has tuberculosis may pose a risk to the health of children in her classroom. However, with proper medication, this person's disease would be contagious for only a two-week period. With an accommodation of two-weeks absence from the classroom, this teacher would not pose a "direct threat."

- the **nature** and **severity** of the potential harm.

  For example: A person with epilepsy, who has lost consciousness during seizures within the past year, might seriously endanger her own life and the lives of others if employed as a bus driver. But this person would not pose a severe threat of harm if employed in a clerical job.

- the **likelihood** that the potential harm will occur.

  For example: An employer may believe that there is a risk of employing an individual with HIV disease as a teacher. However, it is medically established that this disease can only be transmitted through sexual contact, use of infected needles, or other entry into a person's blood stream. There is little or no likelihood that employing this person as a teacher would pose a risk of transmitting this disease.

  and

- the **imminence** of the potential harm.

  For example: A physician's evaluation of an applicant for a heavy labor job that indicated the individual had a disc condition that might worsen in 8 or 10 years would not be sufficient indication of imminent potential harm.

If the perceived risk to health or safety arises from the behavior of an individual with a mental or emotional disability, the employer must identify the specific behavior that would pose the "direct threat".

3. The risk must be current, not one that is speculative or remote
The employer must show that there is a *current* risk—"a high probability of substantial harm"—to health or safety based on the individual's present ability to perform the essential functions of the job. A determination that an individual would pose a "direct threat" cannot be based on speculation about *future* risk. This includes speculation that an individual's disability may become more severe. An assessment of risk cannot be based on speculation that the individual will become unable to perform a job in the future, or that this individual may cause increased health insurance or workers compensation costs, or will have excessive absenteeism. (See *Insurance,* Chapter VII., and *Workers' Compensation,* Chapter IX.)

4. The assessment of risk must be based on objective medical or other evidence related to a particular individual

The determination that an individual applicant or employee with a disability poses a "direct threat" to health or safety must be based on objective, factual evidence related to *that individual's* present ability to safely perform the essential functions of a job. It cannot be based on unfounded assumptions, fears, or stereotypes about the nature or effect of a disability or of disability generally. Nor can such a determination be based on patronizing assumptions that an individual with a disability may endanger himself or herself by performing a particular job.

For example: An employer may not exclude a person with a vision impairment from a job that requires a great deal of reading because of concern that the strain of heavy reading may further impair her sight.

The determination of a "direct threat" to health or safety must be based on a reasonable medical judgment that relies on the most current medical knowledge and/or the best available objective evidence. This may include:

- **input from the individual with a disability;**
- **the experience of this individual in previous jobs;**
- **documentation from medical doctors, psychologists, rehabilitation counselors, physical or occupational therapists, or others who have expertise in the disability involved and/or direct knowledge of the individual with a disability.**

Where the psychological behavior of an employee suggests a threat to safety, **factual evidence** of this behavior also may constitute evidence of a "direct threat." An employee's violent, aggressive, destructive or threatening behavior may provide such evidence.

Employers should be careful to assure that assessments of "direct threat" to health or safety are based on current medical knowledge and other kinds of evidence listed above, rather than relying on generalized and frequently out-of-date assumptions about risk associated with certain disabilities. They should be aware that Federal contractors who have had similar disability nondiscrimination requirements under the Rehabilitation Act have had to make substantial back pay and other financial payments because they excluded individuals with disabilities who were qualified to perform their jobs, based on generalized assumptions that were not supported by evidence about the individual concerned.

Examples of Contractor Cases:

- A highly qualified experienced worker was rejected for a sheet metal job because of a company's general medical policy excluding anyone with epilepsy from this job. The company asserted that this person posed a danger to himself and to others because of the possibility that he might have a seizure on the job. However, this individual had been seizure-free for 6 years and co-workers on a previous job testified that he carefully followed his prescribed medication schedule. The company was found to have discriminated against this individual and was required to hire him, incurring large back pay and other costs.

- An applicant who was deaf in one ear was rejected for an aircraft mechanic job because the company feared that his impairment might cause a future workers' compensation claim. His previous work record gave ample evidence of his ability to perform the aircraft mechanic job. The company was found to have discriminated because it provided no evidence that this person would have been a danger to himself or to others on the job.
- An experienced carpenter was not hired because a blood pressure reading by the company doctor at the end of a physical exam was above the company's general medical standard. However, his own doctor provided evidence of much lower readings, based on measurements of his blood pressure at several times during a physical exam. This doctor testified that the individual could safely perform the carpenter's job because he had only mild hypertension. Other expert medical evidence confirmed that a single blood pressure reading was not sufficient to determine if a person has hypertension, that such a reading clearly was not sufficient to determine if a person could perform a particular job, and that hypertension has very different effects on different people. In this case, it was found that there was merely a slightly elevated risk, and that a remote possibility of future injury was not sufficient to disqualify an otherwise qualified person. (Note that while it is possible that a person with mild hypertension does not have an impairment that "substantially limits a major life activity," in this case the person was excluded because he was "regarded as" having such an impairment. The employer was still required to show that this person posed a "direct threat" to safety.)

"Direct Threat" to Self

An employer may require that an individual not pose a direct threat of harm to his or her own safety or health, as well as to the health or safety of others. However, as emphasized above, such determinations must be strictly based on valid medical analyses or other objective evidence related to this individual, using the factors set out above. A determination that a person might cause harm to himself or herself *cannot* be based on stereotypes, patronizing assumptions about a person with a disability, or generalized fears about risks that might occur if an individual with a disability is placed in a certain job. Any such determination must be based on evidence of specific risk to a particular individual.

For example: An employer would not be required to hire an individual disabled by narcolepsy who frequently and unexpectedly loses consciousness to operate a power saw or other dangerous equipment, if there is no accommodation that would reduce or eliminate the risk of harm. But an advertising agency could not reject an applicant for a copywriter job who has a history of mental illness, based on a generalized fear that working in this high stress job might trigger a relapse of the individual's mental illness. Nor could an employer reject an applicant with a visual or mobility disability because of a generalized fear of risks to this person in the event of a fire or other emergency.

5. If there is a significant risk, reasonable accommodation must be considered
Where there is a significant risk of substantial harm to health or safety, an employer still must consider whether there is a reasonable accommodation that would eliminate this risk or reduce the risk so that it is below the level of a "direct threat."

For example: A deaf bus mechanic was denied employment because the transit authority feared that he had a high probability of being injured by buses moving in and out of the garage. It was not clear that there was, in fact, a "high probability" of harm in this case, but the mechanic suggested an effective accommodation that enabled him to perform his job with little or no risk. He worked in a corner of the garage, facing outward, so that he could see moving buses. A co-worker was designated to alert him with a tap on the shoulder if any dangerous situation should arise.

Direct Threat" and Accommodation in Food Handling Jobs
The ADA includes a specific application of the "direct threat" standard and the obligation for reasonable accommodation in regard to individuals who have infectious or communicable diseases that may be transmitted through the handling of food.

The law provides that the U.S. Department of Health and Human Services (HHS) must prepare and update annually a list of contagious diseases that are transmitted through the handling of food and the methods by which these diseases are transmitted.

When an individual who has one of the listed diseases applies for work or works in a job involving food handling, the employer must consider whether there is a reasonable accommodation that will eliminate the risk of transmitting the disease through handling of food. If there is such an accommodation, and it would not impose an undue hardship, the employer must provide the accommodation.

An employer would not be required to hire a job **applicant** in such a situation if no reasonable accommodation is possible. However, an employer would be required to consider accommodating an **employee** by reassignment to a position that does not require handling of food, if such a position is available, the employee is qualified for it, and it would not pose an undue hardship.

In August 1991, the Centers for Disease Control (CDC) of the Public Health Service in HHS issued a list of infectious and communicable diseases that are transmitted through handling of food, together with information about how these diseases are transmitted. The list of diseases is brief. In conference with established medical opinion, it does not include AIDS or the HIV virus. In issuing the list, the CDC emphasized that the greatest danger of food-transmitted illness comes from contamination of infected food-producing animals and contamination in food processing, rather than from handling of food by persons with infectious or communicable diseases. The CDC also emphasized that proper personal hygiene and sanitation in food-handling jobs were the most important measures to prevent transmission of disease.

The CDC list of diseases that are transmitted through food handling and recommendations for preventing such transmission appears in Appendix

4.6 Health and Safety Requirements of Other Federal or State Laws

The ADA recognizes employers' obligations to comply with requirements of other laws that establish health and safety standards. However, the Act gives greater weight to Federal than to state or local law.

Federal Laws and Regulations

The ADA does not override health and safety requirements established under other Federal laws. If a standard is required by another Federal law, an employer must comply with it and does not have to show that the standard is job related and consistent with business necessity.

> *For example:* An employee who is being hired to drive a vehicle in interstate commerce must meet safety requirements established by the U.S. Department of Transportation. Employers also must conform to health and safety requirements of the U.S. Occupational Safety and Health Administration (OSHA).

However, an employer still has the obligation under the ADA to consider whether there is a reasonable accommodation, consistent with the standards of other Federal laws, that will prevent exclusion of qualified individuals with disabilities who can perform jobs without violating the standards of those laws.

For example: In hiring a person to drive a vehicle in interstate commerce, an employer must conform to existing Department of Transportation regulations that exclude any person with epilepsy, diabetes, and certain other conditions from such a job.

But, for example, if DOT regulations require that a truck have 3 grab bars in specified places, and an otherwise qualified individual with a disability could perform essential job functions with the assistance of 2 additional grab bars, it would be a reasonable accommodation to add these bars, unless this would be an undue hardship.

The Department of Transportation, as directed by Congress, currently is reviewing several motor vehicle standards that require "blanket" exclusions of individuals with diabetes, epilepsy and certain other disabilities.

2. State and Local Laws

The ADA does not override state or local laws designed to protect public health and safety, except where such laws conflict with ADA requirements. This means that if there is a state or local law that would exclude an individual with a disability for a particular job or profession because of a health or safety risk, the employer still must assess whether a particular individual would pose a "direct threat" to health or safety under the ADA standard. If there is such a "direct threat," the employer also must consider whether it could be eliminated or reduced below the level of a "direct threat" by reasonable accommodation. An employer may not rely on the existence of a state or local law that conflicts with ADA requirements as a defense to a charge of discrimination.

> *For example:* A state law that required a school bus driver to have a high level of hearing in both ears without use of a hearing aid was found by a court to violate Section 504 of the Rehabilitation Act, and would violate the ADA. The court found that the driver could perform his job with a hearing aid without a risk to safety.
>
> (See further guidance on Medical Examinations and Inquires in Chapter VI.)

V. NONDISCRIMINATION IN THE HIRING PROCESS: RECRUITMENT; APPLICATIONS; PRE-EMPLOYMENT INQUIRIES; TESTING

This chapter discusses nondiscrimination requirements that apply to recruitment and the job application process, including pre-employment inquiries. Chapter VI. discusses these requirements more specifically in relation to medical inquiries and examinations.

5.1 Overview of Legal Obligations

- An employer must provide an equal opportunity for an individual with a disability to participate in the job application process and to be considered for a job.
- An employer may not make any pre-employment inquiries regarding disability, but may ask questions about the ability to perform specific job functions and may, with certain limitations, ask an individual with a disability to describe or demonstrate how s/he would perform these functions.
- An employer may not require pre-employment medical examinations or medical histories, but may condition a job offer on the results of a post-offer medical examination, if all entering employees in the same job category are required to take this examination.

- Tests for illegal drugs are not medical examinations under the ADA and may be given at any time.
- A test that screens out or tends to screen out a person with a disability on the basis of disability must be job-related and consistent with business necessity.
- Tests must reflect the skills and aptitudes of an individual rather than impaired sensory, manual, or speaking skills, unless those are job-related skills the test is designed to measure.

A careful review of all procedures used in recruiting and selecting employees is advisable to assure nondiscrimination in the hiring process Reasonable accommodation must be provided as needed, to assure that individuals with disabilities have equal opportunities to participate in this process.

5.2 Job Advertisements and Notices

It is advisable that job announcements, advertisements, and other recruitment notices include information on the essential functions of the job. Specific information about essential functions will attract applicants including individuals with disabilities, who have appropriate qualifications.

Employers may wish to indicate in job advertisements and notices that they do not discriminate on the basis of disability or other legally prohibited bases. An employer may wish to include a statement such as "We are an Equal Opportunity Employer. We do not discriminate on the basis of race, religion, color, sex, age, national origin or disability."

Accessibility of Job Information

Information about job openings should be accessible to people with different disabilities. An employer is not obligated to provide written information in various formats in advance, but should make it available in an accessible format on request.

> *For example:* Job information should be available in a location that is accessible to people with mobility impairments. If a job advertisement provides only a telephone number to call for information, a TDD (telecommunication device for the deaf) number should be included, unless a telephone relay service has been established.* Printed job information in an employment office or on employee bulletin boards should be made available, as needed, to persons with visual or other reading impairments. Preparing information in large print will help make it available to some people with visual impairments. Information can be recorded on a cassette or read to applicants with more severe vision impairments and those who have other disabilities which limit reading ability.

* Title IV of the ADA requires all telephone carriers to establish relay services by July 1993, that will enable people who use TDDs to speak directly to anyone through use of a relay operator. Many states already have such services.

5.3 Employment Agencies

Employment agencies are "covered entities" under the ADA, and must comply with all ADA requirements that are applicable to their activities.

The definition of an "employment agency" under the ADA is the same as that under Title VII of the Civil Rights Act. It includes private and public employment agencies and other organizations, such as college placement services, that regularly procure employees for an employer.

When an employer uses an employment agency to recruit, screen, and refer potential employees, both the employer and the employment agency may be liable if there is any violation of ADA requirements.

For example: An employer uses an employment agency to recruit and the agency places a newspaper advertisement with a telephone number that all interested persons must call, because no address is given. However, there is no TDD number. If there is no telephone relay service, and a deaf person is unable to obtain information about a job for which she is qualified and files a discrimination charge, both the employer and the agency may be liable.

An employer should inform an employment agency used to recruit or screen applicants of the mutual obligation to comply with ADA requirements. In particular, these agencies should be informed about requirements regarding qualification standards, pre-employment inquiries, and reasonable accommodation.

If an employer has a contract with an employment agency, the employer may wish to include a provision stating that the agency will conduct its activities in compliance with ADA and other legal nondiscrimination requirements.

5.4 Recruitment

The ADA is a nondiscrimination law. It does not require employers to undertake special activities to recruit people with disabilities. However, it is consistent with the purpose of the ADA for employers to expand their "outreach" to sources of qualified candidates with disabilities. (See *Locating Qualified Individuals with Disabilities* below).

Recruitment activities that have the effect of screening out potential applicants with disabilities may violate the ADA.

For example: If an employer conducts recruitment activity at a college campus, job fair, or other location that is physically inaccessible, or does not make its recruitment activity accessible at such locations to people with visual, hearing or other disabilities, it may be liable if a charge of discrimination is filed.

Locating Qualified Individuals with Disabilities

There are many resources for locating individuals with disabilities who are qualified for different types of jobs. People with disabilities represent a large, underutilized human resource pool. Employers who have actively recruited and hired people with disabilities have found valuable sources of employees for jobs of every kind.

Many of the organizations listed are excellent sources for recruiting qualified individuals with disabilities as well as sources of technical assistance for any accommodations needed. For example, many colleges and universities have coordinators of services for students with disabilities who can be helpful in recruitment and in making accommodations. The Association on Handicapped Student Service Programs in Postsecondary Education can provide information on these resources. Local Independent Living Centers, state and local vocational rehabilitation agencies, organizations such as Goodwill Industries, and many organizations representing people who have specific disabilities are among other recruitment sources.

5.5 Pre-Employment Inquiries

The ADA Prohibits Any Pre-Employment Inquiries About a Disability.

This prohibition is necessary to assure that qualified candidates are not screened out because of their disability before their actual ability to do a job is evaluated. Such protection is particularly important for people with hidden disabilities who frequently are excluded, with no real opportunity to present their qualifications, because of information requested in application forms, medical history forms, job interviews, and pre-employment medical examinations.

The prohibition on pre-employment inquiries about disability does not prevent an employer from obtaining necessary information regarding an applicant's qualifications, including medical information necessary to assess qualifications and assure health and safety on the job.

The ADA requires only that such inquiries be made in two separate stages of the hiring process.

1. Before making a job offer

At this stage, an employer:

- may ask questions about an applicant's ability to perform specific job functions;
- may not make an inquiry about a disability;
- may make a job offer that is conditioned on satisfactory results of a post-offer medical examination or inquiry.

2. After making a conditional job offer and before an individual starts work

At this stage, an employer may conduct a medical examination or ask health-related questions, providing that all candidates who receive a conditional job offer in the same job category are required to take the same examination and/or respond to the same inquiries.

Inquiries that may and may not be made at the pre-offer stage are discussed in the section that follows. Guidance on obtaining and using information from post-offer medical and inquiries and examinations is provided in Chapter VI.

5.5(a) Basic Requirements Regarding Pre-Offer Inquiries

- An employer may not make any pre-employment inquiry about a disability, or about the nature or severity of a disability: on application forms in job interviews in background or reference checks.
- An employer may not make any medical inquiry or conduct any medical examination prior to making a conditional offer of employment.
- An employer may ask a job applicant questions about ability to perform specific job functions, tasks, or duties, as long as these questions are not phrased in terms of a disability. Questions need not be limited to the "essential" functions of the job.
- An employer may ask all applicants to describe or demonstrate how they will perform a job, with or without an accommodation.
- If an individual has a known disability that might interfere with or prevent performance of job functions, s/he may be asked to describe or demonstrate how these functions will be performed, with or without an accommodation, even if other applicants are not asked to do so; however,
- If a known disability would not interfere with performance of job functions, an individual may only be required to describe or demonstrate how s/he will perform a job if this is required of all applicants for the position.
- An employer may condition a job offer on the results of a medical examination or on the responses to medical inquiries if such an examination or inquiry is required of all entering employees in the same job category, regardless of disability; information obtained from such inquiries or examinations must be handled according to the strict confidentiality requirements of the ADA. (See Chapter VI.)

5.5(b) The Job Application Form

A review of job application forms should be a priority before the ADA's effective date, to eliminate any questions related to disability.

SOME EXAMPLES OF QUESTIONS THAT MAY NOT BE ASKED ON APPLICATION FORMS OR IN JOB INTERVIEWS:

- Have you ever had or been treated for any of the following conditions or diseases? (Followed by a checklist of various conditions and diseases.)
- Please list any conditions or diseases for which you have been treated in the past 3 years.

- Have you ever been hospitalized? If so, for what condition?
- Have you ever been treated by a psychiatrist or psychologist? If so, for what condition?
- Have you ever been treated for any mental condition?
- Is there any health-related reason you may not be able to perform the job for which you are applying?
- Have you had a major illness in the last 5 years?
- How many days were you absent from work because of illness last year?

(Preemployment questions about illness may not be asked, because they may reveal the existence of a disability. However, an employer may provide information on its attendance requirements and ask if an applicant will be able to meet these requirements. [See also *The Job Interview* below.])

- Do you have any physical defects which preclude you from performing certain kinds of work? If yes, describe such defects and specific work limitations.
- Do you have any disabilities or impairments which may affect your performance in the position for which you are applying?

(This question should not be asked even if the applicant is requested in a follow-up question to identify accommodations that would enable job performance. Inquiries should not focus on an applicant's disabilities. The applicant may be asked about ability to perform specific job functions, with or without a reasonable accommodation. [See *Information That May be Asked,* below.])

- Are you taking any prescribed drugs?

(Questions about use of prescription drugs are not permitted before a conditional job offer, because the answers to such questions might reveal the existence of certain disabilities which require prescribed medication.)

- Have you ever been treated for drug addiction or alcoholism?

(Information may not be requested regarding treatment for drug or alcohol addiction, because the ADA protects people addicted to drugs who have been successfully rehabilitated, or who are undergoing rehabilitation, from discrimination based on drug addiction. [See Chapter VI for discussion of post-offer inquiries and Chapter VIII for drug and alcohol issues.])

- Have you ever filed for workers' compensation insurance?

(An employer may not ask about an applicant's workers' compensation history at the pre-offer stage, but may obtain such information after making a conditional job offer. Such questions are prohibited because they are likely to reveal the existence of a disability. In addition, it is discriminatory under the ADA not to hire an individual with a disability because of speculation that the individual will cause increased workers' compensation costs. (See Chapter IV, **4.5(3),** and Chapter IX.)

Information about an applicant's ability to perform job tasks, with or without accommodation, can be obtained through the application form and job interview, as explained below. Other needed information may be obtained through medical inquiries or examinations conducted after a conditional offer of employment, as described in Chapter VI.

5.5(c) Exception for Federal Contractors Covered by Section 503 of the Rehabilitation Act and Other Federal Programs Requiring Identification of Disability.

Federal contractors and subcontractors who are covered by the affirmative action requirements of Section 503 of the Rehabilitation Act may invite individuals with disabilities to identify themselves on a job application form or by other pre employment inquiry, to satisfy the affirmative action requirements of Section 503 of the Rehabilitation Act. Employers who request such information must observe Section 503 requirements regarding the manner in which such information is requested and used, and the procedures for maintaining such information as a separate, confidential record, apart from regular personnel records. (For further information, see Office of Federal Contract Compliance Programs.)

A pre-employment inquiry about a disability also is permissible if it is required or necessitated by another Federal law or regulation. For example, a number of programs administered or funded by the U.S. Department of Labor target benefits to individuals with disabilities, such as, disabled veterans, veterans of the Vietnam era, individuals eligible for Targeted Job Tax Credits, and individuals eligible for Job Training Partnership Act assistance. Pre-employment inquiries about disabilities may be necessary under these laws to identify disabled applicants or clients in order to provide the required special services for such persons. These inquiries would not violate the ADA.

5.5(d) Information that May Be Requested on Application Forms or in Interviews

An employer may ask questions to determine whether an applicant can perform specific job functions. The questions should focus on the applicant's ability to perform the job, not on a disability.

> *For example:* An employer could attach a job description to the application form with information about specific job functions. Or the employer may describe the functions. This will make it possible to ask whether the applicant can perform these functions. It also will give an applicant with a disability needed information to request any accommodation required to perform a task. The applicant could be asked:

- Are you able to perform these tasks without an accommodation?

If the applicant indicates that s/he can perform the tasks with an accommodation, s/he may be asked:

- How would you perform the tasks, and with what accommodation(s)?

However, the employer must keep in mind that it cannot refuse to hire a qualified individual with a disability because of this person's need for an accommodation that would be required by the ADA.

An employer may inform applicants on an application form that they may request any needed accommodation to participate in the application process. **For example:** accommodation for a test, a job interview, or a job demonstration.

The employer may wish to provide information on the application form and in the employment office about specific aspects of the job application process, so that applicants may request any needed accommodation. The employer is not required to provide such information, but without it the applicant may have no advance notice of the need to request an accommodation. Since the individual with a disability has the responsibility to request an accommodation and the employer has the responsibility to provide the accommodation (unless it would cause an undue hardship), providing advance information on various application procedures may help avoid last minute problems in making necessary accommodations. This information can be communicated orally or on tape for people who are visually impaired. (See also *Testing,* **5.6** below)

5.5(e) Making Job Applications Accessible

Employers have an obligation to make reasonable accommodations to enable an applicant with a disability to apply for a job. Some of the kinds of accommodations that may be needed have been suggested in the section on *Accessibility of Job Information,* 5.2 above. Individuals with visual or learning disabilities or other mental disabilities also may require assistance in filling out application forms.

5.5(f) The Job Interview

The basic requirements regarding pre-employment inquiries and the types of questions that are prohibited on job application forms apply to the job interview as well. (See 5.5(a) and (b) above.) An interviewer may not ask questions about a disability, but may obtain more specific information about the ability to perform job tasks and about any needed accommodation, as set out below.

To assure that an interview is conducted in a nondiscriminatory manner, interviewers should be well-informed about the ADA's requirements. The employer may wish to provide written guidelines to people who conduct job interviews.

Most employment discrimination against people with disabilities is not intentional. Discrimination most frequently occurs because interviewers and others involved in hiring lack knowledge about the differing capabilities of individuals with disabilities and make decisions based on stereotypes, misconceptions, or unfounded fears. To avoid discrimination in the hiring process, employers may wish to provide "awareness" training for interviewers and others involved in the hiring process. Such training provides factual information about disability and the qualifications of people with disabilities, emphasizes the importance of individualized assessments, and helps interviewers feel more at ease in talking with people who have different disabilities.

The job interview should focus on the *ability* of an applicant to perform the job, not on disability.

> *For example:* If a person has only one arm and an essential function of a job is to drive a car, the interviewer should not ask if or how the disability would affect this person's driving. The person may be asked if s/he has a valid driver's license, and whether s/he can perform any special aspect of driving that is required, such as frequent long-distance trips, with or without an accommodation.

The interviewer also could obtain needed information about an applicant's ability and experience in relation to specific job requirements through statements and questions such as: "Eighty-percent of the time of this sales job must be spent on the road covering a three-state territory. What is your outside selling experience? Do you have a valid driver's license? What is your accident record?"

Where an applicant has a visible disability (for example, uses a wheelchair or a guide dog, or has a missing limb) or has volunteered information about a disability, the interviewer may *not* ask questions about:

- the nature of the disability;
- the severity of the disability;
- the condition causing the disability;
- any prognosis or expectation regarding the condition or disability; or
- whether the individual will need treatment or special leave because of the disability.

The interviewer may describe or demonstrate the specific functions and tasks of the job and ask whether an applicant can perform these functions with or without a reasonable accommodation.

> *For example:* An interviewer could say: "The person in this mailroom clerk position is responsible for receiving incoming mail and packages, sorting the mail, and taking it in a cart to many offices in two buildings, one block apart. The mail clerk also must receive incoming boxes of supplies up to 50 pounds in weight, and place them on storage shelves up to 6 feet in height. Can you perform these tasks? Can you perform them with or without a reasonable accommodation?"

As suggested above, (see **5.5(d)**), the interviewer also may give the applicant a copy of a detailed position description and ask whether s/he can perform the functions described in the position, with or without a reasonable accommodation.

Questions may be asked regarding ability to perform *all* job functions, not merely those that are essential to the job.

For example: A secretarial job may involve the following functions:

1. transcribing dictation and written drafts from the supervisor and other staff into final written documents;
2. proofreading documents for accuracy;
3. developing and maintaining files;
4. scheduling and making arrangements for meetings and conferences;
5. logging documents and correspondence in and out;
6. placing, answering, and referring telephone calls;
7. distributing documents to appropriate staff members;
8. reproducing documents on copying machines; and
9. occasional travel to perform clerical tasks at out of town conferences.

Taking into account the specific activities of the particular office in which this secretary will work, and availability of other staff, the employer has identified functions 1-6 as essential, and functions 7-9 as marginal to this secretary's job. The interviewer may ask questions related to all 9 functions; however, an applicant with limited mobility should not be screened out because of inability to perform the last 3 functions due to her disability. S/he should be evaluated on ability to perform the first 6 functions, with or without accommodation.

Inquiries Related to Ability to Perform Job Functions and Accommodations
An interviewer may obtain information about an applicant's ability to perform essential job functions and about any need for accommodation in several ways, depending on the particular job applicant and the requirements of a particular job:

- The applicant may be asked to describe or demonstrate how s/he will perform specific job functions, **if this is required of everyone applying for a job in this job category, regardless of disability.**

  For example: An employer might require all applicants for a telemarketing job to demonstrate selling ability by taking a simulated telephone sales test, but could not require that a person using a wheelchair take this test if other applicants are not required to take it.

- If an applicant has a **known** disability that would appear to interfere with or prevent performance of a job-related function, s/he may be asked to describe or demonstrate how this function would be performed, even if other applicants do not have to do so.

  For example: If an applicant has one arm and the job requires placing bulky items on shelves up to six feet high, the interviewer could ask the applicant to demonstrate how s/he would perform this function, with or without an accommodation. If the applicant states that s/he can perform this function with a reasonable accommodation, for example, with a step stool fitted with a device to assist lifting, the employer either must provide this accommodation so that the applicant can show that s/he can shelve the items, or let the applicant describe how s/he would do this task.

- However, if an applicant has a known disability that would not interfere with or prevent performance of a job related function, the employer can only ask the applicant to demonstrate how s/he would perform the function if all applicants in the job category are required to do so, regardless of disability.

  For example: If an applicant with one leg applies for a job that involves sorting small parts while seated, s/he may not be required to demonstrate the ability to do this job unless all applicants are required to do so.

If an applicant indicates that s/he cannot perform an essential job function even with an accommodation, the applicant would not be qualified for the job in question.

Inquiries About Attendance

An interviewer may not ask whether an applicant will need or request leave for medical treatment or for other reasons related to a disability.

The interviewer may provide information on the employer's regular work hours, leave policies, and any special attendance needs of the job, and ask if the applicant can meet these requirements (provided that the requirements actually are applied to employees in a particular job).

For example: "Our regular work hours are 9 to 6, five days weekly, but we expect employees in this job to work overtime, evenings, and weekends for 6 weeks during the Christmas season and on certain other holidays. New employees get 1 week of vacation, 7 sick leave days and may take no more than 5 days of unpaid leave per year. Can you meet these requirements?"

Information about previous work attendance records may be obtained on the application form, in the interview or in reference checks, but the questions should not refer to illness or disability.

If an applicant has had a poor attendance record on a previous job, s/he may wish to provide an explanation that includes information related to a disability, but the employer should not ask whether a poor attendance record was due to illness, accident or disability. For example, an applicant might wish to disclose voluntarily that the previous absence record was due to surgery for a medical condition that is now corrected, treatment for cancer that is now in remission or to adjust medication for epilepsy, but that s/he is now fully able to meet all job requirements.

Accommodations for Interviews

The employer must provide an accommodation, if needed, to enable an applicant to have equal opportunity in the interview process. As suggested earlier, the employer may find it helpful to state in an initial job notice, and/or on the job application form, that applicants who need accommodation for an interview should request this in advance.

Needed accommodations for interviews may include:

- an accessible location for people with mobility impairments;
- a sign interpreter for a deaf person;
- a reader for a blind person.

Conducting an Interview

The purpose of a job interview is to obtain appropriate information about the background qualifications and other personal qualities of an applicant in relation to the requirements of a specific job.

This chapter has discussed ways to obtain this information by focusing on the abilities rather than the disability of a disabled applicant. However, there are other aspects of an interview that may create barriers to an accurate and objective assessment of an applicant's job qualifications. The interviewer may not know how to communicate effectively with people who have particular disabilities, or may make negative, incorrect assumptions about the abilities of a person with a disability because s/he misinterprets some external manifestation of the disability.

> *For example.* An interviewer may assume that a person who displays certain characteristics of cerebral palsy, such as indistinct speech, lisping, and involuntary or halting movements, is limited in intelligence. In fact, cerebral palsy does not affect intelligence at all.

If an applicant who is known to have a disability was referred by a rehabilitation agency or other source familiar with the person, it may be helpful to contact the agency to learn more about this individual's ability to perform specific job functions; however, questions should not be asked about the nature or extent of the person's disability.

5.5(g) Background and Reference Checks

Before making a conditional job offer, an employer may not request any information about a job applicant from a previous employer, family member, or other source that it may not itself request of the job applicant.

If an employer uses an outside firm to conduct background checks, the employer should assure that this firm complies with the ADA's prohibitions on pre-employment inquiries. Such a firm is an agent of the employer. The employer is responsible for actions of its agents and may not do anything through a contractual relationship that it may not itself do directly.

Before making a conditional offer of employment, an employer may not ask previous employers or other sources about an applicant's:

- disability;
- illness;

- workers' compensation history;
- or any other questions that the employer itself may not ask of the applicant.

A previous employer may be asked about:

- job functions and tasks performed by the applicant;
- the quality and quantity of work performed;
- how job functions were performed;
- attendance record;
- other job-related issues that do not relate to disability.

If an applicant has a known disability and has indicated that s/he could perform a job with a reasonable accommodation, a previous employer may be asked about accommodations made by that employer.

5.6 Testing

Employers may use any kind of test to determine job qualifications. The ADA has two major requirements in relation to tests:

1. **If a test screens out or tends to screen out an individual with a disability or a class of such individuals on the basis of disability, it must be job-related and consistent with business necessity.**

- This requirement applies to all kinds of tests, including, but not limited to: aptitude tests, tests of knowledge and skill, intelligence tests, agility tests, and job demonstrations.

A test will most likely be an accurate predictor of the job performance of a person with a disability when it most directly or closely measures actual skills and ability needed to do a job. **For example:** a typing test, a sales demonstration test, or other job performance test would indicate what the individual actually could do in performing a job, whereas a test that measured general qualities believed to be desirable in a job may screen out people on the basis of disability who could do the job. **For example,** a standardized test used for a job as a heavy equipment operator might screen out a person with dyslexia or other learning disability who was able to perform all functions of the job itself.

An employer is only required to show that a test is job-related and consistent with business necessity if it screens out a person with a disability *because of* the disability. If a person was screened out for a reason unrelated to disability, ADA requirements do not apply.

> *For example:* If a person with paraplegia who uses a wheelchair is screened out because s/he does not have sufficient speed or accuracy on a typing test, this person probably was not screened out *because of* his or her disability. The employer has no obligation to consider this person for a job which requires fast, accurate typing.

Even if a test is job-related and justified by business necessity, the employer has an obligation to provide a specific reasonable accommodation, if needed. For example, upon request, test sites must be accessible to people who have mobility disabilities. The ADA also has a very specific requirement for accommodation in testing, described below.

2. Accommodation in Testing

The ADA requires that tests be given to people who have impaired sensory, speaking or manual skills in a format and manner that does not require use of the impaired skill, unless the test is designed to measure that skill. (Sensory skills include the abilities to hear, see and to process information.)

The purpose of this requirement is to assure that tests *accurately* reflect a person's job skills, aptitudes, or whatever else the test is supposed to measure, rather than the person's impaired skills.

This requirement applies the reasonable accommodation obligation to testing. It protects people with disabilities from being excluded from jobs that they actually can do because a disability prevents them from taking a test or negatively influences a test result. However, an employer does not have to provide an alternative test format for a person with an impaired skill if the purpose of the test is to measure that skill.

For example:

- A person with dyslexia should be given an opportunity to take a written test orally, if the dyslexia seriously impairs the individual's ability to read. But if ability to read is a job-related function that the test is designed to measure, the employer could require that a person with dyslexia take the written test. However, even in this situation, reasonable accommodation should be considered. The person with dyslexia might be accommodated with a reader, unless the ability to read unaided is an essential job function, unless such an accommodation would not be possible on the job for which s/he is being tested, or would be an undue hardship. For example, the ability to read without help would be essential for a proofreader's job. Or, a dyslexic firefighter applicant might be disqualified if he could not quickly read necessary instructions for dealing with specific toxic substances at the site of a fire when no reader would be available.
- Providing extra time to take a test may be a reasonable accommodation for people with certain disabilities, such as visual impairments, learning disabilities, or mental retardation. On the other hand, an employer could require that an applicant complete a test within an established time frame if speed is one of the skills that the test is designed to measure. However, the results of a timed test should not be used to exclude a person with a disability unless the test measures a *particular* speed necessary to perform an essential function of the job, and there is no reasonable accommodation that would enable this

person to perform that function within prescribed time frames, or the accommodation would cause an undue hardship.

Generally, an employer is only required to provide such an accommodation if it knows, before administering a test, that an accommodation will be needed. Usually, it is the responsibility of the individual with a disability to request any required accommodation for a test. It has been suggested that the employer inform applicants, in advance, of any tests that will be administered as part of the application process so that they may request an accommodation, if needed. (See **5.5(d)** above.) The employer may require that an individual with a disability request an accommodation within a specific time period before administration of the test. The employer also may require that documentation of the need for accommodation accompany such a request.

Occasionally, however, an individual with a disability may not realize in advance that s/he will need an accommodation to take a particular test.

For example: A person with a visual impairment who knows that there will be a written test may not request an accommodation because she has her own specially designed lens that usually is effective for reading printed material. However, when the test is distributed, she finds that her lens is not sufficient, because of unusually low color contrast between the paper and the ink. Under these circumstances, she might request an accommodation and the employer would be obligated to provide one. The employer might provide the test in a higher contrast format at that time, reschedule the test, or make any other effective accommodation that would not impose an undue hardship.

An employer is not required to offer an applicant the specific accommodation requested. This request should be given primary consideration, but the employer is only obligated to provide an effective accommodation. (See Chapter III.) The employer is only required to provide, upon request, an "accessible" test format for individuals whose disabilities impair sensory, manual, or speaking skills needed to take the test, unless the test is designed to measure these skills.

Some Examples of Alternative Test Formats and Accommodations:

- Substituting a written test for an oral test (or written instructions for oral instructions) for people with impaired speaking or hearing skills;
- Administering a test in large print, in Braille, by a reader, or on a computer for people with visual or other reading disabilities;
- Allowing people with visual or learning disabilities or who have limited use of their hands to record test answers by tape recorder, dictation or computer;
- Providing extra time to complete a test for people with certain learning disabilities or impaired writing skills;
- Simplifying test language for people who have limited language skills because of a disability;

- Scheduling rest breaks for people with mental and other disabilities that require such relief;
- Assuring that a test site is accessible to a person with a mobility disability;
- Allowing a person with a mental disability who cannot perform well if there are distractions to take a test in a separate room, if a group test setting is not relevant to the job itself;
- Where it is not possible to test an individual with a disability in an alternative format, an employer may be required, as a reasonable accommodation, to evaluate the skill or ability being tested through some other means, such as an interview, education, work experience, licenses or certification, or a job demonstration for a trial period.

There are a number of technical assistance resources for effective alternative methods of testing people with different disabilities

VI. MEDICAL EXAMINATIONS AND INQUIRIES

6.1 Overview of Legal Obligations

Pre-Employment, Pre-Offer

- An employer may not require a job applicant to take a medical examination, to respond to medical inquiries or to provide information about workers' compensation claims before the employer makes a job offer.

Pre-Employment, Post-Offer

- An employer may condition a job offer on the satisfactory result of a post-offer medical examination or medical inquiry if this is required of all entering employees in the same job category. A post-offer examination or inquiry does not have to be "job-related" and "consistent with business necessity." Questions also may be asked about precious injuries and workers' compensation claims.
- If an individual not hired because a post-offer medical examination or inquiry reveals a disability, the reason(s) for not hiring must be related and necessary for the business. The employer also must. show that no reasonable accommodation was available that would enable this individual to perform the essential job functions, or that accommodation would impose an undue hardship.
- A post-offer medical examination may disqualify an individual who would pose a "direct threat" to health or safety. Such a disqualification is job-related and consistent with business necessity.
- A post-offer medical examination may not disqualify an individual with a disability who is currently able to perform essential job functions because of speculation that the disability may cause a risk of future injury.

Employee Medical Examination and Inquiries

- After a person starts work, a medical examination or inquiry of an employee must be job related and necessary for the business.

- Employers may conduct employee medical examinations where there is evidence of a job performance or safety problem, examinations required by other Federal laws, examinations to determine current "fitness" to perform a particular job and voluntary examinations that are part of employee health programs.

Confidentiality

- Information from all medical examinations and inquiries must be kept apart from general personnel files as a separate, confidential medical record, available only under limited conditions specified in the ADA. (See **6.5** below.)

Drug Testing

- Tests for illegal use of drugs are not medical examinations under the ADA and are not subject to the restrictions on such examinations. (See Chapter VIII.)

6.2 Basic Requirements

The ADA does not prevent employers from obtaining medical and related information necessary to evaluate the ability of applicants and employees to perform essential job functions, or to promote health and safety on the job. However, to protect individuals with disabilities from actions based on such information that are not job-related and consistent with business necessity, including protection of health and safety, the ADA imposes specific and differing obligations on the employer at three stages of the employment process:

1. **Before making a job offer,** an employer may not make any medical inquiry or conduct any medical examination.
2. **After making a conditional job offer,** before a person starts work, an employer may make unrestricted medical inquiries, but may not refuse to hire an individual with a disability based on results of such inquiries, unless the reason for rejection is job related and justified by business necessity.
3. **After employment,** any medical examination or inquiry required of an employee must be job-related and justified by business necessity. Exceptions are voluntary examinations conducted as part of employee health programs and examinations required by other federal laws.

Under the ADA, "medical" documentation concerning the qualifications of an individual with a disability, or whether this individual constitutes a "direct threat" to health and safety, does not mean only information from medical doctors. It may be necessary to obtain information from other sources, such as rehabilitation experts, occupational or physical therapists, psychologists, and others knowledgeable about the individual and the disability concerned. It also may be more relevant to look at the individual's previous work history in making such determinations than to rely on an examination or tests by a physician.

The basic requirements regarding actions based on medical information and inquiries have been set out in Chapter IV. As emphasized there, such actions taken because of a disability **must be job-related** and **consistent with business**

necessity. When an individual is rejected as a **"direct threat"** to health and safety:

- **the employer must be prepared to show a significant current risk of substantial harm (not a speculative or remote risk);**
- **the *specific* risk must be identified;**
- **the risk must be *documented* by objective medical or other factual evidence regarding the particular individual;**
- **even if a genuine significant risk of substantial harm exists, the employer must consider whether it can be eliminated or reduced below the level of a "direct threat" by *reasonable accommodation.***

This chapter discusses in more detail the content and manner of medical examinations and inquiries that may be made, and the documentation that may be required (1) before employment and (2) after employment.

6.3 Examination and Inquiries Before Employment

No Pre-Offer Medical Examination or Inquiry

The ADA prohibits medical inquiries or medical examinations before making a conditional job offer to an applicant. This prohibition is necessary because the results of such inquiries and examinations frequently are used to exclude people with disabilities from jobs they are able to perform.

Some employers have medical policies or rely on doctors' medical assessments that overestimate the impact of a particular condition on a particular individual, and/or underestimate the ability of an individual to cope with his or her condition. Medical policies that focus on disability, rather than the **ability** of a particular person, frequently will be discriminatory under the ADA.

> *For example:* A policy that prohibits employment of *any* individual who has epilepsy, diabetes or a heart condition from a certain type of job, and which does not consider the ability of a *particular* individual, in most cases would violate the ADA. (See Chapter IV.)

Many employers currently use a pre-employment medical questionnaire, a medical history, or a pre-employment medical examination as one step in a several-step selection process. Where this is so, an individual who has a "hidden" disability such as diabetes, epilepsy, heart disease, cancer, or mental illness, and who is rejected for a job, frequently does not know whether the reason for rejection was information revealed by the medical exam or inquiry (which may not have any relation to this person's ability to do the job), or whether the rejection was based on some other aspect of the selection process.

A history of such rejections has discouraged many people with disabilities from applying for jobs, because of fear that they will automatically be rejected when their disability is revealed by a medical examination. The ADA is designed to remove this barrier to employment.

6.4 POST-OFFER EXAMINATIONS AND INQUIRIES PERMITTED

The ADA recognizes that employers may need to conduct medical examinations to determine if an applicant can perform certain jobs effectively and safely. The ADA requires only that such examinations be conducted as a separate, second step of the selection process, after an individual has met all other job pre-requisites. The employer may make a job offer to such an individual, conditioned on the satisfactory outcome of a medical examination or inquiry, providing that the employer requires such examination or inquiry for all entering employees in a particular job category, not merely individuals with known disabilities, or those whom the employer believes may have a disability.

A *post-offer* medical examination does not have to be given to all entering employees in all jobs, only to those in the same job category.

For example: An examination might be given to all entering employees in physical labor jobs, but not to employees entering clerical jobs.

The ADA does not require an employer to justify its requirement of a post-offer medical examination. An employer may wish to conduct a post-offer medical exam or make post-offer medical inquiries for purposes such as:

To determine if an individual currently has the physical or mental qualifications necessary to perform certain jobs:

For example: If a job requires continuous heavy physical exertion, a medical examination may be useful to determine whether an applicant's physical condition will permit him/her to perform the job.

To determine that a person can perform a job without posing a "direct threat" to the health or safety of self or others.

For example:

- A medical examination and evaluation might be required to ensure that prospective construction crane operators do not have disabilities such as uncontrolled seizures that would pose a significant risk to other workers.
- Workers in certain health care jobs may need to be examined to assure that they do not have a current contagious disease or infection that would pose a significant risk of transmission to others, and that could not be accommodated (for example, by giving the individual a delayed starting date until the period of contagion is over).

Compliance with Medical Requirements of Other Federal laws

Employers may comply with medical and safety requirements established under other Federal laws without violating the ADA.

For example: Federal Highway Administration regulations require medical examinations and evaluations of interstate truck drivers, and the Federal Aviation Administration requires examinations for pilots and air controllers.

However, an employer still has an obligation to consider whether there is a reasonable accommodation, consistent with the requirements of other Federal laws, that would not exclude individuals who can perform jobs safely.

Employers also may conduct post-offer medical examinations that are required by state laws, but, as explained in Chapter IV, may not take actions based on such examinations if the state law is inconsistent with ADA requirements. (See *Health and Safety Requirements of Other Federal or State Laws,* **4.6.**)

Information That May Be Requested in Post-Offer Examinations or Inquiries
After making a conditional job offer, an employer may make inquiries or conduct examinations to get any information that it believes to be relevant to a person's ability to perform a job. **For example,** the employer may require a full physical examination. An employer may ask questions that are prohibited as pre-employment inquiries about previous illnesses, diseases or medications. (See Chapter V.)

If a post-offer medical examination is given, it must be administered to *all* persons entering a job category. If a response to an initial medical inquiry (such as a medical history questionnaire) reveals that an applicant has had a previous injury, illness, or medical condition, the employer cannot require the applicant to undergo a medical **examination** unless all applicants in the job category are required to have such examination. However, the ADA does not require that the scope of medical examinations must be identical. An employer may give follow-up tests or examinations where an examination indicates that further information is needed.

For example: All potential employees in a job category must be given a blood test, but if a person's initial test indicates a problem that may affect job performance, Further tests may be given to that person only, in order to get necessary information.

A **post-offer** medical examination or inquiry, made before an individual starts work, need not focus on ability to perform job functions. Such inquiries and examinations themselves, unlike examinations/inquiries of **employees,** do not have to be "job related" and "consistent with business necessity." However, if a conditional job offer is withdrawn because of the results of such examination or inquiry, an employer must be able to show that:

- the reasons for the exclusion are job-related and consistent with business necessity, or the person is being excluded to avoid a "direct threat" to health or safety; and that
- no reasonable accommodation was available that would enable this person to

perform the essential job functions without a significant risk to health or safety, or that such an accommodation would cause undue hardship.

Some examples of post-offer decisions that might be job related and justified by business necessity, and/or where no reasonable accommodation was possible:

- a medical history reveals that the individual has suffered serious multiple re-injuries to his back doing similar work, which have progressively worsened the back condition. Employing this person in this job would incur significant risk that he would further reinjure himself.
- a workers' compensation history indicates multiple claims in recent years which have been denied. An employer might have a legitimate business reason to believe that the person has submitted fraudulent claims. Withdrawing a job offer for this reason would not violate the ADA, because the decision is not based on disability.
- a medical examination reveals an impairment that would require the individual's frequent lengthy absence from work for medical treatment, and the job requires daily availability for the next 3 months. In this situation, the individual is not available to perform the essential functions of the job, and no accommodation is possible.

Examples of discriminatory use of examination results that are *not* job related and justified by business necessity:

- A landscape firm sent an applicant for a laborer's job (who had been doing this kind of work for 20 years) for a physical exam. An x-ray showed that he had a curvature of the spine. The doctor advised the firm not to hire him because there was a risk; that he might injure his back at some time in the future. The doctor provided no specific medical documentation that this would happen or was likely to happen. The company provided no description of the job to the doctor. The job actually involved riding a mechanical mower. This unlawful exclusion was based on speculation about future risk of injury, and was not job-related.
- An individual is rejected from a job because he cannot lift more than 50 pounds. The job requires lifting such a weight only occasionally. The employer has not considered possible accommodations, such as sharing the occasional heavy weight lifting with another employee or providing a device to assist lifting.

Risk Cannot Be Speculative or Remote

The results of a medical examination may not disqualify persons *currently* able to perform essential job functions because of unsubstantiated *speculation* about future risk.

The results of a medical inquiry or examination may not be used to disqualify persons who are *currently* able to perform the essential functions of a job, either with or without an accommodation, because of fear or *speculation* that a disability may indicate a greater risk of future injury, or absenteeism, or may cause future workers' compensation or insurance costs. An employer may use such information to exclude an individual with a disability where there is specific medical documentation, reflecting current medical knowledge, that *this individual* would pose a significant, current risk of substantial harm to health or safety. (See *Standards for Health and Safety: "Direct Threat"* Chapter IV.)

For example:

- An individual who has an abnormal back X-ray may not be disqualified from a job that requires heavy lifting because of fear that she will be more likely to injure her back or cause higher workers' compensation or health insurance costs However, where there is documentation that this individual has injured and re-injured her back in similar jobs, and the back condition has been aggravated further by injury, *and* if there is no reasonable accommodation that would eliminate the risk of reinjury or reduce it to an acceptable level, an employer would be justified in rejecting her for this position.
- If a medical examination reveals that an individual has epilepsy and is seizure-free or has adequate warning of a seizure, it would be unlawful to disqualify this person from a job operating a machine because of fear or speculation that he might pose a risk to himself or others. But if the examination and other medical inquiries reveal that an individual with epilepsy has seizures resulting in loss of consciousness, there could be evidence of significant risk in. employing this person as a machine operator. However, even where the person might endanger himself by operating a machine, an accommodation, such as placing a shield over the machine to protect him, should be considered.

The Doctor's Role

A doctor who conducts medical examinations for an employer should not be responsible for making employment decisions or deciding whether or not it is possible to make a reasonable accommodation for a person with a disability. That responsibility lies with the employer.

The doctor's role should be limited to advising the employer about an individual's functional abilities and limitations in relation to job functions, and about whether the individual meets the employer's health and safety requirements.

Accordingly, employers should provide doctors who conduct such examinations with **specific** information about the job, including the type of information indicated in the discussions of "job descriptions" and "job analysis" in Chapter II. (See **2.3.**)

Often, particularly when an employer uses an outside doctor who is not familiar with actual demands of the job, a doctor may make incorrect assumptions about the nature of the job functions and specific tasks, or about the ability of an individual with a disability to perform these tasks with. a reasonable accommodation. It may be useful for the doctor to visit the job site to see how the job is done.

The employer should inform the doctor that any recommendations or conclusions related to hiring or placement of an individual should focus on only two concerns:

1. Whether this person currently is able to perform this specific job, with or without an accommodation.

This evaluation should look at the individual's specific abilities and limitations in regard to specific job demands.

> *For example:* The evaluation may indicate that a person can lift up to 30 pounds and can reach only 2 feet above the shoulder; the job as usually performed (without accommodation) requires lifting 50 pound crates to shelves that are 6 feet high.

2. Whether this person can perform this job without posing a "direct threat" to the health or safety of the person or others.

The doctor should be informed that the employer must be able to show that an exclusion of an individual with a disability because of a risk to health or safety meets the "direct threat" standard of the ADA, based on "the most current medical knowledge and/or the best available objective evidence about this individual." (See Chapter IV., *Standards Necessary for Health and Safety,* and 6.2 above.)

> *For example:* If a post-offer medical questionnaire indicates that a person has a history of repetitive motion injuries but has had successful surgery with no further problems indicated, and a doctor recommends that the employer reject this candidate because this medical history indicates that she would pose a higher risk of future injury, the employer would violate the ADA if it acted on the doctor's recommendation based only on the history of injuries. In this case, the doctor would not have considered this person's actual current condition as a result of surgery.

A doctor's evaluation of any future risk must be supported by valid medical analyses indicating a high probability of substantial harm if *this individual* performed the particular functions of the particular job in question. Conclusions of general medical studies about work restrictions for people with certain disabilities will not be sufficient evidence, because they do not relate to a particular individual and do not consider reasonable accommodation.

The employer should not rely only on a doctor's opinion, but on the *best available objective evidence.* This may include the experience of the individual with a disability in previous similar jobs, occupations, or non-work activities, the opinions of other doctors with expertise on the particular disability, and the advice of rehabilitation counselors, occupational or physical therapists, and others with direct knowledge of the disability and/or the individual concerned. Organizations such as Independent Living Centers, public and private rehabilitation agencies, and organizations serving people with specific disabilities such as the Epilepsy Foundation!, United Cerebral Palsy Associations, National Head Injury Foundation, and many others can provide such assistance.

Where the doctors report indicates that an individual has a disability that may prevent performance of essential job functions, or that may pose a "direct threat" to health or safety, the employer also may seek his/her advice on possible accommodations that would overcome these disqualifications.

6.5 Confidentiality and Limitations on Use of Medical Information

Although the ADA does not limit the nature or extent of post-offer medical examinations and inquiries, it imposes very *strict limitations on the use of information* obtained from such examinations and inquiries. These limitations also apply to information obtained from examinations or inquiries of employees.

- All information obtained from post-offer medical examinations and inquiries must be collected and maintained on separate forms, in separate medical files and must be treated as a *confidential medical record.* Therefore, an employer should not place any medical-related material in an employee's personnel file. The employer should take steps to guarantee the security of the employee's medical information, including:
  —keeping the information in a medical file in a separate, locked cabinet, apart from the location of personnel files; and
  —designating a specific person or persons to have access to the medical file.
- All medical-related information must be kept confidential, with the following exceptions:
  —Supervisors and managers may be informed about necessary restrictions on the work or duties of an employee and necessary accommodations;
  —First aid and safety personnel may be informed, when appropriate, if the disability might require emergency treatment or if any specific procedures are needed in the case of fire or other evacuations.
  —Government officials investigating compliance with the ADA and other Federal and state laws prohibiting discrimination on the basis of disability or handicap should be provided relevant information on request. (Other Federal laws and regulations also may require disclosure of relevant medical information.)
  —Relevant information may be provided to state workers' compensation offices or "second injury" funds, in accordance with state workers' compensation laws. (See Chapter IX., *Workers' Compensation and Work-Related Injury.*)

— Relevant information may be provided to insurance companies where the company requires a medical examination to provide health or life insurance for employees. (See H*ealth Insurance and Other Benefit Plans,* Chapter VII.)

6.6 Employee Medical Examinations and Inquiries

The ADA's requirements concerning medical examinations and inquiries of employees(are more stringent than those affecting applicants who are being evaluated for employment after a conditional job offer. In order for a medical examination or inquiry to be made of an employee, it must be job related and consistent with business necessity. The need for the examination may be triggered by some evidence of problems related to job performance or safety, or an examination may be necessary to determine whether individuals in physically demanding jobs continue to be fit for duty. In either case, the scope of the examination also must be job-related.

For example:

- An attorney could not be required to submit to a medical examination or inquiry just because her leg had been amputated. The essential functions of an attorney's job do not require use of both legs; therefore such an inquiry would not be job related.
- An employer. may require a warehouse laborer, whose back impairment affects the ability to lift, to be examined by an orthopedist, but may not require this employee to submit to an HIV test where the test is not related to either the essential functions of his job or to his impairment.

Medical examinations or inquiries may be job related and necessary under several circumstances:

- **When an employee is having difficulty performing his or her job effectively.** In such cases, a medical examination may be necessary to determine if s/he can perform essential job functions with or without an accommodation.

  For example: If an employee falls asleep on the job, has excessive absenteeism, or exhibits other performance problems, an examination may be needed to determine if the problem is caused by an underlying medical condition, and whether medical treatment is needed. If the examination reveals an impairment that is a disability under the ADA, the employer must consider possible reasonable accommodations. If the impairment is not a disability, the employer is not required to make an accommodation.

  For example: An employee may complain of headaches caused by noise at the worksite. A medical examination may indicate that there is no medically discernible mental or physiological disorder causing the headaches. This employee would not be "an individual with a disability" under the ADA, and the employer would have no obligation to provide an accommodation. The employer may voluntarily take steps to improve the noise situation, particularly if other employees also suffer from noise, but would have no obligation to do so under the ADA.

- **When An Employee Becomes Disabled**

An employee who is injured on or off the job, who becomes ill, or suffers any other condition that meets the ADA definition of "disability," is protected by the Act if s/he can perform the essential functions of the job with or without reasonable accommodation.

Employers are accustomed to dealing with injured workers through the workers' compensation process and disability management programs, but they have different, although not necessarily conflicting obligations under the ADA. The relationship between ADA, workers' compensation requirements and medical examinations and inquiries is discussed in Chapter IX.

Under the ADA, medical information or medical examinations may be required when an employee suffers an injury on the job. Such an examination or inquiry also may be required when an employee wishes to return to work after an injury or illness, if it is job related and consistent with business necessity:

—to determine if the individual meets the ADA definition of "individual with a disability," if an accommodation has been requested.

—to determine if the person can perform essential functions of the job currently held, (or held before the injury or illness), with or without reasonable accommodation, and without posing a "direct threat" to health or safety that cannot be reduced or eliminated by reasonable accommodation.

—to identify an effective accommodation that would enable the person to perform essential job functions in the current (previous) job, or in a vacant job for which the person is qualified (with or without accommodation). (See Chapter IX.)

- **Examination Necessary for Reasonable Accommodation**

A medical examination may be required if an employee requests an accommodation on the basis of disability. An accommodation may be needed in an employee's existing job, or if the employee is being transferred or promoted to a different job. Medical information may be needed to determine if the employee has a disability covered by the ADA and is entitled to an accommodation, and if so, to help identify an effective accommodation.

Medical inquiries related to an employee's disability and functional limitations may include consultations with knowledgeable professional sources, such as occupational and physical therapists, rehabilitation specialists, and organizations with expertise in adaptations for specific disabilities.

- **Medical Examinations, Screening and Monitoring Required by Other Laws**

Employers may conduct periodic examinations and other medical screening and monitoring required by federal, state or local laws. As indicated in Chapter IV, the ADA recognizes that an action taken to comply with another Federal law is job-related and consistent with business necessity; however, requirements of state and local laws do not necessarily meet this standard unless they are consistent with the ADA.

For example: Employers may conduct medical examinations and medical monitoring required by:

- The U.S. Department of Transportation for interstate bus and truck drivers, railroad engineers, airline pilots and air controllers;
- The Occupational Safety and Health Act:
- The Federal Mine Health and Safety Act;
- Other statutes that require employees exposed to toxic or hazardous substances to be medically monitored at specific intervals.

However, if a state or local law required that employees in a particular job be periodically tested for AIDS or the HIV virus, the ADA would prohibit such an examination unless an employer can show that it is job-related and consistent with business necessity, or required to avoid a direct threat to health or safety. (See Chapter IV.)

- **Voluntary "Wellness" and Health Screening Programs**

An employer may conduct voluntary medical examinations and inquiries as part of an employee health program (such as medical screening for high blood pressure, weight control, and cancer detection), providing that:

- participation in the program is voluntary;
- information obtained is maintained according to the confidentiality requirements of the ADA (See **6.5**); and
- this information is not used to discriminate against an employee.

Information from Medical Inquiries May Not be Used to Discriminate

An employer may not use information obtained from an employee medical examination or inquiry to discriminate against the employee in any employment practice. (See Chapter VII.)

Confidentiality

All information obtained from employee medical examinations and inquiries must be maintained and used in accordance with ADA confidentiality requirements. (See **6.6** above.)

VII. NONDISCRIMINATION IN OTHER EMPLOYMENT PRACTICES

7.1 Introduction

The nondiscrimination requirements of the ADA apply to all employment practices and activities. The preceding chapters have explained these requirements as they apply to job qualification and selection standards, the hiring process, and medical examinations and inquiries. This chapter discusses the application of nondiscrimination requirements to other employment practices and activities.

In most cases, an employer need only apply the basic nondiscrimination principles already emphasized; however, there are also some special requirements applicable to certain employment activities. This chapter discusses:

- the ADA's prohibition of discrimination on the basis of a **relationship or association with** an individual with a disability; nondiscrimination requirements affecting:
- **promotion, assignment, training, evaluation, discipline, advancement opportunity and discharge;**
- **compensation, insurance, leave, and other benefits and privileges of employment;**
- **and contractual relationships.**

7.2 Overview of Legal Obligations

- An employer may not discriminate against a qualified individual with a disability because of the disability, in any employment practice, or any term, condition or benefit of employment.
- An employer may not deny an employment opportunity because an individual, with or without a disability, **has a relationship or association with** an individual who has a disability.
- An employer may not participate in a contractual or other arrangement that subjects the employer's qualified applicant or employee with a disability to discrimination.
- An employer may not discriminate or retaliate against any individual, whether or not the individual is disabled, because the individual has opposed a discriminatory practice, filed a discrimination charge, or participated in any way in enforcing the ADA.

7.3 Nondiscrimination in all Employment Practice

The ADA prohibits discrimination against a qualified individual with a disability on the basis of disability in the following employment practices:

- Recruitment, advertising, and job application procedures;
- Hiring, upgrading, promotion, award of tenure, demotion, transfer, layoff, termination, right of return from layoff, and rehiring;

- Rates of pay or any other form of compensation, and changes in compensation;
- Job assignments, job classifications, organizational structures, position descriptions, lines of progression, and seniority lists;
- Leaves of absence, sick leave, or any other leave;
- Fringe benefits available by virtue of employment, whether or not administered by the covered entity;
- Selection and financial support for training, including: apprenticeships, professional meetings, conferences, and other related activities, and selection for leaves of absence to pursue training;
- Activities sponsored by a covered entity including social and recreational programs; and
- Any other term, condition, or privilege of employment.

Nondiscrimination, as applied to all employment practices, means that:

- an individual with a disability should have equal access to any employment opportunity available to a similarly situated individual who is not disabled;
- employment decisions concerning an employee or applicant should be based on objective factual evidence about the particular individual, not on assumptions or stereotypes about the individual's disability;
- the qualifications of an individual with a disability may be evaluated on ability to perform all job-related functions, with or without reasonable accommodation. However, an individual may not be excluded from a job because a disability prevents performance of marginal job functions;
- an employer must provide a reasonable accommodation that will enable an individual with a disability to have an equal opportunity in every aspect of employment, unless a particular accommodation would impose an undue hardship;
- an employer may not use an employment practice or policy that screens out or tends to screen out an individual with a disability or a class of individuals with disabilities, *unless* the practice or policy is job related and consistent with business necessity and the individual cannot be accommodated without undue hardship;
- an employer may not limit, segregate, or classify an individual with a disability in any way that negatively affects the individual in terms of job opportunity and advancement;
- an individual with a disability should not because of a disability be treated differently than a similarly situated individual in any aspect of employment, except when a reasonable accommodation is needed to provide an equal employment opportunity, or when another Federal law or regulation requires different treatment.

These requirements are discussed in this chapter as they apply to various employment practices. The prohibition against retaliation is discussed in Chapter X.

7.4. Nondiscrimination and Relationship or Association with an Individual with a Disability

The ADA specifically provides that an employer or other covered entity may not deny an employment opportunity or benefit to an individual, whether or not that individual is disabled, because that individual has a **known relationship or association** with an individual who has a disability. Nor may an employer discriminate in any other way against an individual, whether or not disabled, because that individual has such a relationship or association.

The term "relationship or association" refers to family relationships and any other social or business relationship or association. Therefore, this provision of the law prohibits employers from making employment decisions based on concerns about the disability of a family member of an applicant or employee, or anyone else with whom this person has a relationship or association.

For example: An employer may not:

- refuse to hire or fire an individual because the individual has a spouse, child, or other dependent who has a disability. The employer may not assume that the individual will be unreliable, have to use leave time, or be away from work in order to care for the family member with a disability;
- refuse to hire or fire an individual because s/he has a spouse, child or other dependent who has a disability that is either not covered by the employer's current health insurance plan or that may cause future increased health care costs;
- refuse to insure, or subject an individual to different terms or conditions of insurance, solely because the individual has a spouse, child, or other dependent who has a disability;
- refuse to hire or fire an individual because the individual has a relationship or association with a person or persons who have disabilities.

For example: an employer cannot fire an employee because s/he does volunteer work with people who have AIDS.

This provision of the law prohibits discrimination in employment decisions concerning an individual, whether the individual is or is not disabled, because of a known relationship or association with an individual with a disability. However, an employer is not obligated to provide a reasonable accommodation to a non disabled individual, because this person has a relationship or association with a disabled individual. The obligation to make a reasonable accommodation applies only to qualified individuals with disabilities.

For example: The ADA does not require that an employer provide an employee who is not disabled with a modified work schedule as an accommodation, to enable the employee to care for a spouse or child with a disability.

7.5. Nondiscrimination and Opportunity for Advancement

The nondiscrimination requirements that apply to initial selection apply to 811 aspects of employment, including opportunities for advancement. For example, an employer may not discriminate in promotion, job classification, evaluation, disciplinary action, opportunities for training, or participation in meetings and conferences. In particular, an employer:

- should not assume that an individual is not interested in, or not qualified for, advancement because of disability;
- should not deny a promotion because of the need to make an accommodation, unless the accommodation would cause an undue hardship;
- should not place individuals with disabilities in separate lines of progression or in segregated units or locations that limit opportunity for advancement;
- should assure that supervisors and managers who make decisions regarding promotion and advancement are aware of ADA nondiscrimination requirements.

7.6. TRAINING

Employees with disabilities must be provided equal opportunities to participate in training to improve job performance and provide opportunity for advancement. Training opportunities cannot be denied because of the need to make a reasonable accommodation, unless the accommodation would be an undue hardship. Accommodations that may be necessary, depending on the needs of particular individuals, may include:

- accessible locations and facilities for people with mobility disabilities;
- interpreters and note-takers for employees who are deaf;
- materials in accessible formats and/or readers for people who are visually impaired, for people with learning disabilities, and for people with mental retardation;
- if audiovisual materials are used, captions for people who are deaf, and voice-overs for people who are visually impaired;
- good lighting on an interpreter, and good general illumination for people with visual impairments and other disabilities;
- clarification of concepts presented in training for people who have reading or other disabilities;
- individualized instruction for people with mental retardation and certain other disabilities.

If an employer contracts for training with a training company, or contracts for training facilities such as hotels or conference centers, the employer is responsible for assuring accessibility and other needed accommodations.

It is advisable that any contract with a company or facility used for training include a provision requiring the other party to provide needed accommodations. However, if the contractor does not do so, the employer remains responsible for providing the accommodation, unless it would cause an undue hardship.

For example: Suppose a company with which an employer has contracted proposes to conduct training at an inaccessible location. The employer is responsible for providing an accommodation that would enable an employee who uses a wheelchair to obtain this training. The employer might do this by: requiring the training company to relocate the program to an accessible site; requiring the company to make the site (including all facilities used by trainees) accessible; making the site accessible or providing resources that enable the training company to do so; contracting with another training company that uses accessible sites; or providing any other accommodation (such as temporary ramps) that would not impose an undue hardship. If it is impossible to make an accommodation because the need is only discovered when an employee arrives at the training site, the employer may have to provide accessible training at a later date.

Or, for example: An employer contracts with a hotel to hold a conference for its employees. The employer must assure physical and communications accessibility for employees with disabilities, including accessibility of guest rooms and all meeting and other rooms used by attendees. The employer may assure accessibility by inspecting the site, or may ask a local disability group with accessibility expertise (such as an Independent Living Center) to do so. The employer remains responsible for assuring accessibility. However, if the hotel breaches a contract provision requiring accessibility, the hotel may be liable to the employer under regular (non-ADA) breach of contract law. The hotel also may be liable under Title III of the ADA, which requires accessibility in public accommodations.

7.7 Evaluations. Discipline and Discharge

- An employer can hold employees with disabilities to the same standards of production/performance as other similarly situated employees without disabilities for performing essential job functions (with or without reasonable accommodation).
- An employer also can hold employees with disabilities to the same standards of production/performance as other employees regarding marginal job functions, *unless* the disability affects the ability to perform these marginal functions. If the ability to perform marginal functions is affected by the disability, the employer must provide some type of reasonable accommodation such as job restructuring (unless to do so would be an undue hardship).
- A disabled employee who needs an accommodation (that is not an undue hardship for an employer) in order to perform a job function should not be evaluated on his/her ability to perform the function without the accommoda-

tion, and should not be downgraded because such an accommodation is needed to perform the function.

- An employer should not give employees with disabilities "special treatment." They should not be evaluated on a lower standard or disciplined less severely than any other employee. This is not equal employment opportunity.
- An employer must provide an employee with a disability with reasonable accommodation necessary to enable the employee to participate in the evaluation process (for example, counseling or an interpreter).
- If an employee with a disability is not performing well, an employer may require medical and other professional inquiries that are job-related and consistent with business necessity to discover whether the disability is causing the poor performance, and whether any reasonable accommodation or additional accommodation is needed. (See Chapter VI.)
- An employer may take the same disciplinary action against employees with disabilities as it takes against other similarly situated employees, if the illegal use of drugs or alcohol use affects job performance and/or attendance. (See Chapter VIII.)
- An employer may not discipline or terminate an employee with a disability if the employer has refused to provide a requested reasonable accommodation that did not constitute an undue hardship, and the reason for unsatisfactory performance was the lack of accommodation.

7.8. Compensation

- An employer cannot reduce pay to an employee with a disability because of the elimination of a marginal job function or because it has provided a reasonable accommodation, such as specialized or modified equipment. The employer can give the employee with a disability other marginal functions that s/he can perform.
- An employee who is reassigned to a lower paying job or provided a part-time job as an accommodation may be paid the lower amount that would apply to such positions, consistent with the employer's regular compensation practices.

7.9. Health Insurance and Other Employee Benefit Plans

As discussed above, an employer or other covered entity may not limit, segregate or classify an individual with a disability, on the basis of disability, in a manner that adversely affects the individual's employment. This prohibition applies to the provision and administration of health insurance and other benefit plans, such as life insurance and pension plans.

This means that:

- If an employer provides insurance or other benefit plans to its employees, it must provide the same coverage to its employees with disabilities.

Employees with disabilities must be given equal access to whatever insurance or benefit plans the employer provides.

- An employer cannot deny insurance to an individual with a disability or subject an individual with a disability to different terms or conditions of insurance, based on disability alone, if the disability does not pose increased insurance risks. Nor may the employer enter into any contract or agreement with an insurance company or other entity that has such effect.
- An employer cannot fire or refuse to hire an individual with a disability because the employer's current health insurance plan does not cover the individual's disability, or because the individual may increase the employer's future health care costs.
- An employer cannot fire or refuse to hire an individual (whether or not that individual has a disability) because the individual has a family member or dependent with a disability that is not covered by the employer's current health insurance plan, or that may increase the employer's future health care costs.

While establishing these protections for employees with disabilities, the ADA permits employers to provide insurance plans that comply with existing Federal and state insurance requirements, even if provisions of these plans have an adverse affect on people with disabilities, provided that the provisions are not used as a subterfuge to evade the purpose of the ADA.

Specifically, the ADA provides that:

- Where an employer provides health insurance through an insurance carrier that is regulated by state law, it may provide coverage in accordance with accepted principles of risk assessment and/or risk classification, as required or permitted by such law, even if this causes limitations in coverage for individuals with disabilities.
- Similarly, self-insured plans which are not subject to state law may provide coverage in a manner that is consistent with basic accepted principles of insurance risk classification, even if this results in limitations in coverage to individuals with disabilities.

In each case, such activity is permitted only if it is not being used as a subterfuge to evade the intent of the ADA. Whether or not an activity is being used as a subterfuge will be determined regardless of the date that the insurance plan or employee benefit plan was adopted.

This means that:

- An employer may continue to offer health insurance plans that contain pre-existing condition exclusions, even if this adversely affects individuals with disabilities, unless these exclusions are being used as a subterfuge to evade the purpose of the ADA.
- An employer may continue to offer health insurance plans that limit coverage for certain *procedures,* and/or limit particular *treatments* to a specified

number per year, even if these restrictions adversely affect individuals with disabilities, as long as the restrictions are uniformly applied to all insured individuals, regardless of the disability.

For example, an employer can offer a health insurance plan that limits coverage of blood transfusions to five transfusions per year for all employees, even though an employee with hemophilia may require more than five transfusions per year. However, the employer could not deny this employee coverage for another, otherwise covered procedure, because the plan will not pay for the additional blood transfusions that the procedure would require.

- An employer may continue to offer health insurance plans that limit reimbursements for certain types of drugs or procedures, even if these restrictions adversely affect individuals with disabilities, as long as the restrictions are uniformly applied without regard to disability.

For example, an employer can offer a health insurance plan that does not cover experimental drugs or procedures, as long as this restriction is applied to all insured individuals.

7.10 Leave

- An employer may establish attendance and leave policies that are uniformly applied to all employees, regardless of disability, but may not refuse leave needed by an employee with a disability if other employees get such leave.
- An employer may be required to make adjustments' in leave policy as a reasonable accommodation. The employer is not obligated to provide additional paid leave, but accommodations may include leave flexibility and unpaid leave. (See Chapter III.)
- A uniformly applied leave policy does not violate the ADA because it has a more severe effect on an individual because of his/her disability. However, if an individual with a disability requests a modification of such a policy as a reasonable accommodation, an employer may be required to provide it, unless it would impose an undue hardship.

For example: If an employer has 8 policy providing 2 weeks paid leave for all employees, with no other provision for sick leave and a "no leave" policy for the first 6 months of employment, an employee with a disability who cannot get leave for needed medical treatment could not successfully charge that the employer's policy is discriminatory on its face. However, this individual could request leave without pay or advance leave as a reasonable accommodation. Such leave should be provided, unless the employer can show undue hardship: *For example,* an employer might be able to show that it is necessary for the operation of the business that this employee be available for the time period when leave is requested.

- An employer is not required to give leave as a reasonable accommodation to an employee who has a relationship with an individual with a disability to enable the employee to care for that individual. (See p. 8 above.)

7.11 Contractual or Other Relationships

An employer may not do anything through a contractual relationship that it cannot do directly. This applies to any contracts, including contracts with:

- training organizations (see above);
- insurers (see above);
- employment agencies and agencies used for background checks (see Chapter V);
- labor unions (see below).

7.11(a) Collective Bargaining Agreements

Labor unions are covered by the ADA and have the same obligation as the employer to comply with its requirements. An employer also is prohibited by the ADA from taking any action through a labor union contract that it may not take itself.

For example: If a union contract contained physical requirements for a particular job that screened out people with disabilities who were qualified to perform the job, and these requirements are not job-related and consistent with business necessity, they could be challenged as discriminatory by a qualified individual with a disability.

The terms of a collective bargaining agreement may be relevant in determining whether a particular accommodation would cause an employer undue hardship.

For example: If the collective bargaining agreement reserves certain jobs for employees with a given amount of seniority, this may be considered as a factor in determining whether it would be an undue hardship to reassign an individual with a disability who does not have seniority to a vacant job.

Where a collective bargaining agreement identifies functions that must be performed in a particular job, the agreement, like a job description, may be considered as evidence of what the employer and union consider to be a job's essential functions. However, just because a function is listed in a union agreement does not mean that it is an essential function. The agreement, like the job description, will be considered along with other types of evidence. (See Chapter II.)

The Congressional Committee Reports accompanying the ADA advised employers and unions that they could carry out their responsibilities under the Act, and avoid conflicts between the bargaining agreement and the employer's duty to provide reasonable accommodation, by adding a provision to agreements negotiated after the effective date of the ADA, permitting the employer to take all actions necessary to comply with the Act.

7.12 Nondiscrimination in Other Benefits and Privileges of Employment

Nondiscrimination requirements, including the obligation to make reasonable accommodation, apply to all social or recreational activities provided or conducted by an employer, to any transportation provided by an employer for its employees or applicants, and to all other benefits and privileges of employment.

This means that:

- Employees with disabilities must have an equal opportunity to attend and participate in any social functions conducted or sponsored by an employer. Functions such as parties, picnics, shows, and award ceremonies should be held in accessible locations, and interpreters or other accommodation should be provided when necessary.
- Employees with disabilities must have equal access to break rooms, lounges, cafeterias, and any other non-work facilities that are provided by an employer for use by its employees.
- Employees with disabilities must have equal access to an exercise room, gymnasium, or health club provided by an employer for use by its employees. However, an employer would not have to eliminate facilities provided for employees because a disabled employee cannot use certain equipment or amenities because of his/her disability. *For example,* an employer would not have to remove certain exercise machines simply because an employee who is a paraplegic could not use them.
- Employees with disabilities must be given an equal opportunity to participate in employer-sponsored sports teams, leagues, or recreational activities such as hiking or biking clubs. However, the employer does not have to discontinue such activities because a disabled employee cannot fully participate due to his/her disability. *For example,* an employer would not have to discontinue the company biking club simply because a blind employee is unable to ride a bicycle.

Any transportation provided by an employer for use by its employees must be accessible to employees with a disability. This includes transportation between employer facilities, transportation to or from mass transit and transportation provided on a occasional basis to employer-sponsored events.

VIII. DRUG AND ALCOHOL ABUSE

8.1 Introduction

The ADA specifically permits employers to ensure that the workplace is free from the illegal use of drugs and the use of alcohol, and to comply with other

Federal laws and regulations regarding alcohol and drug use. At the same time, the ADA provides limited protection from discrimination for recovering drug addicts and for alcoholics.

8.2 Overview of Legal Obligations

- An individual who is currently engaging in the illegal use of drugs is not an "individual with a disability" when the employer acts on the basis of such use.
- An employer may prohibit the illegal use of drugs and the use of alcohol at the workplace.
- It is not a violation of the ADA for an employer to give tests for the illegal use of drugs.
- An employer may discharge or deny employment to persons who currently engage in the illegal use of drugs.
- An employer may not discriminate against a drug addict who is not currently using drugs and who has been rehabilitated, because of a history of drug addiction.
- A person who is an alcoholic is an "individual with a disability" under the ADA.
- An employer may discipline, discharge or deny employment to an alcoholic whose use of alcohol impairs job performance or conduct to the extent that s/he is not a "qualified individual with a disability."
- Employees who use drugs or alcohol may be required to meet the same standards of performance and conduct that are set for other employees.
- Employees may be required to follow the Drug-Free Workplace Act of 1988 and rules set by Federal agencies pertaining to drug and alcohol use in the workplace.

8.3 Illegal Use of Drugs

An employer may discharge or deny employment to current illegal users of drugs, on the basis of such drug use, without fear of being held liable for disability discrimination. Current illegal users of drugs are not "individuals with disabilities" under the ADA.

The illegal use of drugs includes the use, possession, or distribution of drugs which are unlawful under the Controlled Substances Act. It includes the use of illegal drugs and the illegal use of prescription drugs that are 'controlled substances'.

> *For example:* Amphetamines can be legally prescribed drugs. However, amphetamines, by law, are "controlled substances" because of their abuse and potential for abuse. If a person takes amphetamines without a prescription, that person is using drugs illegally, even though they could be prescribed by a physician.

The illegal use of drugs does not include drugs taken under supervision of a licensed health care professional, including experimental drugs for people with AIDS, epilepsy, or mental illness.

For example: A person who takes morphine for the control of pain caused by cancer is not using a drug illegally if it is taken under the supervision of a licensed physician. Similarly, a participant in a methadone maintenance treatment program cannot be discriminated against by an employer based upon the individual's lawful use of methadone.

An individual who illegally uses drugs but also has a disability, such as epilepsy, is only protected by the ADA from discrimination on the basis of the disability (epilepsy). An employer can discharge or deny employment to such an individual on the basis of his/her illegal use of drugs.

What Does "Current" Drug Use Mean?

If an individual tests positive on a test for the illegal use of drugs, the individual will be considered a current drug user under the ADA where the test correctly indicates that the individual is engaging in the illegal use of a controlled substance.

"Current" drug use means that the illegal use of drugs occurred recently enough to justify an employer's reasonable belief that involvement with drugs is an on-going problem. It is not limited to the day of use, or recent weeks or days, in terms of an employment action. It is determined on a case-by-case basis.

For example: An applicant or employee who tests positive for an illegal drug cannot immediately enter a drug.g rehabilitation program and seek to avoid the possibility of discipline or termination by claiming that s/he now is in rehabilitation and is no longer using drugs illegally. A person who tests positive for illegal use of drugs is not entitled to the protection that may be available to former users who have been or are in rehabilitation (see below).

8.4 Alcoholism

While a current illegal user of drugs has no protection under the ADA if the employer acts on the basis of such use, a person who currently-uses alcohol is not automatically denied protection simply because of the alcohol use. An alcoholic is a person with a disability under the ADA and may be entitled to consideration of accommodation, if s/he is qualified to perform the essential functions of a job. However, an employer may discipline, discharge or deny employment to an alcoholic whose use of alcohol adversely affects job performance or conduct to the extent that s/he is not "qualified."

For example: If an individual who has alcoholism often is late to work or is unable to perform the responsibilities of his/her job, an employer can take disciplinary action on the basis of the poor job performance and conduct. However, an employer may not discipline an alcoholic employee more severely than it does other employees for the same performance or conduct.

8.5 Recovering Drug Addicts

Persons addicted to drugs, but who are no longer using drugs illegally and are receiving treatment for drug addiction or who have been rehabilitated successfully, are protected by the ADA from discrimination on the basis of past drug addiction.

For example: An addict who is currently in a drug rehabilitation program and has not used drugs illegally for some time is not excluded from the protection of the ADA. This person will be protected by the ADA because s/he has a history of addiction, or if s/he is "regarded as" being addicted. Similarly, an addict who is rehabilitated or who has successfully completed a supervised rehabilitation program and is no longer illegally using drugs is not excluded from the ADA.

However, a person who casually used drugs illegally in the past, but did not become addicted is not an individual with a disability based on the past drug use. In order for a person to be "substantially limited" because of drug use, s/he must be addicted to the drug.

To ensure that drug use is not recurring, an employer may request evidence that an individual is participating in a drug rehabilitation program or may request the results of a drug test (see below).

A "rehabilitation program" may include in-patient, out-patient, or employee assistance programs, or recognized self-help programs such as Narcotics Anonymous.

8.6 Persons "Regarded As" Addicts and Illegal Drug Users

Individuals who are not illegally using drugs, but who are erroneously perceived as being addicts and as currently using drugs illegally, are protected by the ADA.

For example: If an employer perceived someone to be addicted to illegal drugs based upon rumor and the groggy appearance of the individual, but the rumor was false and the appearance was a side-effect of a lawfully prescribed medication, this individual would be "regarded as" an individual with a disability (a drug addict) and would be protected from discrimination based upon that false assumption. If an employer did not regard the individual as an addict, but simply as a social user of illegal drugs, the individual would not be "regarded as" an individual with a disability and would not be protected by the ADA.

As with other disabilities, an individual who claims that s/he was discriminated against because of past or perceived illegal drug addiction, may be asked to prove that s/he has a record of, or is regarded as having, an addiction to drugs.

8.7 Efforts to Prohibit Drug and Alcohol Use in the Workplace

The ADA does not prevent efforts to combat the use of drugs and alcohol in the workplace

The ADA does not interfere with employers' programs to combat the use of drugs and alcohol in the workplace. The Act specifically provides that an employer may:

- prohibit the use of drugs and alcohol in the workplace.
- require that employees not be under the influence of alcohol or drugs in the workplace.

  For example: An employer can require that employees not come to work or return from lunch under the influence of alcohol, or drugs used illegally.

- Require that employees who illegally use drugs or alcohol meet the same qualification and performance standards applied to other employees. Unsatisfactory behavior such as absenteeism, tardiness, poor job performance, or accidents caused by alcohol or illegal drug use need not be accepted nor accommodated.

  For example: If an employee is often late or does not show up for work because of alcoholism, an employer can take direct action based on the conduct. However, an employer would violate the ADA if it imposed greater sanctions on such an alcoholic employee than it did on other employees for the some misconduct.

While the ADA permits an employer to discipline or discharge an employee for illegal use of drugs or where alcoholism results in poor performance or misconduct, the Act does not require this. Many employers have established employee assistance programs for employees who abuse drugs or alcohol that are helpful to both employee and employer. However, the ADA does not *require* an employer to provide an opportunity for rehabilitation in place of discipline or discharge to such employees. The ADA may, however, require consideration of reasonable accommodation for a drug addict who is rehabilitated and not using drugs or an alcoholic who remains a "qualified individual with a disability." For example, a modified work schedule, to permit the individual to attend an ongoing self-help program, might be a reasonable accommodation for such an employee.

An employer can fire or refuse to hire a person with a past history of illegal drug use, even if the person no longer uses drugs, in specific occupations, such as law enforcement, when an employer can show that this policy is job-related and consistent with business necessity.

For example: A law enforcement agency might be able to show that excluding an individual with a history of illegal drug use from a police officer position was necessary, because such illegal conduct would undermine the credibility of the officer as a witness for the prosecution in a criminal case.

However, even in this case, exclusion of a person with a history of illegal drug use might not be justified automatically as a business necessity, if an applicant with such a history could demonstrate an extensive period of successful performance as a police officer since the time of drug use.

An employer also may fire or refuse to hire an individual with a history of alcoholism or illegal drug use if it can demonstrate that the individual poses a "direct threat" to health or safety because of the high probability that s/he would return to the illegal drug use or alcohol abuse. The employer must be able to demonstrate that such use would result in a high probability of substantial harm to the individual or others which could not be reduced or eliminated with a reasonable accommodation. Examples of accommodations in such cases might be to require periodic drug or alcohol tests, to modify job duties or to provide increased supervision.

An employer cannot prove a "high probability" of substantial harm simply by referring to statistics indicating the likelihood that addicts or alcoholics in general have a specific probability of suffering a relapse. A showing of "significant risk of substantial harm" must be based upon an assessment of the particular individual and his/her history of substance abuse and the specific nature of the job to be performed.

For example: An employer could justify excluding an individual who is an alcoholic with a history of returning to alcohol abuse from a job as a ship captain.

8.8 Pre-employment Inquiries About Drug and Alcohol Use

An employer may make certain pre-employment, pre-offer inquiries regarding use of alcohol or the illegal use of drugs. An employer may ask whether an applicant drinks alcohol or whether he or she is currently using drugs illegally. However, an employer may not ask whether an applicant is a drug addict or alcoholic, nor inquire whether s/he has ever been in a drug or alcohol rehabilitation program. (See also *Pre-Employment Inquiries,* Chapter V.)

After a conditional offer of employment, an employer may ask any questions concerning past or present drug or alcohol use. However, the employer may not use such information to exclude an individual with a disability, on the basis of a disability, unless it can show that the reason for exclusion is job-related and consistent with business necessity, and that legitimate job criteria cannot be met with a reasonable accommodation. (For more information on pre-employment medical inquiries, see Chapter VI.)

8.9 Drug Testing

An employer may conduct tests to detect illegal use of drugs. The ADA does not prohibit, require, or encourage drug tests. Drug tests are not considered medical examinations, and an *applicant* can be required to take a drug test before a conditional offer of employment has been made. An *employee* also can be required to take a drug test, whether or not such a test is job-related and necessary for the business. (On the other hand, a test to determine an individual's blood alcohol level would be a "medical examination" and only could be required by an employer in conformity with the ADA.)

An employer may refuse to hire an applicant or discharge or discipline an employee based upon a test result that indicates the illegal use of drugs. The employer may take these actions even if an applicant or employee claims that s/he recently stopped illegally using drugs.

Employers may comply with applicable Federal, State, or local laws regulating when and how drug tests may be used, what drug tests may be used, and confidentiality. Drug tests must be conducted to detect *illegal use of* drugs. However, tests for illegal use of drugs also may reveal the presence of lawfully-used drugs. If a person is excluded from a job because the employer erroneously "regarded" him/her to be an addict currently using drugs illegally when a drug test revealed the presence of a lawfully prescribed drug, the employer would be liable under the ADA. To avoid such potential liability, the employer would have to determine whether the individual was using a legally prescribed drug. Because the employer may not ask what prescription drugs an individual is taking before making a conditional job offer, one way to avoid liability is to conduct drug tests after making an offer, even though such tests may be given at anytime under the ADA. Since applicants who test positive for illegal drugs are not covered by the ADA, an employer can withdraw an offer of employment on the basis of illegal drug use.

If the results of a drug test indicate the presence of a lawfully prescribed drug, such information must be kept confidential, in the some way as any medical record. If the results reveal information about a disability in addition to information about drug use, the disability-related information is to be treated as a confidential medical record. (See confidentiality requirements regarding medical inquiries and examinations in Chapter VI.)

> *For example:* If drug test results indicate that an individual is HIV positive, or that a person has epilepsy or diabetes because use of a related prescribed medicine is revealed, this information must remain confidential.

8.10 Laws and Regulations Concerning Drugs and Alcohol

An employer may comply with other Federal laws and regulations concerning the use of drugs and alcohol, including the Drug-Free Workplace Act of 1988; regulations applicable to particular types of employment, such as law enforcement positions; regulations of the Department of Transportation for airline employees, interstate motor carrier drivers and railroad engineers; and regulations for safety sensitive positions established by the Department of Defense and the Nuclear Regulatory Commission. Employers may continue to require that their applicants and employees comply with such Federal laws and regulations.

For example: A trucking company can take appropriate action if an applicant or employee tests positive on a drug test required by Department of Transportation regulations or refuses to take such a drug test.

IX. WORKERS' COMPENSATION AND WORK-RELATED INJURY

9.1 Overview of Legal Obligations

- An employer may not inquire into an applicant's workers' compensation history before making a conditional offer of employment.
- After making a conditional job offer, an employer may ask about a person's workers' compensation history in a medical inquiry or examination that is required of all applicants in the same job category.
- An employer may not base an employment decision on the speculation that an applicant may cause increased workers' compensation costs in the future. However, an employer may refuse to hire, or may discharge an individual who is not currently able to perform a job without posing a significant risk of substantial harm to the health or safety of the individual or others, if the risk cannot be eliminated or reduced by reasonable accommodation. (See *Standards Necessary for Health and safety: A "Direct Threat"*, Chapter IV.)
- An employer may submit medical information and records concerning employees and applicants (obtained after a conditional job offer) to state workers' compensation offices and "second injury" funds without violating ADA confidentiality requirements.
- Only injured workers who meet the ADA's definition of an "individual with a disability" will be considered disabled under the ADA, regardless of whether they satisfy criteria for receiving benefits under workers' compensation or other disability laws. A worker also must be "qualified" (with or without reasonable accommodation) to be protected by the ADA.

9.2 Is a Worker Injured on the Job Protected by the ADA?

Whether an injured worker is protected by the ADA will depend on whether or not the person meets the ADA definitions of an "individual with a disability" and "qualified individual with a disability." (See Chapter II.) The person must have an impairment that "substantially limits a major life activity," have a "record of' or be "regarded as" having such an impairment. S/he also must be able to perform the essential functions of a job currently held or desired, with or without an accommodation.

Clearly, not every employee injured on the job will meet the ADA definition. Work-related injuries do not always cause physical or mental impairments severe enough to "substantially limit" a major life activity. Also, many on-the-job injuries cause non-chronic impairments which heal within a short period of time with little or no long-term or permanent impact. Such injuries, in most circumstances, are not considered disabilities under the ADA.

The fact that an employee is awarded workers' compensation benefits, or is assigned a high workers' compensation disability rating, does not automatically establish that this person is protected by the ADA. In most cases, the definition of disability under state workers' compensation laws differs from that under the ADA, because the state laws serve a different purpose. Workers' compensation laws are designed to provide needed assistance to workers who suffer many kinds of injuries, whereas the ADA's purpose is to protect people from discrimination on the basis of disability.

Thus, many injured workers who qualify for benefits under workers' compensation or other disability benefits laws may not be protected by the ADA. An employer must consider work-related injuries on a case-by-case basis to know if a worker is protected by the ADA. Many job injuries are not "disabling" under the ADA, but it also is possible that an impairment which is not "substantially limiting" in one circumstance could result in, or lead to, disability in other circumstances.

> *For example:* Suppose a construction worker falls from a ladder and breaks a leg and the leg heals normally within a few months. Although this worker may be awarded workers' compensation benefits for the injury, he would not be considered a person with 8 disability under the ADA. The impairment suffered from the injury did not "substantially limit" a major life activity, since the injury healed within a short period and had little or no long-term impact. However, if the worker's leg took significantly longer to heal than the usual healing period for this type of injury, and during this period the worker could not walk, s/he would be considered to have a disability. Or, if the injury caused a permanent limp, the worker might be considered disabled under the ADA if the limp substantially limited his walking, as compared to the average person in the general population.

An employee who was seriously injured while working for a former employer, and was unable to work for a year because of the injury, would have a *"record of"* a substantially limiting impairment. If an employer refused to hire or promote this person on the basis of that record, even if s/he had recovered in whole or in part from the injury this would be a violation of the ADA.

If an impairment or condition caused by an on-the-job injury does not substantially limit an employee's ability to work, but the employer regards the individual as having an impairment that makes him/her unable to perform a class of jobs, such as "heavy labor," this individual would be *"regarded"* by the employer as having a disability. An employer who refused to hire or discharged an individual because of this perception would violate the ADA.

Of course, in each of the examples above, the employer would only be liable for discrimination if the individual was qualified for the position held or desired, with or without an accommodation.

9.3 What Can an Employer Do to Avoid Increased Workers' Compensation Costs and Comply with the ADA?

The ADA allows an employer to take reasonable steps to avoid increased workers' compensation liability while protecting persons with disabilities against exclusion from jobs they can safely perform.

Steps the Employer May Take

After making a conditional job offer, an employer may inquire about a person's workers' compensation history in a medical inquiry or examination that is required of all applicants in the same job category. However, an employer may not require an applicant to have a medical examination because a response to a medical inquiry (as opposed to results from a medical examination) discloses a previous on-the-job injury, unless all applicants in the same job category are required to have the examination. (See Chapter V.)

The employer may use information from medical inquiries and examinations for various purposes, such as:

- to verify employment history;
- to screen out applicants with a history of fraudulent workers' compensation claims;
- to provide information to state officials as required by state laws regulating workers' compensation and "second injury" funds;
- to screen out individuals who would pose a "direct threat" to health or safety of themselves or others, which could not be reduced to an acceptable level or eliminated by a reasonable accommodation. (See Chapter IV.)

9.4 What Can an Employer Do When a Worker Is Injured on the Job?

Medical Examinations

An employer may only make medical examinations or inquiries of an employee regarding disability if such examinations are job-related and consistent with business necessity. If a worker has an on-the-job injury which appears to affect his/her ability to do essential job functions, a medical examination or inquiry is job-related and consistent with business necessity. A medical examination or inquiry also may be necessary to provide reasonable accommodation. (See Chapter VI.)

When a worker wishes to return to work after absence due to accident or illness, s/he can only be required to have a "job-related" medical examination, not a full physical exam, as a condition of returning to work.

The ADA prohibits an employer from discriminating against a person with a disability who is "qualified" for a desired job. The employer cannot refuse to let an individual with a disability return to work because the worker is not fully recovered from injury, unless s/he: (1) cannot perform the essential functions of the job s/he holds or desires with or without an accommodation; or (2) would pose a significant risk of substantial harm that could not be reduced to an acceptable level with reasonable accommodation. (See Chapter IV.) Since reasonable accommodation may include reassignment to a vacant position, an employer may be required to consider an employee's qualifications to perform other vacant jobs for which s/he is qualified, as well as the job held when injured.

"Light Duty" Jobs

Many employers have established "light duty" positions to respond to medical restrictions on workers recovering from job-related injuries, in order to reduce workers' compensation liability. Such positions usually place few physical demands on an employee and may include tasks such as answering the telephone and simple administrative work. An employee's placement in such a position is often limited by the employer to a specific period of time.

The ADA does not require an employer to create a "light duty" position unless the "heavy duty" tasks an injured worker can no longer perform are *marginal* job functions which may be reallocated to co-workers as part of the reasonable accommodation of job-restructuring. In most cases however, "light duty" positions involve a totally different job from the job that a worker performed before the injury. Creating such positions by job restructuring is not required by the ADA. However, if an employer already has a vacant light duty position for which an injured worker is qualified, it might be a reasonable accommodation to reassign the worker to that position. If the position was created as a temporary job, a reassignment to that position need only be for a temporary period.

When an employer places an injured worker in a temporary "light duty" position, that worker is "otherwise qualified" for that position for the term of that position; a worker's qualifications must be gauged in relation to the position occupied, not in relation to the job held prior to the injury. It may be necessary to provide additional reasonable accommodation to enable an injured worker in a light duty position to perform the essential functions of that position.

> *For example:* Suppose a telephone line repair worker broke both legs and fractured her knee joints in a fall. The treating physician states that the worker will not be able to walk, even with crutches, for at least nine months. She therefore has a "disability." Currently using a wheelchair, and unable to do her previous job, she is placed in a "light duty" position to process paperwork associated with line repairs. However, the office to which she is assigned is

not wheelchair accessible. It would be a reasonable accommodation to place the employee in an office that is accessible. Or, the office could be made accessible by widening the office door, if this would not be an undue hardship. The employer also might have to modify the employee's work schedule so that she could attend weekly physical therapy sessions.

Medical information may be very useful to an employer who must decide whether an injured worker can come back to work, in what job, and, if necessary, with what accommodations. A physician may provide an employer with relevant information about an employee's functional abilities, limitations, and work restrictions. This information will be useful in determining how to return the employee to productive work, but the employer bears the ultimate responsibility for deciding whether the individual is qualified, with or without a reasonable accommodation. Therefore, an employer cannot avoid liability if it relies on a physician's advice which is not consistent with ADA requirements.

9.5 Do the ADA's Pre-Employment Inquiry and Confidentiality Restrictions Prevent an Employer from Filing Second Injury Fund Claims?

Most states have established "second injury" funds designed to remove financial disincentives in hiring employees with a disability. Without a second injury fund, if a worker suffered increased disability from a work related injury because of a pre-existing condition, the employer would have to pay the full cost. The second injury fund provisions limit the amount the employer must pay in these circumstances, and provide for the balance to be paid out of a common fund.

Many second injury funds require an employer to certify that it knew at the time of hire that the employee had a pre-existing injury. The ADA does not prohibit employers from obtaining information about pre-existing injuries and providing needed information to second injury funds. As discussed in Chapter VI., an employer may make such medical inquiries and require a medical examination *after a conditional offer of employment,* and before a person starts work, so long as the examination or inquiry is made of all applicants in the same job category. Although the ADA generally requires that medical information obtained from such examinations or inquiries be kept confidential, information may be submitted to second injury funds or state workers' compensation authorities as required by state workers' compensation laws.

9.6 Compliance with State and Federal Workers' Compensation Laws

a. Federal Laws

It may be a defense to a charge of discrimination under the ADA that a challenged action is required by another Federal law or regulation, or that another Federal law prohibits an action that otherwise would be required by the ADA. This defense is not valid, however, if the Federal standard does not require the discriminatory action, or if there is a way that an employer can comply with both legal requirements.

b. State Laws

ADA requirements supersede any *conflicting* state workers' compensation laws.

For example: Some state workers' compensation statutes make an employer liable for paying additional benefits if an injury occurs because the employer assigned a person to a position likely to jeopardize the person's health or safety, or exacerbate an earlier workers' compensation injury. Some of these laws may permit or require an employer to exclude a disabled individual from employment in cases where the ADA would not permit such exclusion. In these cases, the ADA takes precedence over the state law. An employer could not assert, as a valid defense to a charge of discrimination, that it failed to hire or return to work an individual with a disability because doing so would violate a state workers' compensation law that required exclusion of this individual.

9.7 Does Filing a Workers' Compensation Claim Prevent an Injured Worker from Filing a Charge Under the ADA?

Filing a workers' compensation claim does not prevent an injured worker from filing a charge under the ADA. "Exclusivity" clauses in state workers' compensation laws bar all other civil remedies related to an injury that has been compensated by a workers' compensation system. However, these clauses do not prohibit a qualified individual with a disability from filing a discrimination charge with EEOC, or filing a suit under the ADA, if issued a "right to sue" letter by EEOC. (See Chapter X.)

9.8 What if an Employee Provides False Information About His/Her Health or Physical Condition?

An employer may refuse to hire or may fire a person who knowingly provides a false answer to a lawful post-offer inquiry about his/her condition or workers' compensation history.

Some state workers' compensation laws release an employer from its obligation to pay benefits if a worker falsely represents his/her health or physical condition at the time of hire and is later injured as a result. The ADA does not prevent use of this defense to a workers' compensation claim. The ADA requires only that information requests about health or workers compensation history are made as part of a post-offer medical examination or inquiry. (See Chapter VI.)

X. ENFORCEMENT PROVISIONS

10.1 Introduction

Title I of the ADA is enforced by the Equal Employment Opportunity Commission (EEOC) under the same procedures used to enforce Title VII of the Civil Rights Acts of 1964. The Commission receives and investigates charges of discrimination and seeks through conciliation to resolve any discrimination found and obtain full relief for the affected individual. If conciliation is not successful, the EEOC may file a suit or issue a "right to sue" letter to the person who filed the charge. Throughout the enforcement process, EEOC makes every effort to resolve issues through conciliation and to avoid litigation.

The Commission also recognizes that differences and disputes about the ADA requirements may arise between employers and people with disabilities as a result of misunderstandings. Such disputes frequently can be resolved more effectively through informal negotiation or mediation procedures, rather than through the formal enforcement process of the ADA. Accordingly, EEOC will encourage efforts to settle such differences through alternative dispute resolution, provided that such efforts do not deprive any individual of legal rights granted by the statute.

10. 2 Overview of Enforcement Provisions

- A job applicant or employee who believes s/he has been discriminated against on the basis of disability in employment by a private, state, or local government employer, labor union, employment agency, or joint labor management committee can file a charge with EEOC.
- An individual, whether disabled or not, also may file a charge if s/he believes that s/he has been discriminated against because of an association with a person with a known disability, or believes that s/he has suffered retaliation because of filing a charge or assisting in opposing a discriminatory practice. (See *Retaliation* below.) Another person or organization also may file a charge on behalf of such applicant or employee.
- The entity charged with violating the ADA should receive written notification of the charge within 10 days after it is filed.
- EEOC will investigate charges of discrimination. If EEOC believes that discrimination occurred, it will attempt to resolve the charge through conciliation and obtain full relief for the aggrieved individual consistent with EEOC's standards for remedies.
- If conciliation fails, EEOC will file suit or issue a "right to sue" letter to the person who filed the charge. (If the charge involves a state or local government agency, EEOC will refer the case to the Department of Justice for consideration of litigation or issuance of a "right to sue" letter.)
- Remedies for violations of Title I of the ADA include hiring, reinstatement, promotion, back pay, front pay, restored benefits, reasonable accommodation, attorneys' fees, expert witness fees, and court costs. Compensatory and punitive damages also may be available in cases of intentional discrimination or where an employer fails to make a good faith effort to provide a reasonable accommodation.
- Employers may not retaliate against any applicant or employee who files a

charge, participates in an EEOC investigation or opposes an unlawful employment practice.

10. 3 Questions and Answers on the ADA Enforcement Process

When do the ADA's employment enforcement provisions become effective?

Charges of discrimination can be filed against employers with 25 or more employees and other covered entities beginning July 26, 1992. The alleged discriminatory act(s) must have occurred on or after July 26, 1992.

Charges can be filed against employers with 15 or more employees beginning July 26, 1994. The alleged discriminatory act(s) must have occurred on or after July 26, 1994, if the charge is against an employer with 15 to 24 employees.

Who can file charges of discrimination?

An applicant or employee who feels that s/he has been discriminated against in employment on the basis of disability can file a charge with EEOC. An individual, group or organization also can file a charge on behalf of another person. An individual, group or organization that files a charge is called the "charging party."

How are charges of discrimination filed?

A person who feels s/he has been discriminated against, or other potential "charging party" should contact the nearest EEOC office. If there is no EEOC office nearby, call, toll free 1-800-669-4000 (voice) or 1-800-800-3302 (TDD).

What are the time limits for filing charges of discrimination?

A charge of discrimination on the basis of disability must be filed with EEOC within *180 days* of the alleged discriminatory act.

If there is a state or local fair employment practices agency that enforces a law prohibiting the same alleged discriminatory practice, it is possible that charges may be filed with EEOC up to *300 days* after the alleged discriminatory act. However, to protect legal rights, it is recommended that EEOC be contacted promptly when discrimination is believed to have occurred.

How is a charge of discrimination filed?

A charge can be filed in person, by telephone, or by mail. If an individual does not live near an EEOC office, the charge can be filed by telephone and verified by mail. The type of information that will be requested from a charging party may include:

- the charging party's name, address, and telephone number (if a charge is filed on behalf of another individual, his/her identity may be kept confidential, unless required for a court action);
- the employer's name, address, telephone number, and number of employees;

- the basis or bases of the discrimination claimed by the individual (e.g., disability, race, color, religion, sex, national origin, age, retaliation);
- the issue or issues involved in the alleged discriminatory act(s) (e.g., hiring, promotion, wages, terms and conditions of employment, discharge);
- identification of the charging party's alleged disability (e.g., the physical or mental impairment and how it affects major life activities, the record of disability the employer relied upon, or how the employer regarded the individual as disabled);
- the date of the alleged discriminatory act(s);
- details of what allegedly happened; and
- identity of witnesses who have knowledge of the alleged discriminatory act(s).

Charging parties also may submit additional oral or written evidence on their behalf.

EEOC has work-sharing agreements with many state and local fair employment agencies. Depending on the agreement, some charges may be sent to a state or local agency for investigation; others may be investigated directly by EEOC. (See also *Coordination Procedures to Avoid Duplicate Complaint Processing under the ADA and the Rehabilitation Act,* below.)

Can a charging party file a charge on more than one basis?
EEOC also enforces other laws that bar employment discrimination based on race, color, religion, sex, national origin, and age (persons 40 years of age and older). An individual with a disability can file a charge of discrimination on more than one basis.

> *For example:* A cashier who is a paraplegic may claim that she was discriminated against by an employer based on both her sex and her disability. She can file a single charge claiming both disability and sex discrimination.

Can an individual file a lawsuit against an employer?
An individual can file a lawsuit against an employer, but s/he must first file the charge with EEOC. The charging party can request a "right to sue" letter from the EEOC 180 days after the charge was first filed with the Commission. A charging party will then have 90 days to file suit after receiving the notice of right to sue. If the charging party files suit, EEOC will ordinarily dismiss the original charges filed with the Commission. "Right to sue" letters also are issued when EEOC does not believe discrimination occurred or when conciliation attempts fail and EEOC decides not to sue on the charging party's behalf (see below).

Are charging parties protected from retaliation?
It is unlawful for an employer or other covered entity to retaliate against someone who files a charge of discrimination, participates in an investigation, or

opposes discriminatory practices. Individuals who believe that they have been retaliated against should contact EEOC immediately. Even if an individual has already filed a charge of discrimination, s/he can file a new charge based on retaliation.

How does EEOC process charges of discrimination?

- A charge of employment discrimination may be filed with EEOC against a private employer, state or local government, employment agency, labor union or joint labor management committee. When a charge has been filed, EEOC calls these covered entities "respondents."
- Within 10 days after receipt of a charge, EEOC sends written notification of receipt to the respondent and the charging party.
- EEOC begins its investigation by reviewing information received from the charging party and requesting information from the respondent. Information requested from the respondent initially, and in the course of the investigation, may include:
  - — specific information on the issues raised in the charge;
  - — the identity of witnesses who can provide evidence about issues in the charge;
  - — information about the business operation, employment process, and workplace; and
  - — personnel and payroll records.

(Note: All or part of the data-gathering portion of an investigation may be conducted on-site, depending on the circumstances.)

- A respondent also may submit additional oral or written evidence on its own behalf.
- EEOC also will interview witnesses who have knowledge of the alleged discriminatory act(s).
- EEOC may dismiss a charge during the course of the investigation for various reasons. For example, it may find that the respondent is not covered by the ADA, or that the charge is not timely filed.
- EEOC may request additional information from the respondent and the charging party. They may be asked to participate in a fact-finding conference to review the allegations, obtain additional evidence, and, if appropriate, seek to resolve the charge through a negotiated settlement.
- The charging party and respondent will be informed of the preliminary findings of the investigation—that is, whether there is cause to believe that discrimination has occurred and the type of relief that may be necessary. Both parties will be provided opportunity to submit further information.
- After reviewing all information, the Commission sends an official "Letter of Determination" to the charging party and the respondent, stating whether it has or has not found "reasonable cause" to believe that discrimination occurred.

What if the EEOC concludes that no discrimination occurred?
If the investigation finds no cause to believe discrimination occurred, EEOC will take no further action. EEOC will issue a "right to sue" letter to the charging party, who may irritate a private suit.

What if the EEOC concludes that discrimination occurred?
If the investigation shows that there is reasonable cause to believe that discrimination occurred, EEOC will attempt to resolve the issue through conciliation and to obtain full relief consistent with EEOC's standards for remedies for the charging party. (See *Relief Available to Charging Party,* below.) EEOC also can request an employer to post a notice in the workplace stating that the discrimination has been corrected and that it has stopped the discriminatory practice.

What happens if conciliation fails?
At all stages of the enforcement process, EEOC will try to resolve a charge without a costly lawsuit.

If EEOC has found cause to believe that discrimination occurred, but cannot resolve the issue through conciliation, the case will be considered for litigation. If EEOC decides to litigate, a lawsuit will be filed in federal district court. If the Commission decides not to litigate, it will send the charging party a "right-to-sue" letter. The charging party may then initiate a private civil suit within 90 days, if desired. If conciliation fails on a charge against a state or local government, EEOC will refer the case to the Department of Justice for consideration of litigation or issuance of a "right to sue" letter.

10.4 Coordination Procedures to Avoid duplicative complaints Processing Under the ADA and the Rehabilitation Act

The ADA requires EEOC and the federal agencies responsible for Section 503 and Section 504 of the Rehabilitation Act of 1973 to establish coordination procedures to avoid duplication and to assure consistent standards in processing complaints that fall within the overlapping jurisdiction of both laws. EEOC and the Office of Federal Contract Compliance in the Department of Labor (OFCCP) have issued a joint regulation establishing such procedures for complaints against employers covered by the ADA who are also federal contractors or subcontractors (Published in the *Federal Register* of January 24, 1992.) EEOC and the Department of Justice also will issue a joint regulation establishing procedures for complaints against employers covered by the ADA who are recipients of federal financial assistance.

The joint EEOC-OFCCP rule provides that a complaint of discrimination on the basis of disability filed with OFCCP under Section 503 will be considered a charge filed simultaneously under the ADA if the complaint fails within the ADA's jurisdiction. This will ensure that an individual's ADA rights are preserved. OFCCP will process such complaints/charge for EEOC, with certain exceptions specified in the regulation, where OFCCP will refer the charge to

EEOC. OFCCP also will refer to EEOC for litigation review any complaint/charge where a violation has been found, conciliation fails, and OFCCP decides not to pursue administrative enforcement.

EEOC will refer to OFCCP ADA charges that fall under Section 503 jurisdiction when the Commission finds cause to believe that discrimination has occurred but decides not to litigate, for any administrative action that OFCCP finds appropriate. Where a charge involves both allegations of discrimination and violation of OFCCP's affirmative action requirements, EEOC generally will refer the charge to OFCCP for processing and resolution.

(Note: Procedures established in an EEOC-Department of Justice joint rule on processing complaints that are within ADA and Section 504 jurisdiction will be summarized in a future supplement to this *Manual,* when a final regulation has been issued.)

10.5 Remedies

The "relief' or remedies available for employment discrimination, whether caused by intentional acts or by practices that have a discriminatory effect, may include hiring, reinstatement, promotion, back pay, front pay, reasonable accommodation, or other actions that will make an individual "whole" (in the condition s/he would have been but for the discrimination). Remedies also may include payment of attorneys' fees, expert witness fees and court costs.

Compensatory and punitive damages also may be available where intentional discrimination is found. Damages may be available to compensate for actual monetary losses, for future monetary losses, for mental anguish and inconvenience. Punitive damages also may be available if an employer acted with malice or reckless indifference. The total amount of punitive damages and compensatory damages for future monetary loss and emotional injury for each individual is limited, based upon the size of the employer, using the following schedule:

NUMBER OF EMPLOYEES	DAMAGES WILL NOT EXCEED
15-100	$ 50 000
101-200	100,000
201-500	200,000
500 and more	300,000

Punitive damages are not available against state or local governments.

In cases concerning reasonable accommodation, compensatory or punitive damages may not be awarded to the charging party if an employer can demonstrate that "good faith" efforts were made to provide reasonable accommodation.

What are EEOC's obligations to make the charge process accessible to and usable by individuals with disabilities?

EEOC is required by Section 504 of the Rehabilitation Act of 1973, as amended, to make all of its programs and activities accessible to and usable by individuals with disabilities. EEOC has an obligation to provide services or devices necessary to enable an individual with a disability to participate in the charge filing process. For example, upon request, EEOC will provide an interpreter when necessary for a charging party who is hearing impaired. People with visual or manual disabilities can request on-site assistance in filling out a "charge of discrimination" form and affidavits. EEOC will provide access to the charge process as needed by each individual with a disability, on a case-by-case basis.

Notes

[1] 135 Cong. Rec. S10789 (Sept. 8, 1989); *Washington Post,* Sept. 8, 1989, p. A1.
[2] H. R. 12154, 92nd Cong., 1st Sess., 117 Cong. Rec. 45945 (1971).
[3] S. 3044, 92nd Cong., 2nd Sess., 118 Cong. Rec. 525 (1972).
[4] U.S. Commission on Civil Rights, *Accommodating the Spectrum of Individual Abilities,* Appendix B, pp. 169–172 (U.S. Gov. Printing Office, Washington, D.C., 1983).
[5] See "Small Business and Local Government Groups Question Cost of Federal Bill for Disabled," Daily Lab. Rep. (BNA) No. 209, at c-6 (Oct. 31, 1989).
[6] Id.
[7] ADA Section 305.
[8] ADA Sections 101(5), 108, 42 U.S.C. 12111.
[9] ADA Section 204(a), 42 U.S.C. 12134.
[10] Id.
[11] ADA Sections 203(a), 306(a), 42 U.S.C. 12186.
[12] ADA Section 102(a), 42 U.S.C. 12112.
[13] Id.
[14] ADA Section 101(8).
[15]EEOC Interpretive Rules, 56 Fed. Reg. 35 (July 26, 1991).
[16] 42 F. R. 22686 (May 4, 1977); S. Rep. 101–116; H. Rep. 101–485, Part 2, 51.
[17] Subtitle A, Section 3(2). The ADA departed from the Rehabilitation Act of 1973 and other legislation in using the term "disability" rather than "handicap."
[18] 29 U.S.C. Section 706(8) (Supp. V. 1975).
[19] S. Rep. at page 26, 135 Cong. Rep. S10 (Daily ed., Sept. 7, 1989).
[20] 28 C.F.R. Section 41.31.
[21]28 C.F.R. Section 41.31. This provision is adopted by and reiterated in the Senate Report at page 22.
[22] See *Jasany v. U.S. Postal Service,* 755 F. 2d 1244 (6th Cir. 1985).
[23] 497 F. Supp. 1088 (D. Haw. 1980).
[24] S. Rep. 101–116, 23; H. Rep. 101–485, Part 2, 52–53.
[25] 780 F. 2d 64, 66 (D.C. Cir. 1985).
[26] *Kohl by Kohl v. Woodhaven Learning Center,* 672 F. Supp. 1221 (W.D. Mo. 1987).
[27]*Bey v. Bolger,* 540 F. Supp. 910 (ED Pa. 1982).
[28] *Mahoney v. Ortiz,* 645 F. Supp. 22 (SD NY 1986).
[29] 45 C.F.R. 84.3(j)(2)(iv), quoted from H. Rep. 101–485, Part 3, 29; S. Rep. 101–116, 23:H. Rep. 101–485, Part 2, 53; See also *School Board of Nassau County, Florida v. Arline,* 107 S. Ct. 1123 (1987) (leading case).

[30] EEOC Interpretive Guidelines, 56 Fed. Reg. 35, 742 (July 26, 1991).
[31] S. Comm. on Lab. and Hum. Resources Rep. at 24; H. Comm. on Educ. and Lab. Rep. at 53; H. Comm. on Jud. Rep. at 30–31.
[32] 29 C.F.R. Section 1630.2(1).
[33] ADA Section 101(8).
[34] H. Comm. on Educ. and Lab. Rep. at 64.
[35] *Guinn v. Bolger,* 598 F. Supp. 196 (DDC 1984); *Treadway v. Alexander,* 707 F. 2d 473, 476 n. 5 (11th Cir. 1983); *Prewitt v. US Postal Serv.,* 662 F. 2d 292, 298 (5th Cir. 1981); *Coleman v. Darden,* 595 F. 2d 533 (10th Cir. 1979).
[36] EEOC Interpretive Rules, supra, note 9.
[37] Id.
[38] ADA Section 103(b).
[39] EEOC Interpretive Guidelines.
[40] Id.
[41] 56 Fed. Reg. 35,745 (July 26, 1991); See also *Davis v. Meese,* 692 F. Supp. 505 (ED Pa. 1988) (Rehabilitation Act decision).
[42] ADA Section (9).
[43] EEOC Interpretive Guidelines.
[44] Id.
[45] See *Gruegging v. Burke,* 48 Fair Empl. Prac. Cas. (BNA) 140 (DDC 1987); *Bento v. ITO Corp.,* 599 F. Supp. 731 (DRI 1984).
[46] EEOC Interpretive Guidelines, 56 Fed. Reg. 35,744 (July 26, 1991); See also Rehabilitation Act decisions including *Harrison v. March,* 46 Fair Empl. Prac. Cas. (BNA) 971 (WD Mo. 1988); *Wallace v. Veteran Admin.,* 683 F. Supp. 758 (D. Kan. 1988).
[47] ADA Section 101(10)(a).
[48] EEOC Interpretive Guidelines.
[49] S. Comm. on Lab. and Hum. Resources Rep. at 38; H. Comm. on Jud. Rep. at 42.
[50] OFCCP Reg., 41 C.F.R. Section 60-741.6(c). See also *OFCCP v. EE Black, Ltd.,* 19 Fair Empl. Prac. Cas. (BNA) 1642 (DOL 1979), aff'd, 23 Fair Empl. Prac. Cas. (BNA) 1254 (D. Haw. 1980).
[51] ADA Section 102(C)(2).
[52] ADA Section 102(c)(2)(A).
[53] EEOC Interpretive Guidelines, 56 Fed. Reg. 35,751 (July 26, 1991). Federally mandated periodic examinations include such laws as the Rehabilitation Act, Occupational Safety and Health Act, Federal Coal Mine Health Act, and numerous transportation laws.
[54] ADA Section 102(c).
[55] ADA Section 511(b).
[56] ADA Sections 103(d)(1) and (2).
[57] Id.
[58] ADA Section 103(d)(1).
[59] ADA Section 201(1).
[60] S. Rep 101–116, 21; H. Rep 101–485, Part 2; Part 3, 26–27.
[61] ADA Section 302.
[62] ADA Section 302(b)(2)(A)(iv).
[63] ADA Section 301(9).
[64] Department of Justice Regulations, 28 C.F.R. Section 36.403(f)(1).
[65] ADA Section 303(a)(1). This exception is very narrow in scope and only applies in rare and unusual circumstances. This is another new concept but parallels the "physical integrity" exception under the Fair Housing Amendment Act.

[66] S. Rep 101–116, 69; H. Rep 101–485 Part 2, 117–118. This section also includes the committees' views concerning accessibility requirements to particular circumstances and types of facilities.
[67] ADA Section 3(1).
[68] Report of the House Committee on Energy and Commerce on the Americans with Disabilities Act of 1990, H. R. Rep. No. 485, 101st Cong., 2d Sess., (1990) (hereinafter cited as H. Comm. on Energy and Comm. Rep.); H. Comm. on Educ. and Lab. Rep., supra.; S. Comm. on Lab. and Hum. Resources Rep., supra.
[69] ADA Section 501.
[70] ADA Sections 511(a), (b); Section 508. There is some indication that many of the conditions excluded from the disability classification under the ADA may be considered a covered handicap under the Rehabilitation Act. See *Rezza v. US Dept. of Justice,* 46 Fair Empl. Prac. Cas. (BNA) 1336 (ED Pa. 1988) (compulsive gambling); *Fields v. Lyng,* 48 Fair Empl. Prac. Cas. (BNA) 1037 (D. Md. 1988) (kleptomania).
[71] ADA Sections 102(b)(4) and 302(b)(1)(E).
[72] H. Rep. 101–485, Part 2, 51.
[73] ADA Section 102(b)(4).
[74] H. Rep. 101–485, Part 2, 61–62; Part 3, 38–39.
[75] ADA Section 105.
[76] EEOC Interpretive Guidelines.
[77] Id.
[78] ADA Section 103(c)(2).
[79] ADA Section 501(c). See also Senate Report accompanying S. 933.
[80] Civil Rights Act of 1991, Section 102.
[81] S. Rep. 101–116, 21; H. Rep. 101–485 Part 2, 51; Part 3, 28.
[82] ADA Sections 505 and 513.
[83] ADA Section 101(2), 42 U.S.C. 12111.
[84] ADA Sections 509(a)(1), (b), (c)(2), 42 U.S.C. 12209.
[85] ADA Section 101(5)(B), 42 U.S.C. 12111.
[86] H. Rep. 101–485, Part 2, p. 51.
[87] *Technical Assistance Manual for the Americans with Disabilities Act,* EEOC, pages 1–3.
[88] EEOC Interpretive Guidelines, 56 Fed. Reg. 35,740 (July 26, 1991); Report of the Senate Comm. on Labor and Human Resources on the Americans with Disabilities Act of 1989, S. Rep. No. 116, 101st Cong., 1st Sess. (1989).
[89] S. Comm. on Lab. and Hum. Resources Rep. at 22.
[90] Technical Assistance Manual, supra.
[91] Id.
[92] H. Comm. on Educ. and Lab. Rep. at 52; S. Comm. on Lab. and Hum. Resources Comm. at 22, 136 Cong. Rec. S9697 (July 13, 1990). See also Technical Assistance Manual, supra.
[93] Technical Assistance Manual, supra.
[94] Id.
[95] Id.
[96] Id.
[97] Id.
[98] Id.
[99] ADA Section
[100] EEOC Regs. at 29 C.F.R. Sec. 1630.2(o)(1).
[101] EEOC Interpretive Guidelines, 56 Fed. Reg. 35,744 (July 26, 1991).
[102] ADA Section 101(9)(B); EEOC Regs. at 29 C.F.R. Sec. 1630.2(n)(2).

[103] ADA Section 101(10(a); EEOC Technical Assistance Manual, supra.
[104] EEOC Technical Assistance Manual, supra.
[105] ADA Section 101(10)(B); EEOC Technical Assistance Manual, supra.
[106] ADA Section 102(c)(1).
[107] ADA Section 103(b).
[108] ADA Section 101(c); 29 C.F.R. Sec. 1530.2(r).
[109] H. Comm. on Educ. and Lab. Rep. at 56; 29 C.F.R. Sec. 1630.2(r).
[110] 56 Fed. Reg. 35,745 (July 26, 1991).
[111] 480 U.S. 273 (1987).
[112] Id.
[113] ADA Section 103(d)(3).
[114] H. Comm. on Educ. and Lab. Rep. at 59, 137.
[115] ADA Section 102(b)(2); EEOC Technical Assistance Manual, supra.
[116] EEOC Technical Assistance Manual, supra.
[117] ADA Section 503(a) and (b).
[118] EEOC Technical Assistance Manual, supra.
[119] Id.
[120] Id.
[121] 29 U.S.C. Sec. 794.
[122] ADA Section 301(8).
[123] ADA Section 301(7).
[124] ADA Section 3(1).
[125] See Kentucky Department of Vocational Rehabilitation Accessibility Checklist, 1990. [Based on Kentucky Standards for Accessibility and American National Standards (ANSI A117.1)].
[126] The Americans with Disabilities Act, BNA Special Report, 1990.
[127] Id.
[128] ADA Section 302(b)(s)(A).
[129] 47 U.S.C. 201 et. seq.
[130]H. Comm. on Educ. and Lab. Rep. at 59.
[131] EEOC Interpretive Guidelines, 56 Fed. Reg. 35,753 (July 26, 1991).
[132] House Resolution 558 of the 100th Congress as agreed on October 4, 1988.
[133] ADA Section 513.
[134] ADA Section 501(b).
[135] ADA Section 102(b)(6).
[136] EEOC Regs. at 29 C.F.R. Sec. 1630.10.
[137] S. Rep. 101–116, 69; H. Rep 101–485 Part 2, 117–118.
[138] ADA Section 301(9).
[139] ADA Section 301(9).
[140] 28 C.F.R. Sec. 36.304.
[141] Justice Department Regulations, 28 C.F.R. Sec. 36.402(f)(2).
[142] See Justice Department Regulations, 28 C.F.R. Sec. 36.401(c).
[143] I.R.C. Sec. 162.
[144] Treas. Regs. Sec. 1.190-1(b); I.R.C. Sec. 263.1016(a)(1).
[145] See I.R.C. Sec. 51.
[146] U.S. Department of Justice, Civil Rights Division, Office on the Americans with Disabilities Act, *Americans with Disabilities Act: Questions and Answers,* 1991.

Index